UNDERSTANDING
John le Carré

Understanding Contemporary British Literature
Matthew J. Bruccoli, Series Editor

UNDERSTANDING
JOHN
le Carré

John L. Cobbs

UNIVERSITY OF SOUTH CAROLINA PRESS

© 1998 University of South Carolina

Published in Columbia, South Carolina, by the
University of South Carolina Press

Manufactured in the United States of America

02 01 00 99 98   5 4 3 2 1

Library of Congress Cataloging-in-Publication Data

Cobbs, John L.
  Understanding John le Carré / John L. Cobbs.
    p. cm. — (Understanding contemporary British literature)
  Includes bibliographical references and index.
  ISBN 1–57003–168–1
  1. Le Carré, John, 1931– —Criticism and interpretation.
  2. Spystories, English—History and criticism. I. Title. II. Series.
  PR6062.E33Z66 1998
  823'.914—dc21   97–4863

For Kathy
For, sith a womman was so pacient
Unto a mortal man, wel moore us oghte
Receyven al in gree that God us sent.

Chaucer

CONTENTS

Contents

EDITOR'S PREFACE

The volumes of *Understanding Contemporary British Literature* have been planned as guides or companions for students as well as good nonacademic readers. The editor and publisher perceive a need for these volumes because much of the influential contemporary literature makes special demands. Uninitiated readers encounter difficulty in approaching works that depart from the traditional forms and techniques of prose and poetry. Literature relies on conventions, but the conventions keep evolving; new writers form their own conventions—which in time may become familiar. Put simply, *UCBL* provides instruction in how to read certain contemporary writers—identifying and explicating their material, themes, use of language, point of view, structures, symbolism, and responses to experience.

The word *understanding* in the titles was deliberately chosen. Many willing readers lack an adequate understanding of how contemporary literature works—that is, what the author is attempting to express and the means by which it is conveyed. Although the criticism and analysis in the series have been aimed at a level of general accessibility, these introductory volumes are meant to be applied in conjunction with the works they cover. They do not provide a substitute for the works and authors they introduce but, rather, prepare the reader for more profitable literary experiences.

M. J. B.

ACKNOWLEDGMENTS

I have been fortunate during the time I was writing this book to have had valuable feedback from many of John le Carré's admirers. Most of these chapters were, in part at least, suggested, explored, and developed in discussions—academic or casual—varying from professional conferences to lunchroom chats.

I am particularly grateful to Merritt Moseley of the University of North Carolina, Asheville, and Joseph Sitterson of Georgetown University, who encouraged me to undertake this study and talked me through the early stages. Jim Applewhite and the faculty of the English department at Kutztown University were enormously supportive, particularly in the last weeks of the process when my teaching and editing were seriously hampered by illness. Matt Bruccoli, series editor at the University of South Carolina Press, was a constant source of suggestion and stimulation. I am especially indebted to Kathryn Wixon and Hank Noordam of Muhlenberg College for reading the manuscript and helping me to separate the wheat from the chaff.

UNDERSTANDING
John le Carré

CHAPTER ONE

Biography and Career

Most writers of thrillers are born and live far from the fantasy worlds that they create, and their lives have little direct bearing on their fiction. Some of John le Carré's life, however, might have sprung from the pages of one of his novels, just as much in those novels surely derived from his life. Like Ian Fleming and the far less significant American Howard Hunt—who was a spy novelist as well as a Watergate conspirator—le Carré may really have been involved in espionage. At least he was once a minor member of the British intelligence community. The image of him as a dashing spy with a mysterious past, however, is purely the product of an admiring public insisting on reading a writer's life in his fiction, and vice versa. John le Carré may or may not have been a low-level spy for a short time, but almost everything else about him is a matter of record.

He was born David John Moore Cornwell, 19 October 1931, on the south coast of England—Thomas Hardy country. His mother deserted the family early, perhaps understandably, considering the personality and psychology of his father. Ronnie Cornwell was a colorful con man, social climber, and speculator who lived alternately in mansions or jails during le Carré's youth, depending on the success of his current scams. In an early biographical account the newly successful novelist described Ronnie Cornwell, half-accurately, as, "a wealthy businessman of sporting tastes, who owned racehorses and once sought election to Parliament as a liberal."[1] What that early thumbnail sketch did not mention was that Ronnie had also gone to jail for fraud and had spent his life posing and strutting and conniving to project a gentility that he had neither been born to nor earned. From a poor family of humble and morally simplistic, straightlaced dissenters, Ronnie Cornwell was determined to project himself and his sons into the gentry, or at least to appear to be part of it. More recently, Le Carré has been franker about his father's mottled character. Ronnie was "like Gatsby," his son said of him after his death; "he lived in a contradictory world."[2]

Le Carré went off to boarding school at age five, very young even in a country that sent its boys off early. Perhaps it was a growing awareness of his father's dishonesty which led the future novelist to reject the world of Sherborne, the respectable public school in which Ronnie eventually placed him. Certainly, he was not happy there: the vulnerable, terribly lonely little Bill Roach, the "watcher" of *Tinker, Tailor, Soldier, Spy,* borrows much from the lonely schoolboy le Carré must have been. The hypocrisy and snobbery at Carne, the self-consciously elite school of *A Murder of Quality,* is patterned largely after Sherborne, although undoubtedly the author's teaching stint at even more elite Eton served as a model too. Happy or not, le Carré won the Sherborne school prize for English verse then fled to Europe when he was sixteen to escape both his father and the public school system. Once safely there, David Cornwell, yet to be John le Carré, forged a new self—one not based on fawning adaptability, role-playing, and social climbing. He studied languages at the University of Berne, developing a mastery of German and German culture which would profoundly influence his work. Returning to England in 1949, he joined the army, and his skill in languages won him an assignment in army intelligence in postwar Vienna, where both the skulduggery of the Cold War and its ghastly effects on civilians came home to the young man, for among his jobs was debriefing British officers and interviewing refugees. Several of his fictional protagonists would grow up in the service, including Jonathan Pine of *The Night Manager.* It may have been at this time that le Carré was actually recruited by "Her Majesty's Secret Service," but he has been characteristically unforthcoming about whether he was actually an undercover agent in training for years before he officially joined the British Foreign Service in 1958. Le Carré has always been steadfastly reticent about acknowledging whether he ever was a "spy," although he confesses to considerable inside knowledge of the "profession." "Look at it like this," he told the London *Daily Telegraph*'s James Cameron, who asked him directly if he had been "at one time on the game himself," "if you or I write a novel about a brothel-keeper people wouldn't assume that we'd *been* brothel keepers."[3] Cameron discreetly did not suggest that the suspicion might depend on how realistically an author described a brothel.

In the meantime le Carré returned to England and "read modern languages" (as pursuing a course of academic study is called in England) at Lincoln College, Oxford. He married Alison Sharpe, the daughter of a field marshal in the Royal Air Force (RAF), in 1954 and produced three sons with her before the long-moribund marriage ended in divorce in 1971.[4] Personally reserved and discreet about his personal life, le Carré has said virtually nothing publicly about this first marriage, and critics have found little evidence of its effect on his writings, with the probable exception of the faltering marriage and chaotic adulterous affair described in the atypical romance *The Naive and Sentimental Lover* (1971).

Le Carré took a prestigious "first" degree in Modern Languages at Oxford in 1956 then taught French and German at Eton, regarded as England's most elite boarding school, of which he later wrote: "Eton, at its worst, is unbelievably frightful. It is intolerant, chauvinistic, bigoted, ignorant. At its best it is enlightened, adaptable, fluent, and curiously democratic."[5]

Le Carré's scholarly excellence is something that his readers, and particularly his critics, often forget when categorizing him as a spy novelist, and therefore an "entertainer" rather than a teacher and edifier, which is the role of serious writers. Le Carré could easily have been a university don or have written the sort of highly esoteric novels packed ostentatiously with history, aesthetics, and philosophy which John Fowles handles so well (and is so well rewarded by elitist reviewers for not producing "page-turners"). Le Carré's works are actually packed with intellectual apparatus and arcana as well as linguistic legerdemain—but not flamboyantly. Critics could ruminate endlessly, for example, simply on the symbolism of his names and titles.

One name that is of particular interest is John le Carré itself, which he once claimed to have snatched at random off a shop billboard. He later admitted that he liked the aristocratic "Norman" sound of the French, perhaps coupled with the highly generic commonplace English *John.* One also wonders about the implications of his choosing to write as "John the Square" (*carré* is "square" in French) or perhaps playing on the alternate French use of *carré* to mean solid and sound.

The decision to write under a pen name was a natural one, primarily because there was a question of conflict when he published *Call for the Dead*. Since the novelist was still working for the Foreign Office, and perhaps British intelligence, anonymity was essential. Beyond that purely practical consideration, contradiction and duplicity had been hallmarks of the novelist's young life for all his formative years. The pressure of being the son of a man who was sometimes a candidate for Parliament, sometimes in jail, impressed upon the young Cornwell the need to be flexible as well as closemouthed. He began to think of himself as a sort of social spy, fitting in to a spectrum of social groups from the snobbish blue bloods whom he met and lived with at school to his father's Cockney tout friends from the track (both types would figure vividly in *A Perfect Spy,* and in fact that novel's portrait of young Magnus up to the time he leaves for Europe in his mid-teens is an accurate picture of the author's youth). "I, from very early, lived a secret life, an inward life, became extremely secretive. . . . I seemed to go about in disguise," le Carré remembered years later.[6] A good deal of this tortured progress through the grim world of English class warfare found its way directly into other le Carré's novels, but much of *A Perfect Spy* is very close to autobiography. The tarnished father figure of Ricky Pym in that book seems almost indistinguishable from Ronnie Cornwell, and Magnus Pym's childhood in the fluctuating care of this con man is basically le Carré's own. As for the adult Magnus, he seems to be a dishonest doppelgänger, a damaged alter ego that le Carré might have become had he not only tried desperately to please his father—which he did—but followed in his shifty footsteps as well.

As his shuffling back and forth from grifters and bookies to Ascot "Aristos" indicates, Ronnie Cornwell's checkered life gave his son another priceless piece of equipment for a novelist:

constantly changing environments and exposure to a wide variety of people. Along with the duplicity and the role-playing, le Carré's rootless childhood gave him the chance to observe the full spectrum of British society and to feel comfortable, if defensive, moving from one segment of it to another. This background of wandering—often scrambling—between jet sets and demimondes, gave le Carré a grasp of class warfare which he would never forget as a writer, and he always remembered, almost like a Marxist, that class was the basis of the Cold War.

American critics—working out of a society that often pretends that "class" not only doesn't matter but doesn't even exist—have been slow to recognize the importance of class consciousness in le Carré. Class is not simply window dressing designed to give his British characters a convincing verisimilitude, any more than the creaky machinery of the Circus tradecraft (called the "Circus" for its offices in Piccadilly Circus in London), with its arcane jargon, is simply verbal "apparatus" to make spying seem real. The snobbery of Bill Haydon, the gaucherie of Ricky Tarr, the social importance of Smiley's Oxford degree as opposed to Bill Bland's "red brick" one—all reflect an understanding of class distinctions and their often traumatic impact on human psychology which le Carré picked up during these years half-in and half-out of social respectability. This aching consciousness of class and its importance for men and women living and working within British society was intensified for le Carré when he taught a year at Eton; although he may never have accepted it, he cannot have forgotten the duke of Wellington's remark, so dear to the British ruling class, that "the battle of Waterloo was won on the playing fields of Eton."

Biography and Career

Le Carré's actual participation in British intelligence remains to be detailed by his first comprehensive biographer. Today, a third of a century after he left the Foreign Service, the novelist seems no more inclined to elaborate upon whether he was or was not an actual *spy* than when success brought him enough money to leave the service and fame brought a rash of requests for personal interviews. He actually wrote his first two short novels, *Call for the Dead* (1961) and *A Murder of Quality* (1962), while commuting to work. In them he laid out in depth the character of George Smiley, the "anti-spy," who would become, with James Bond, the most famous agent in literary history. He appears in the first chapter of *Call for the Dead,* "A Brief History of George Smiley," essentially as he would be in later, larger novels— already rumpled, cuckolded, socially awkward if not exactly insecure, and decidedly the antithesis of suave James Bond or all the sleek Oxford and Cambridge men whom le Carré had known in the Secret Service. As he put it, "When I first began writing, Ian Fleming was riding high and the picture of the spy was that of a character who could have affairs with women, drive a fast car, who used gadgetry and gimmickry to escape."[7] Smiley was sketched as le Carré's statement of protest against the British intelligence establishment, and it was doubtless a satisfying irony for his creator that this pudgy, unfashionable emblem of reality came to be so visible an image of the messy world of espionage for the vast reading public.

The publication of *The Spy Who Came in from the Cold* in 1963 marked the first of several felicitous conjunctions between the writing of le Carré's novels and political tides that boosted their sales—although much of this timeliness is due to le Carré's acuity in keeping his fiction up to date. The cresting of the Bond craze had left the public hungry for a more realistic form of spy story, a trend that was to be continued with the success of Len Deighton's *Funeral in Berlin* the following year. The Cuban missile crisis, coupled with the provocative building of the Berlin Wall and the bellicose stance of President Kennedy in the United States and Premier Khrushchev in the USSR, made the public aware that the Cold War was more dangerous than many had thought during the halcyon Eisenhower years. The sensational sex-and-secrets scandal of British secretary of state for war John Profumo in the spring of 1963 was followed by the highly publicized defection of British aristocratic spy Kim Philby to Russia, along with the revelation of great depths of communist infiltration of British intelligence. (Philby would furnish the material for a le Carré book of his own in *Tinker, Tailor, Soldier, Spy* a decade later). All in all, it was a hot year in the Cold War, and le Carré undoubtedly reaped the dividends, but the foundation of *The Spy Who Came in from the Cold*'s stunning success was the encomium of its preliminary reviews. It garnered raves from virtually all readers, including many of the most respected literary voices in England, as well as the word-of-mouth reputation the book quickly earned as perhaps the best spy story ever written.

Whatever the reasons, the novel changed le Carré's life permanently. It made him rich and famous, and his greatest battles as a writer were to be fought trying to come to terms with that fame and keep it from ruining him as an artist.[8] He did so admirably but not without difficulty. His literary career has had predictable artistic ups and downs, although the former have overwhelmingly dominated. Almost without exception le Carré's novels have sold very well, and for the most part they have received the kind of praise and literary prizes normally reserved for "serious" literature. There is not a more successful serious writer of fiction in England, perhaps in the world.

The end of the Cold War, which many commentators felt would strip him of his only subject, left le Carré determined to expand his scope. He had already begun working away from the European standoff between the democracies and the communists by taking notes for a novel about a new arena of conflict. He had always been a careful writer, meticulous about his facts and the verisimilitude of his scenes, but for his new novel he resorted to extensive travel and research. The book was *The Little Drummer Girl* (1983), and in it he turned away from Europe and the British intelligence establishment (always called "the Circus" in the Smiley books) and examined the Arab/Israeli struggle, not surprisingly finding no saints, few devils, and many victims in a struggle that has corrupted or destroyed everyone involved.

In *A Perfect Spy* (1986), published three years later, he returned to Europe and drew heavily on his own life to examine what might have happened to him had he followed his father's example and failed to find either direction or an informing morality. Then, in *The Russia House* (1989) and *The Secret Pilgrim* (1990), he wrote two novels that were essentially codas for the Cold War conflict, although the second was more a gathering of short stories and sketches, ending appropriately with George Smiley and an old Circus friend, Ned, declaring the Cold War finished. Le Carré dealt with the aftermath of the forty-year struggle in *Our Game* (1995), another extraordinarily topical book, which explored the disintegration of the Soviet empire as Russian troops and Chechnyan guerrilla fighters shot it out in the streets of Grozny, the capital of a Caucasus republic trying desperately to separate itself from a disintegrating Soviet Union itself trying desperately to hold onto as much of its old self as brutal suppression could enforce. In between these two Cold War coda novels le Carré wrote *The Night Manager* (1995), a widely praised story of an intrepid British agent employed to expose a vicious international arms dealer, "the worst man in the world." That this hyperbolic title applies to neither a communist nor a representative of any government or philosophy shows how the moral polarities of le Carré's world have changed since he handed in his identity card a third of a century ago, because he didn't have to be a spy anymore, because he was rich. If, that is, he ever were a spy.

In his long and productive career as a novelist there was one period of serious personal and professional difficulty—the time of adjustment leading up to the writing and publication of le Carré's one non-espionage novel and his one popular and critical failure. Although both novels that followed *The Spy Who Came in from the Cold*—*The Looking-Glass War* (1965) and *A Small Town in Germany* (1968)—received favorable reviews and sold well, le Carré was stung by suggestions that he could write nothing but spy fiction. Accordingly, he produced a purely romantic novel about the psychology of love and friendship, *The Naive and Sentimental Lover* (1971). The book was based on a triangular relationship he had developed with his close friend, Scottish writer James Kennaway, the author of *Tunes of Glory,* and Kennaway's wife, Susan. The affair was not only messy but

Biography and Career

public, with a few highly visible drunken scenes. Such behavior seemed totally out of character for le Carré, who had a lifetime of personal reserve and strict regard for privacy. Kennaway died in a car wreck; his wife published a discussion of the affair; and le Carré fictionalized the encounter in *The Naive and Sentimental Lover.* The novel was a critical disaster, and le Carré felt bitterly that he had been pigeonholed as a writer of popular entertainments rather than an artist. He was not so bitter, however, that he did not take the lesson to heart. While he was licking his wounds, he fortunately also started work on a revival of Smiley and the Circus, *Tinker, Tailor, Soldier, Spy* (1974). Many of the devotees who regard le Carré as the finest novelist of espionage in the history of the language, perhaps of any language, feel this novel is the true heart of his canon.

Tinker, Tailor, Soldier, Spy was the first long novel featuring George Smiley. So celebrated was the master spy to become that many readers are surprised to realize that the unassuming, portly genius is a dominant figure in only four of le Carré's fifteen novels. Smiley first appears in the short but dense *Call for the Dead* in 1961 and again in a relatively conventional detective role in *A Murder of Quality,* published a year later. Even in the "Karla trilogy" (*Tinker, Tailor, Soldier, Spy; The Honourable Schoolboy;* and *Smiley's People*), Smiley is peripheral to the middle volume, and he is a minor character in *The Spy Who Came in from the Cold* in 1963 and similarly in *The Looking-Glass War* published two years later. Given le Carré's reticence, the public is unlikely to know whether only the Kennaway debacle and the failure of *The Naive and Sentimental Lover* brought Smiley out of retirement or whether le Carré would have realized without prompting that he had created one of the great characters of British literature and then left him languishing on the shelf for a decade. Regardless, critical and popular reception of *Tinker, Tailor, Soldier, Spy* has been totally gratifying, and every novel he has written since has been similarly received.

For a serious writer and artist he has been phenomenally successful, and he accepts his success gracefully. "Basically, I've been incredibly lucky," he says. "I've had a wonderful life."[9] He has also been wealthy for a third of a century now. What is critical, perhaps, is that he cannot ever have been accused of being among the "idle rich." His productivity, if not phenomenal along the lines of Dickens or Trollope, has been far more even in terms of consistent high quality, for he has published a first-rate novel every two or three years for a third of a century. Although some are obviously better than others, few critics—or readers—will claim that a single one is genuinely shoddy. The structural grab bag of *The Secret Pilgrim* may lack the internal integrity to pass muster as a true novel, but it contains some finely turned stories, and *The Honourable Schoolboy*—perhaps the only le Carré book to be widely *overpraised* on publication—has some of the author's most vivid and powerful descriptive writing. Each of his novels, from *Call for the Dead* to *Our Game,* has been based on scrupulous research and verification and hands-on personal knowledge of his subject. Nothing is more reflective of his writing career than the fact that he traveled five times to Southeast Asia to research *The Honourable Schoolboy* and that he was pinned down by automatic weapons fire during one of those trips; he jotted his impressions of the incident on file cards as the bullets flew over his head.[10] It is representative of perhaps the most remarkable aspect of John le Carré's remarkably fruitful career: although like all artists, he has produced greater and lesser works of art, his overall level of achievement has been remarkably high. It has been argued by his many admirers and grudgingly admitted by most of his few detractors that he has never written a truly *bad* novel.

CHAPTER TWO

Overview

John le Carré, like Ernest Hemingway, is a writer whose enormous popularity and intriguing public image as a "real spy" make it easier to understand him as a phenomenon than as an artist. Unlike Hemingway, however, in le Carré's case the popularity is far more significant than the profile, because the writer is an inherently private and reserved man and because he writes in a genre traditionally taken lightly by the reading public and professional critics. Not that David Cornwell has encouraged the public to romanticize his authorial alter ego, John le Carré. He has never tried to hide behind his pseudonym, which he uses only professionally, nor has he ever tried to be a "Great Unknown," like Sir Walter Scott, or a mysterious hermit of the Thomas Pynchon and J. D. Salinger variety. Still, le Carré makes it a policy not to grant interviews to critics in the process of analyzing his writing, and he has assiduously avoided the kind of mass media publicity which his mammoth sales figures might attract. Writers of comparable popularity, like Stephen King in the United States, tend to be constantly on view in tabloids and on television. Not so le Carré.

On the other hand, admirers of the writer's fiction as works of art often forget that this man is arguably the most successful serious British author since World War II. Purely in terms of sales, such commercially viable producers of "literature" as the late Sir Kingsley Amis (or his currently highly marketable son Martin) and John Fowles don't even come close. *The Spy Who*

Overview

Came in from the Cold has sold tens of millions of copies in more than twenty languages, and a half-dozen other le Carré books have done almost as well. Most of his fifteen novels have been made into films or multi-episode television dramas. The public impression has been further blurred by the nature of le Carré's chosen genre, the spy thriller—although applying the label "thriller" to novels that even skilled readers comfortable with Faulkner, Joyce, and Beckett find challenging is questionable. Regardless, the knowledge that le Carré worked in British intelligence and *may* have been something like a spy, coupled with his craggy good looks and obvious knowledge of some of the more dramatic dark corners of the modern world, have produced a slightly rakish and sensational image that is distracting when considering the purely literary quality of his writing.

Le Carré's dominant subject has, of course, been espionage. This genre is unfashionable among "highbrow" writers (and critics), and the only other major literary artist to work seriously within the subject since Joseph Conrad early in this century has been le Carré's literary predecessor Graham Greene, a writer so fastidious about preserving the pristine category of "high art" that he felt compelled to call even such a serious spy novel as his own *Brighton Rock* an "entertainment." Much of this effete attitude toward thrillers is a legacy of the generations of realist writers and literary commentators who, from the middle of the nineteenth century, pilloried romanticism in general and "derring-do" romanticism in particular as dishonest fantasy. Mark Twain's assault on "Sir Walter Scottism" and his withering parody of Dumas in Tom and Huck's "evasion" at the end of *Huckleberry Finn* pointed the way toward twentieth-century contempt for anything that smacked of adventure-for-adventure's sake; Hemingway, who did plenty of pure adventure writing and produced at least one thriller in *For Whom the Bell Tolls,* was only covering his tracks when he wrote that all American literature derived from *Huckleberry Finn.*

The Cold War has been le Carré's donnée from the beginning of his career as a writer of fiction, and in one form or another it has informed every novel he has written except *The Naive and Sentimental Lover.* Ten of his fifteen novels have an immediate setting within the forty-year struggle between the Western democracies and communism. Even such of his later "post–Cold War" works as *The Little Drummer Girl* and *The Night Manager* deal with a world of violence, conflict, terrorism, and crime, which are determined by the mind-set of the East-West apposition, whether in Europe or worldwide, which developed at the close of World War II and shaped the political destiny of the entire Third World thereafter. Charlie in *The Little Drummer Girl* becomes a killer and a seductress because it is useful for the Western-backed Israelis to have her kill an Eastern-backed Palestinian in a region whose recent history cannot be separated from that of Central Europe. The apparently apolitical post–Cold War thriller *The Night Manager* is a study of characters who carry fundamentally Cold War cat-and-mouse psychologies of terrorism and antiterrorism onto a stage on which glasnost and the collapse of communism have made Cold Warriors obsolete.

Despite its dominance of human history following World War II, the Cold War has received short shrift in the literature of Western writers. It is a bitter irony that the great novels defining the struggle have come from behind the Iron Curtain, where

objective expression was either forbidden or severely curtailed.
It may well be an ultimate reproach to the myopia of Western
European and American literature that the major novelists of the
Cold War are Solzhenitsyn, Kundera, Havel, and other courageous artists in communist countries who defined tyranny at risk
of their lives when Western writers, working freely under the
benevolent tolerance of democracy, were delineating subjects
who measured out their lives with coffee spoons. Before the rise
of modernism in the early twentieth century, mainstream Western novelists were often almost obsessively political and social
historians: Tolstoy, Dickens, Balzac, Zola, Cervantes, Stendhal,
Mann. Even between the world wars Joyce, Galsworthy, Waugh,
Mann, and Rolland pursued the novel of society, politics, and
history. In the postwar period, though, le Carré not only swims
against the mainstream of the twentieth-century psychological
and experimental novel, but, as a serious writer of literature rather
than simply a popular entertainer, he is nearly alone in doing so.

In terms of influences and affinities, hints of virtually all the
English literature of adventure and detection appear throughout
his work, for le Carré is deeply educated and a voracious reader.
Certainly, Kipling affected him, as he did most twentieth-century
English writers, for better or worse; Kipling's *Kim* (1904), the
story of the training of a British spy, is particularly important.
Beyond that Dickens's novels obviously loom large in terms of
delineation of society and class as well as being models for plots
rooted in murky and often sinister ambiguity, as with *Bleak
House* and *Great Expectations.* Le Carré's reading background
also obviously included pioneer spy story writer John Buchan as
well as Somerset Maugham's Ashenden stories and, undoubt-

edly, that most important and influential literary influence on all British and American popular literature of detection, espionage, and pure adventure—Sherlock Holmes. The Holmesian penchant for pondering and unraveling the meaning of obscure and complex reality is especially significant. Another important influence in le Carré's case was his study of the German romantics, Goethe and Schiller in particular, in whom he specialized when he took an academically rigorous "First" degree in modern languages at Oxford.

Two other recent English novelists pointed the way in espionage fiction and strongly influenced le Carré: Joseph Conrad and Graham Greene. Conrad's impact is the more significant, because le Carré has acknowledged his debt to that great explorer of international themes and because, of all the Victorian and turn-of-the-century masters of the novel, Conrad comes closest to le Carré in treating espionage directly. *The Secret Agent* and *Under Western Eyes* are major forerunners of le Carré's fiction and virtually the only such works written by an enshrined "great" novelist. Both of these novels, and many other Conrad novels and stories as well, explore themes central to le Carré's fiction: the angst of conflicting loyalties, the corruption of bureaucracy, the tension between the individual and the state, personal betrayal rationalized by misguided idealism, and ultimately the almost naturalist pathos of vulnerable humanity in the grip of amoral and impersonal political and social institutions. Perhaps more important for le Carré is Conrad's refusal to allow political themes to distort art, either by forcing it into a stuffy academic rhetoric or by cheapening it through slick sensationalism. As le Carré admiringly quoted Conrad, the aim of art is "to make you hear, to make you feel, it is before all to make you *see.*"[1]

Greene is an even more immediate and obvious literary antecedent, since his career as an espionage writer overlaps le Carré's, and his later "entertainments," such as *The Comedians* and *Travels with My Aunt,* actually anticipate the world of post–Cold War espionage in which seriocomic regional chaos pre-empts East-West polarities. These are international thrillers in which the fundamental political apposition is no longer the traditional East-West one of le Carré's early novels. Even in his most political works, however, Greene was never given to scrutinizing the Cold War too closely and candidly, probably because of his overt sympathy for communism—particularly in his youth (when he was briefly a member of the Party, probably the only non-Russian novelist of espionage to have that credential). Neither spying per se or spy catching, the heart of the true espionage novel, have ever been central even to the Greene novels most about espionage. Of his best *The Third Man* is a psychological study of postwar corruption, *The Quiet American* a political/sociological discussion of colonialism and revolution in Southeast Asia, and *Our Man in Havana* a charming burlesque of incompetent intelligence operations in Cuba.

One of Greene's late novels, *The Human Factor* (1978), is particularly relevant to le Carré, although by that time the younger writer had been the more productive and successful novelist for fifteen years, and the question of which writer influences the other becomes academic. *The Human Factor* is Greene's version of the notorious defection to Russia in 1963 of British agent Kim Philby, much as *Tinker, Tailor, Soldier, Spy* is le Carré's. Greene's character Maurice Castle is more directly drawn on Philby than Bill Haydon is in le Carré's novel, and *The Human Factor* is, for obvious reasons, far more sympathetic to him than le Carré is to his portrait of the traitor. Haydon is basically despicable, although Smiley, through whom we most thoroughly see him, tries to rationalize Haydon's treason. Like Haydon, Maurice Castle is a British intelligence officer who betrays his country, but Greene makes Castle sympathetic, a man of conscience who commits treason for the woman he loves (whereas Haydon betrays his mistress and his friend to commit treason) and who ends an exile in Moscow, sadly aware of the tyranny of the Russians with whom he has made his ungodly bargain.

If the Cold War is primarily only a stage for such "entertainments" for Graham Greene, it is the arena of human psychological identity for le Carré, for at the heart of the Cold War is the conception of division and, as a corollary of that, of doubling. Every le Carré novel is about people divided against each other and themselves in one way or another. Most obviously, these divisions are political, and the East-West confrontation is the basis of le Carré's books from *Call for the Dead* in 1961 to *Smiley's People* in 1980. With the exception of *The Naive and Sentimental Lover,* all le Carré's novels during that generation range the Soviets on one side and the Western democracies, represented primarily by the British, on the other. These works, which conclude with Smiley's ambivalent triumph in the last volume of *The Quest for Karla* in 1980, present a bleak picture of stalemate between the two major blocs, like the trench warfare of World War I, with intense concentrations of effort and suffering being expended to produce relatively minor overall shifts in power.

Unlike many espionage novelists—Frederick Forsyth, Robert Ludlum, or Ken Follett—who weave plots in which the destiny of the Western world, and therefore all humanity, hinges upon a single operation, often upon the heroism or brilliance of a single spy, le Carré's East-West novels make few claims for the importance of secret agents or their work, on either side. Lost in contemplation of the intelligence and virtue of George Smiley, or the basilisk gaze of Karla fixing his evil eye on the Circus, the reader forgets to ask just how much difference either of these men makes. Smiley, however, knows that it is "sheer pride to think that the whole world depends on one fat spy." Most of the energy of the intelligence apparatus of both sides, in fact, seems to go into struggling with each other. The two finest le Carré novels of this period, *The Spy Who Came in from the Cold* and *Tinker, Tailor, Soldier, Spy,* are about moles, one British and one Russian, and the elaborate efforts necessary to protect the one in the former and to expose the other in the latter. The culmination of the three famous Karla novels, *Smiley's People,* focuses with frightening intensity on the increasingly narrow duel between Smiley and Karla, with the prize being a purely psychological coup for the West. Nothing could be more indicative of the personal nature of the struggle than the fact that the ultimate victory or defeat is measured to a considerable degree by something as symbolic as Karla's throwing away Ann's cigarette lighter, which he took from Smiley when they first locked horns. Without doubt there are major consequences of the webs these men weave, but for the most part they are not explored in le Carré's fiction. Quite the contrary, for the bureaucrats who serve as the liaisons between the Circus and the "overt world," as Ned calls it in the last line of *The Secret Pilgrim,* are so vainglorious and occupied with dignifying the trivial that the reader tends to dismiss their claims about the critical nature of anything.

If, in le Carré's divided world, one truth is that the elaborate intelligence machinery doesn't matter very much, the obverse is that it does—to human beings. One thing le Carré repeatedly points out is that, although institutions may kill for power or pride or sport, people pay in suffering and death. Agents die more often than other people, and often more unpleasantly, but there are plenty of victims in the overt world too. From the boyish German guards whom Leamas and Leiser kill in East Germany (before both men also die) to the agents of the blown networks Haydon betrays to the slaughtered General Vladimir, whose death puts Smiley back on the trail of Karla, intelligence work litters the world indiscriminately with the corpses of the involved and the innocent. A willingness to kill is almost a prerequisite for spying, and Smiley's discomfort about his part in the deaths of Dieter Frey and Bill Haydon may be interpreted as conscience by the reader but is surely weakness by the standards of a hard-shelled intelligence professional like Karla.

Beyond the issue of the effectiveness of intelligence and espionage—and le Carré himself seems to have serious reservations about this in hindsight—lies the more important issue of the Cold War itself as a subject for fiction. A century or more ago politics on the international scale was one of the great themes of fiction, as *War and Peace, The Charterhouse of Parma,* and dozens of other major novels attest. But with the twentieth century serious fiction shifted toward the psychological, the novel of inner rather than outer development. Kafka, Joyce, Lawrence, and Faulkner turned toward the individual mind as the great subject of fiction, and even writers intensely conscious of political forces, such as Camus, tended to treat them primarily as aspects of the self. For writers like Faulkner who still focused on social themes, the sense of community often reduced itself to regionalism, and society became a Mississippi hamlet, a village in Devonshire, or the surrealistic streets of a dozen European cities through which wander Leopold Bloom or Monsieur K. In all these works it is psychology that determines the texture, tone, and appearance of political reality. Reality is what we *think* we see—"the ineluctable modality of the visible," as Joyce calls it when Stephen Dedalus closes his eyes and the physical world ceases to exist. Not only are political forces created by the minds that perceive them, but the true focus of fiction is on the perception itself. The mind shapes the political world.

Le Carré reverses the equation, maintaining that individual human minds and lives are shaped by the political forces that act upon them. There are, to be sure, powerful correspondences between psychologies that produce dramatic similarities in behavior. Hence, Smiley and Karla are doppelgängers—alter egos—one mind shaped by the East, the other by the West, but both the product of systems of thought and social organization that are not dissimilar, in that each exercises a tyranny over the individuals in its grasp. On both sides of the divide individuals struggle to be themselves despite the dispassionate power of the institutions that mold them working relentlessly either to dehumanize them or to crush them. Those institutions are the monolithic concepts of organization which shape our world. Governments, bureaucracies, political and social institutions—all with ritualized patterns of behavior—bind human beings in a vice of convention and restrict creativity, spontaneity, and spiritual fulfillment.

"Spiritual fulfillment" is a tricky concept in le Carré's fiction. Most of his major characters have a clear impulse toward the ideal, whether it be Karla's lockstep ideology or Smiley's benevolent sense of genteel humanism, represented by his idealization of a never-never land of German intellectual romanticism. Yet any formalization of how that idealism might manifest itself in the real world is lacking. One concept, and correspondingly one institution, which has almost no place in le Carré's extended study of the forces shaping the modern world is God and the institutionalized forms of God in religions. In this sense, at least, le Carré's vision is akin to that of a Marxist, since it seems simply to ignore theology as a significant issue in the moral framework of Western civilization in the twentieth century. In none of the fifteen novels that form the le Carré canon do either religion or theological questions play a significant part. Occasionally, religious orientation is mentioned as one of the factors that shape psychology, as in the story of Hansen in *The Secret Pilgrim,* in which the narrator Ned attributes some of the renegade agent's aberration to his Jesuit upbringing (231). Casual attribution, however, does not constitute significance, and there is nothing in le Carré even remotely comparable to the importance of Catholicism to the characters of Evelyn Waugh or Graham Greene.

Lack of religion, however, does not necessarily mean that le Carré is presenting a world of moral nihilism nor that he sees all ideologies as equally morally corrupt in the relativism of the postwar world. Leftist critics who have read into his novels an equivocal and undifferentiated condemnation of both capitalism and communism—and who point with glee to his declaration of a lukewarm socialism in terms of political affiliation—fail to take into account the novelist's overt lifelong affection for England and his bristling contempt for those who betray the country. Surely, le Carré has profound reservations about both the hypocrisies and the occasional brutalities of Western intelligence procedures. Correspondingly, he is often savagely satirical when writing about the British class system, American materialism, and the narrowness of capitalist chauvinism, especially in terms of demonizing the enemy and failing to appreciate his or her virtues. His mockery of the speech and behavior habits of characters as diverse as the oily British clubman Roddy Martindale in *Tinker, Tailor, Soldier, Spy* and the working-class bully-boy Mutt-and-Jeff team of British police brutalists Inspector Bryant and Sergeant Luck in *Our Game* is unequivocal in its condemnation of the defects of Western psychologies gone wrong.

So deft is le Carré in mocking the mannerisms of British class and American classlessness that it often seems that he reserves *all* his deftest barbs for characterizing the hypocrisies, affectations, and duplicities of characters on "our side." Much of this, however, is because for le Carré, as for many writers of espionage fiction, the very definition of "the enemy" is as a faceless unknown—or, in the case of a "mole" like Bill Haydon, unknown as an enemy. One who becomes truly familiar is, almost by definition, no longer an enemy. The problem of identifying with the enemy can make for powerful espionage literature, but it also propels the fiction into the complex area of becoming a psychological study of the spy rather than of the process of spying. This is what happens in the three novels of the Karla Trilogy—*Tinker, Tailor, Soldier, Spy; The Honourable Schoolboy;* and *Smiley's People*—in which the most powerful dramatic nuances are rooted in Smiley's psychological difficulty in pursuing an enemy who increasingly has a human face for him. Similarly, much of the effect of *The Honourable Schoolboy* and *The Little Drummer Girl* derives from the increasing perception by the predatory English agents that their targets—Drake Koh in the former and Khalil in the latter—are human beings whose evil, if not excusable, can be understood as the product of idealism, exaggerated and rationalized, and whose defects are mitigated by human virtues. In short, "they," like "us," are human beings, and the novel moves from being simply a study of the process of detection to one of psychological morality.

Le Carré's willingness to consider the enemy sympathetically, coupled with his deftness in skewering British affection and hypocrisy with the acuity of a master caricaturist, have left him open to charges of calling down a plague upon both East and West alike, of seeing no moral distinction between them. Still, there is no ambivalence about le Carré's preferences. In all his life and writings he has been brutally candid about the wretched quality of communist life as well as communist morals. His own familiarity with the Russians, in particular during his time as an intelligence officer and his studies—as a writer who does scrupulous background research of communist dishonesty and brutality and his contacts as a traveler and a member of the international intellectual community—have made him repeatedly express his recognition of the total failure of communism to produce a successful economic, political, or moral society. Nothing is more representative of le Carré's ultimate willingness to take sides in the Cold War than his "loathing" (le Carré's own word) of the notorious treason of British intelligence officer Kim Philby. This was an attitude that le Carré voiced when Philby defected in 1963, then ten years later in a scathing introduction to *The Philby*

Conspiracy, a book that exhaustively detailed Philby's moral bankruptcy, and more than a decade after that, when le Carré was writing *Our Game,* after the Cold War had sputtered and died. Despite the Roddy Martindales, le Carré unequivocally prefers British morals to Russian.

As for his attitude toward Americans and the position of the United States concerning the Cold War, he is a bit more ambivalent. In *Tinker, Tailor, Soldier, Spy* that staunchest of British spies, Jim Prideaux—who is unquestionably a good man—says of the Americans beside whom he must fight not only the Russians but also the treachery of his own people: "To the west, America . . . full of greedy fools fouling up their inheritance." But Jim, though decent, is also not particularly intelligent and has the moral tunnel vision of a charging John Bull. Furthermore, his experience with Americans, like that of most le Carré characters, has been almost exclusively with the kind of Americans active in intelligence work. Critics of le Carré's caustic treatment of Americans need to consider that, whereas through the author's jaded eyes the reader sees all sorts of conditions of English people—from the foursquare reliability of the retired policeman, Mendel, to the despicable aristocratic robber baron Bradshaw—perforce in *British* novels with *British* settings and characters "foreigners" will only appear in roles that interface with their British counterparts, and those counterparts happen to be spies. Perhaps le Carré doesn't dislike Americans, but only *American spies,* who are logically the most likely to appear in a British spy novel. Those who accuse le Carré of "America bashing" should consider the relevant sections of *A Perfect Spy* in which Magnus Pym, an Englishman betraying his American allies, reflects on the decency of the very folk upon whom he is spying.

Understanding John le Carré

Much of le Carré's apparent antipathy toward not only Americans but also the more objectionable characteristics of the English, too, derives from an aspect of his talent that has often been critically ignored in the rush to pigeonhole him as a writer of espionage thrillers. For John le Carré, along with many of the greatest of English novelists, is preeminently a social commentator and writer of novels of manners. Like Fielding, Austen, Dickens, and Trollope, he is concerned with establishing patterns of behavior and examining the ways in which an individual character does or does not fit those patterns.

As is the case with many other modern British novelists—notably Hardy, Lawrence, Forster, and Waugh—study of patterns of behavior often boils down to examination of the English class system, that pervasive milieu that governs all British life and is inseparable from any consideration of it in literature. In this matter le Carré's ambivalence, given his singular upbringing, is particularly significant. With his father as a role model—one that he fortunately largely rejected before reaching manhood—le Carré found himself straddling the class borders between gentility and social nonentity. With the keen eye of a natural observer, or a spy, he noted each nuance of class distinction, from the accent of a Cockney policeman to the clubby jargon of an Oxonian cabinet minister, and eventually carried it into a sweeping portrait of British class behavior. Nor is his keen eye for class affectations and mannerisms simply a gift for one-sided caricature: le Carré's most important characters often transcend class distinctions. Smiley is a gentleman, but his background is vague; certainly, he is "less well-born" than his wife, Ann, who is the daughter of an earl. The same amorphous quality characterizes the class standing of Charlie in *The Little Drummer Girl,* Barley Blair in *The Russia House,* and Jerry Westerby in *The Honourable Schoolboy.* Only with Magnus Pym in *A Perfect Spy* does the author reveal virtually *everything* important about who a character is and where he came from; of course, that is because Magnus is a fusion of le Carré himself and his father, Ronnie Cornwell.

Class is important, but still it is only an arena of social Darwinism in which human psychology develops. Most of le Carré's main themes are psychological. The leitmotifs are predictable, often in an almost classically Freudian sense: betrayal, fatherhood, search for identity, fear of failure, alienation, and alter egos—already a considerable body of critical literature traces each of these themes through the novelist's work. Despite the diversity of le Carré's characters, settings, and plots, there is a similar pattern to each of his novels.

The protagonist of each is an essentially moral human being, be it George Smiley or Charlie or Tim Cranmer, in *Our Game.* He or she is "moral" in existential terms, capable of making moral choices and believing that those choices matter, which certainly does *not* mean that the choices will be morally correct. Some characters, like Magnus in *A Perfect Spy,* will clearly choose wrongly; others, like Cranmer, seem to choose well. Because of the confusing, threatening, and ambiguous nature of the political and social world through which this character moves, he or she is a spy, a role that discourages moral behavior. This spying is usually literal in le Carré's fiction—that is, the person spies deliberately and by profession. Inevitably, the person who *spies* becomes a *spy;* the trade is corrupting and, ultimately, morally compromising. Even as decent a character as George Smiley is eventually compromised, as the bittersweet ending of *Smiley's People* makes clear. Worse, the spy finds that the compromise may have been futile, or the questions of right and wrong are so blurred in the confusing world of espionage that moral distinctions become ambivalent.

One moral distinction that is very clear in le Carré's novels is that between individuals and institutions. If people hold to recognition of the value of human beings, and of love between them, then moral behavior is possible. Smiley's love for his faithless wife, Ann, Charlie's for Joseph, Barley Blair's for Katya, in *The Russia House*—all have the potential for transcending the terrible soullessness of a world in which institutions lack souls and people can only protect themselves by clinging to one another as Matthew Arnold implores them to do in "Dover Beach."

A plea for the simplicity of human love and commitment in apposition to a world of ritualized institutions that tyrannize individuals and drive such love to the wall may seem a singular dominant theme for a novelist who has made his reputation as a writer of espionage thrillers. But then, as every reader of his fiction knows, John le Carré can hardly be pigeonholed as a writer of anything but quality. C. P. Snow, a British novelist of no small reputation also concerned with the state of vulnerable humanity threatened by impersonal institutions and ideologies, predicted early in John le Carré's career that the young writer of thrillers would become, simply, "one of the best contemporary novelists." Few readers would deny the fulfillment of that prophecy.

CHAPTER THREE

Loomings

Call for the Dead and *A Murder of Quality*

The majority of John le Carré's millions of readers today can scarcely remember a time when he was not famous or when each new book was not read as part of an ongoing series with many recognizable characters and settings and familiar approaches to the subject of espionage. There was, of course, such a time, and *Call for the Dead* (1961) and *A Murder of Quality* (1962) are products of it. Of the two *A Murder of Quality* is a readable detective story, a cut above Agatha Christie—professional, enjoyable, but short on substantiality. *Call for the Dead,* however, is what cinematographers would call "the establishing shot," the critical introductory image that sets the tone—in this case for the most important series in the history of espionage fiction. No one had any such idea when it was published in 1961, least of all its thirty-year-old author, who wrote the novel commuting on the train and who expected to continue to earn his modest living at the Foreign Office for a long time. *The Spy Who Came in from the Cold* made John le Carré's fortune in 1963, but all the singular elements of his dark vision were formulated two or three years earlier with his first novel.

Call for the Dead

The analogy of the cinematic "establishing shot," which sets the tone of a film, is particularly appropriate to *Call for the Dead,*

for the pervasive ambiance of the novel—one of plodding meth-
odology masking covert brutality, of shabby quotidian existence
masking issues of horrible import—grew out of the author's
frustration with the bureaucratic drudgery of his work in British
Intelligence, MI5. "I began writing because I was going mad with
boredom," he remembered a third of a century later."[1]

Everything in *Call for the Dead* hinges on the importance of
that which is apparently trivial. The critical phone call that the
murdered man requested the night before his death, thereby
indicating that he did not plan to die or commit suicide, is only
one example of the work's compacting great significance into
unassuming packages. The whole novella itself is the prime
example of this, for it is deceptively slight. Yet in a hundred and
twenty-five pages it manages to present or suggest most of the
major themes of le Carré's Cold War fiction, introduce several of
the most important characters of that oeuvre, and suggest that the
murder of Samuel Fennan is only the tip of a rotten iceberg of
espionage, treachery, and murder. In another ten or more novels
le Carré will expose and explore that iceberg, spinning story after
story out of this slim volume. *The Spy Who Came in from the Cold*
is the story of a British plot against the detestable murderer
Mundt, who begins his career as a double agent during *Call for
the Dead.* Smiley's guilt and regret over his killing of Dieter Frey
in *Call for the Dead* will haunt him through every story that
follows. The trauma to the Circus of discovering this first security
leak in Elsa Fennan will expand into the paranoia of Control's
vendetta against Fiedler in *The Spy* then poison the atmosphere
of *Tinker, Tailor, Soldier, Spy* and carry over into later novels.
Most important of all, perhaps, is the theme established in *Call*

for the Dead that the evils of the present derive from the evils of the past. The deaths of this novel are rooted in the Nazi death camps, and Elsa Fennen's fears and Dieter Frey's hopes for a new order to replace the savagery of the old triggers the new round of plotting, betrayal, and killing which will mark every novel not only of the Circus cycle but of all le Carré's writing. Elsa and Dieter are desperately trying to find rebirth in the postwar world, but the unresolved horrors of modern history rise up to strike them down. It is not coincidental that le Carré did not—as careless readers often think he did—put an article at the beginning of his title. *Call for the Dead* may well be an imperative, and it could serve as a roll call summoning the ghosts of the past, like Hamlet's father, to new reckonings in the present.

This is the novel that introduces George Smiley and adds to the caravan of memorable characters in English literature. Smiley's character was based on several men whom le Carré knew,[2] perhaps most directly the author's friend and fellow intelligence officer John Bingham, also a writer who "looked a bit like Smiley and wrote his thrillers in the lunch hour."[3] All the major traits of Smiley's personality and psychology are established in *Call for the Dead*.[4] So is a good deal of his background, which is perhaps more important in this novel than any other. As *Call for the Dead* details, Smiley would have been a university professor of German literature, passing on to the future his love for the lush idealism of Heine and the German romantics. The opening chapter of the novel, "A Brief History of George Smiley," is a tidy thumbnail introduction to him.[5] He is by nature a shy, scholarly man, unsuited to action and most comfortable channeling his passion and love of beauty vicariously in the classroom. But the

Nazis and the war tore him out of that ivory tower and forced him to embrace life in the real world. It also led him to try to embrace love and beauty the same way, by idolizing and marrying the beautiful, aristocratic Ann Sercomb. For the rest of his professional life he is compelled to wander in that real world, yearning for the idealized world of art and scholarship, trying doggedly to carry its values into his work and his life. Repeatedly in future novels he will cling plaintively to totemic remnants of that vanished life that the Circus lured him from with the siren call of duty, from the copy of Grimmelshausen's *Simplicissimus* which he is about to sell in *Tinker, Tailor, Soldier, Spy* (and, in a Freudian lapse of memory, leaves at his club) to the delicate ceramic shepherdess whose beauty reminds him of Ann.

It is the dichotomy between Ann's amoral establishment hauteur and Smiley's vulnerable unaristocratic morality which lays the groundwork for a study of the debilitating effect of class consciousness on the English character which will pervade all of le Carré's books, from the sinister treachery of upper-class Bill Haydon's betrayal not only of his class but also of his country in *Tinker, Tailor, Soldier, Spy* to Jonathan Pine's compulsive need for social acceptance which informs the action of *The Night Manager.*

No le Carré character's life so represents the damage of class consciousness as does that of George Smiley, and yet no character's class is as difficult to define. Despite his insistent lack of glamour (like "a bullfrog in a sou'wester"), his shyness, and his total inability to plug into the mainstream of camaraderie, which signals success in the modern world, Smiley brings to the espionage business two qualities that protect him through life and eventually bring him qualified victory, both in *Call for the Dead* and in all his later battles for the British Intelligence Service. Those qualities are a penetrating intelligence and an absolute refusal to play the public relations games that characterize all his superiors and most of his colleagues. From this novel's media-conscious Maston, whose greatest qualification for the job of British intelligence chief seems to be that he is rumored to be "the first man to have played power tennis at Wimbledon," to the technological administrators who will take over in the wake of the failures described in *The Russia House,* the men at the top are slick manipulators marked only by ambition, whose sole facility is for looking good. Smiley looks terrible, but he solves cases. As is easy for both the readers and his adversaries to forget, he also has good fundamental survival skills, nowhere exhibited more dramatically than when he is about to open the door of his own house and has a dangerous intruder open it before him then saves himself by claiming to be dropping off "Mr. Smiley's laundry."

There is a third quality that is less obvious—at least in *Call for the Dead*—and that is Smiley's decency and capacity for loyalty. As the opening chapter makes clear, British society is flabbergasted by the beautiful and wealthy Ann's marrying so unlikely a man, but Ann knows as well as the reader will the depths of goodness in him. Nor does she ever lose her respect for Smiley or her need for him. She knows, perhaps, that it is her twisted psychology that drives her to other men, but her appreciation of Smiley's strength and love will keep her asking him to take her back. Years in their future as a couple, in *Smiley's People,* it is he, not she, who will end the relationship. Smiley's decency is, in the long run, his most valuable weapon as a spy, for it binds to him men and women who will *not* betray him or shortchange him professionally for advancement or appearance. In *Call for the Dead* it gains Smiley the invaluable support of Mendal and Guillam. In the future it will bring the love of a few other staunch loyalists who will be the weapons he will use to bring down Karla. "Smiley's people" are the salt of the earth. Often unpretentious, like Mendel, they, like the "proles" in *1984,* are the hope of Western civilization. Actually, considering his unprepossessing appearance, Smiley himself is tough, if not physically skilled. As the laundry incident indicates, his reflexes are good, and he is not afraid to confront even such thugs as the intimidating garage owner Adam Scarr. Before the case is solved he bounces back from a bad beating and manages to kill his younger, stronger adversary Dieter Frey, although whether his skill has anything to do with it is a moot point.

Smiley is the unlikely representative of the good in one of the great polarities of le Carré's writing—the disparity between the virtue of the individual and the corruption of the general, particularly when that "general" is represented by an institution like the Circus. The Circus here and throughout is an organization staffed by many good people—Guillam, Samuel Fennan, and Smiley himself—which is empowered to fight the good fight. Often, however, the Circus fumbles or actually does wrong, because power corrupts, and institutional power especially corrupts, and, when it corrupts almost automatically, it does so under the deceptive guise of cooperation.

Almost as dangerous as the celebration of the institution is the celebration of idealistic concepts in whose name evil may be justified. In *Call for the Dead* this is represented by Dieter Frey's communism and vision of a Europe reborn in inspirational splendor in the glory of socialism. Dieter has, of course, done what most idealists in le Carré have done; he has substituted his own will for the dream, becoming the dictator not only of Else Fennan's heart but of all the disciples who come under his charismatic spell. Collective idealism, suffering from its abstraction and lack of the strength of individual love, for le Carré is susceptible to degeneration into demagoguery. The apostles of communal philosophies must ultimately control the implementation of those philosophies by becoming tyrants and tyrants based on hero worship. Students of Lenin, Stalin, Mao, Castro, and virtually every other twentieth-century dictator would agree.

The charismatic ideologue Dieter Frey is the Byronic heroic figure of *Call for the Dead,* "the living component of all our romantic dreams, he stood at the mast with Conrad, sought the lost Greece with Byron and with Goethe visited the shades of classical and medieval hells" (104). And he is the symbol of every communist "man on horseback" of the postwar world who sacrificed humanity to ideology and made idealism an exercise in egotism. "He was the same improbably romantic with the magic of a charlatan; the same unforgettable figure which had struggled over the ruins of Germany, implacable of purpose, satanic in fulfillment, dark and swift like the Gods of the North" (106).

What is remarkable about *Call for the Dead* is that, in spite of its comprehensive introduction of many of the major themes of le Carré's Cold War fiction, it is far more a detective story than a novel of espionage. This is most apparent considering that, unlike the rest of Smiley's Cold War fiction, there is almost no delineation of the character and ideology of the enemy. The communist menace is almost entirely embodied in the characters of Dieter Frey and Hans-Dieter Mundt (their sharing of the same given name points to their dual nature as aspects of the same nature, Frey representing the deceptively seductive mind of communism, Mundt the sinister muscle). It is not accidental that their code names are "Mr. Robinson" and "Freitag" (German for "Friday"), drawn from *Robinson Crusoe*'s pairing of the brilliant manipulator/visionary narrator and his primitive, muscle-bound servant. The fundamental motivation for Else Fennan's treason is personal love of Frey, although the fear that drives her to that attraction is bound up in her oppression by fascism. Mundt, who will become so much the two-faced symbol of both communist bureaucracy and the corrupt willingness of the Circus to use a vicious tool to subvert it, in *Call for the Dead* is largely a faceless villain who kills and escapes (although le Carré will suggest in *The Spy Who Came in from the Cold* that the reason for his suspicious escape is an unholy bargain with Control). The accent in this book is on detecting and then tracking a killer. Through a typical le Carré twist the "bad" killer Mundt escapes and is replaced by the "good" killer Frey, thereby making the final confrontation with Smiley far more meaningful than the simple bringing to justice of a criminal. The complexities of the novel of espionage, however, are more suggested than inherent in the close of *Call for the Dead,* as Smiley broods over Frey's ambiguous death. For the time being a crime has been solved, and the victorious detective has possession of the field.

The plot of *Call for the Dead* focuses on an apparently simple paradox of the sort that impelled a dozen Sherlock Holmes adventures: an apparent suicide has left orders that he receive a wake-up call from a telephone service. But with proper Holmesian eloquence—through the rhetoric of verifiable objective particulars—the dead here speak with more veracity than the voices of lying appearance. That the suicide is that of a compromised Foreign Office official, that it seems that the Circus is trying to cover up the whole unpleasant incident, that the dead official's wife has a record of pro-communist sympathizing, that a former agent of George Smiley's who is now a communist—through a plethora of similar "coincidences," not the least of which is the mysterious "call for the dead," Smiley determines not only that murder has been done, that the Circus is both corrupt and inept, but that he himself has been forced to kill a friend whom he once trusted and who trusted him. In short, that the spying life is a messy and ambiguous one in which things are often not what they seem—including oneself. Feeling how weary, stale, flat, and unprofitable to him seem all the uses of this world, Smiley refuses to "bury" the case and resigns from the Circus in a sort of muted protest. He will return.

A Murder of Quality

If *Call for the Dead* owes much in terms of plot development to the ingenuity of Arthur Conan Doyle, le Carré's next novel, *A Murder of Quality,* owes even more, for the English "public" school setting (meaning a private boarding school in England) might have been drawn from Sherlock Holmes's cases at the Priory School or Huxtables. *A Murder of Quality* is a far simpler novel and, entertaining as it is, requires little more than a mention in a brief study of le Carré's major fiction. It is at heart a fine example of the "tea cozy" school of mannerly English detective story writing, right down to the setting of a snobbish elite boarding school for the training of the aristocracy, the villain in the person of a sophisticated and traditional master who turns out to be a velvet Satan, and the cast of hearty English schoolboys proffering information that may or may not be relevant. One thinks at once of Dorothy Sayers's *Gaudy Night* and Sherlock Holmes in "The Adventure of the Priory School," but the prototypes are numerous. The real original of the public school Carne in this novel was Sherborne, where le Carré was bitterly unhappy as a child, and probably to a lesser extent Eton, where he taught modern languages, although le Carré's account of Eton's "barbarisms" was tempered by respect for its quality. Years after writing *A Murder of Quality,* in an introduction to the Lamplighter Edition of the novel, le Carré suggested the sources for Carne: "an outrage at my Sherborne schooling, a fascination with the mores of the Etonian class, an attraction to it all, a revulsion from it, a bestiary of frightening adults drawn from the timid chambers of my institutional and largely parentless childhood, and a spiritual brutality towards young minds that in this far-from-perfect story takes the form of bloody violence."[6] English boarding schools as cruel crucibles forming the character of British heroes (and villains) have figured in English literature from *Tom Brown's School Days* to *David Copperfield.* The setting finds its way directly into le Carré's fiction not only as Carne in *A Murder of Quality* but as Thursgood's in *Tinker, Tailor, Soldier, Spy.* With Carne even more than with Thursgood's, the emphasis is on tradition and class, and the horror of murder is intensified in contrast to its pristine setting. The venerable traditions and rules of Carne are only a "whited sepulchre," and the leonine head of the guilty master Fielding reveals the skull beneath the skin in the traditional final confrontation scene in which Smiley proves irrevocably that he must be the murderer of Stella Rode, the apparently virtuous wife of an unpopular master. That the crime was one of lust as well as self-protection and that Stella herself was a corrupt betrayer add to the impression of the genteel Smiley stripping the veneer from the sanctuaries of the upper class to reveal the rot beneath.

Here for the first time in le Carré's fiction the author's singular stance vis-à-vis the British class struggle reveals itself. Smiley, who has the manners of a true gentleman but whose standing as a member of the upper classes is ambiguous and tenuous at best, becomes a social naturalist, tearing off the masks of gentility and revealing the bestial and basic impulses hidden by apparent propriety. The revelation of Fielding's guilt is interesting in terms of its relation to Smiley's victories in other novels. In the final confrontation scene Fielding, who has been reserved and gentlemanly watching Smiley unroll the evidence that will doom him, suddenly cracks and screams, "My God, man, I'll hang!" as his accuser is obviously stricken with the implications of the human consequences of his detective work. The fact that Stella Rode was a scheming virago preying on Fielding makes the master's fate especially painful to the kindly Smiley.

The web of deceit in *A Murder of Quality* is intricately tangled and the intelligence that Smiley displays in practicing the art of Sherlockian deduction in unraveling it is immense, but never again would a le Carré protagonist play on so small a field and with such limited international implications.[7] Ahead lay novels in which the fate of the world was, if not at stake, constantly a consideration. For Smiley, however, the pattern of hollow and painful victories persists through future novels. With the exception of the sui generis romance *The Naive and Sentimental Lover* and *A Small Town in Germany,* le Carré ends the other seven Smiley novels from *Call for the Dead* to *Smiley's People* with Smiley presiding over a scene that *should* be one of victory for him and therefore for "the Service" as well. Yet each triumph proves to be not only Pyrrhic but sometimes disastrous. The unexpected slaughter of Leamas ends *The Spy Who Came in from the Cold,* the capture of Leiser *The Looking-Glass War,* and the death of Jerry Westerby and betrayal by the CIA spoil Smiley's triumph in catching Nelson Ko in *The Honourable Schoolboy.* Whether he is playing detective or spy, or usually both at the same time, there are no moments of unqualified triumph for Smiley but only the bittersweet compensation of having pursued the truth and played fairer than his quarry. Sherlock Holmes and Watson may savor a sense of righteousness upon bringing miscreants to their just rewards; Smiley feels only an awareness of the price they, and he, pay for the victory.

Always, too, Smiley is afflicted with the capacity to see both sides of any issue and to recognize the best impulses that led his adversaries to their worst deeds. In both *Call for the Dead* and *A Murder of Quality* this is the case, although neither novel offers the kind of scope which allows Smiley the real contemplation of the enemy's virtues which he will develop in his struggle with Karla. Still, he recognizes that in trapping Fielding he has brought a man of some character to his destruction, and it pains him. The death of Dieter Frey is an even more grievous victory for Smiley (and it may have much to do with his resigning from the Circus after that case.) He is almost willing to see Dieter as the visionary hero and himself as the villain for slaying the dreamer. "Dieter, mercurial, absolute, had fought to build a civilisation. Smiley, rationalistic, protective, had fought to prevent him. 'Oh, God,' said Smiley aloud, 'who was then the gentleman . . .?'" (118). Smiley is echoing an old working-class ditty sung by British levelers to mock the aristocracy: "When Adam delved and Eve span, who was then the gentleman?" What masochistic Smiley, always ready to take blame upon his conscience, has forgotten is that Dieter didn't die for trying to "build a civilisation"; he died for murdering a woman who trusted him. But, then, Smiley can hardly accept the moral responsibility for that.

Thematically, this painful ambivalence of resolution is what ties these initial novels together as an introduction to le Carré's canon and, particularly, to the Smiley novels. *Call for the Dead* introduces George Smiley as a spy who detects, *A Murder of Quality* introduces him as a detective taking a holiday from spying. Both works establish him as a humanist compelled to function as a ruthless naturalist but suffering existentialist pangs of remorse at the angst of the human condition.

CHAPTER FOUR

The Spy Who Came in from the Cold

It is no more possible to deal completely objectively with *The Spy Who Came in from the Cold* (1963) as a work of art than with *Uncle Tom's Cabin, Gone with the Wind,* or *The Godfather.* Each has a popular profile so massive as to obscure aesthetic questions. *The Spy Who Came in from the Cold* is the most popular and influential spy novel of all literary history in any language. With more than forty million copies in print world-wide, it continues to sell briskly in more than twenty languages and is now required reading for college courses in both popular culture and "serious" literature. Its immediate success on publication in 1963 transformed John le Carré in a few months from an unknown to a writer of international acclaim, rivaled in the espionage genre only by Ian Fleming, whose death the next year left le Carré virtually unchallenged.[1] Among serious writers who had essayed the genre, only Graham Greene and Eric Ambler merited comparison; Ambler had written nothing but spy thrillers, but his best work was well in the past, and he was never a serious challenge for consideration as anything but high-grade entertainment; Greene, for years a perennial contender for the Nobel Prize, had written only a handful of true espionage novels, most of which on examination proved to be "something else."

Fleming's spectacular popularity undoubtedly fueled le Carré's, as did the aggressive Cold Warrior charisma of John F.

Kennedy, the Cuban missile crisis, the furor over the defection of Kim Philby, the economic and social success of West Germany amid rising pressure for German reunification, as well as such subtle influences as the fortuitous sponsorship of Graham Greene, whose declaration that *The Spy Who Came in from the Cold* was "the best spy story I have ever read" (prominently printed on the cover of both the hardback and paperback editions of the novel) lifted the opprobrium of intellectuals usually reserved for "cheap popular" fiction of the James Bond stripe.[2] Certainly, it was a very fine piece of fiction. There are few first novels—and, considering the author's obscurity after publishing only two slight novellas, this was a "first novel"—which can print on their dust jackets not only Greene's encomium but raves by Daphne du Maurier ("I think the book is first-rate"), Alec Waugh ("An absolute spellbinder. I could not put it down until I had read the last page"), and J. B. Priestley ("Superbly constructed, with an atmosphere of chilly hell").[3] It was the power of the James Bond phenomenon, however, which made *The Spy Who Came in from the Cold* such an the extraordinary success and spotlighted a brilliant work that might not even have found a publisher in a less spy-conscious decade. A third of a century later it is difficult to remember the frantic "Bondo-mania," as it was labeled in the tabloids, which swept the Western world in the early 1960s. Sean Connery as Bond was on the cover of *Life,* and Fleming's latest, *On Her Majesty's Secret Service* (1962), topped the best-seller lists.

The perpetuation of the Bond books after Ian Fleming's death in 1964 (by the expedient of "franchising" the character to mystery writer John Gardener) and the endless procession of blandly photogenic clotheshorse Bonds in films after Connery refused to continue in the role have accented the purely caricature nature of Fleming's superspy hero. In these tawdry spin-offs the Bond character continues, painted in broad cartoon brush strokes as Fleming originally created him. Tireless sexual athlete, world-class gourmet (despite a British civil servant salary), expert in repartee, master of a cornucopia of tricky technology, specialist in dozens of ways of killing, and ultimately as invulnerable to shot and shell (not to mention slings and arrows) as Dick Tracy, Bond was strictly the "puff piece" of spy fiction—but a puff piece made highly visible by success and promotion.

With Bond swollen out of all proportion in the media, the stage was set for the corrective antidote of Alec Leamas, a "realistic" spy. Leamas is gritty even in comparison with le Carré's other fictional spies, notably George Smiley. Whereas Smiley had a deliberately obscure background and lacked so-phisticated glibness, there was always an urbane upper-class aura of good manners about him. A man who took a first at Oxford in baroque German literature, who married a gorgeous aristocrat, and who sat at the right hand of Control, the Circus's prince of darkness, was hardly a "common man," despite his rumpled, but hardly off-the-rack, suits. Leamas, however, is the genuine article, right out of the corner pub. Facility with languages is a prerequisite for spy work, but he picked his up in his father's machine shop in Holland. Failed as a very small shopkeeper, Leamas is the epitome of the Circus "fieldman," a nuts-and-bolts agent who works in enemy territory. Divorced and out of touch with his family, short, chunky, and powerful, in polyester suits, he is a hard drinker, able to belt back enough to be convincing as an alcoholic. Significantly, he is totally unintellectual. He works slowly and methodically, with a plodding by-the-numbers memory and solid but unimaginative "tradecraft." He virtually never reads for pleasure and is suspicious of those, like Liz Gold, who do. He is growly, laconic, awkward in social situations, and gruffly defensive to compensate. The failure of his German network, which reaches its violent end as Karl Riemeck is shot before his eyes, is the apotheosis of a lifetime of petty failure which has left him cynical, bitter, and tired.[4]

By the time he falls into Control's spidery web, Leamas is damaged lower-class goods. Control is hardly asking him to stretch his personality in playing a down-and-out malcontent. Leamas as a belligerent alcoholic—the kind of man who might be caught with his hand in the till of the Banking Section, where he has been exiled for incompetence—is not too far a cry from the real Leamas: even within the seedy world of spies, an also-ran. So perfect is Leamas for the part that even the reader, who is partner from the beginning to Control's plan to use Leamas for a clandestine scheme, ostensibly to undermine Hans-Dieter Mundt, is likely to forget that everything Leamas does is part of a deliberate deception. It can be argued, of course, that the gritty believability of Leamas's act as one of life's surly rejects is simply that, brilliant acting, but le Carré gives more than enough information about the man, both in terms of his personal history and his thoughts, to reveal that Control is only typecasting when he chooses him to play the part of a sullen working-class "bloke" come to the butt ends of his days and therefore vulnerable to foreign overtures.

Much of the genius of *The Spy Who Came in from the Cold* lies in this careful characterization of a man psychologically on the skids. The interview in chapter 2 in which Control asks

Leamas to go out "into the cold" one more time is sufficiently vague in terms of specifics so that the agent's subsequent behavior is always problematical. Exactly what Control wants him to do is so vaguely defined that for much of the novel it is unclear whether he is doing it or not. How much of the highly convincing part he plays—the alcoholism, the belligerence, the attack on the grocer, prison—is really an act? The reader, too, is out "in the cold," for le Carré doesn't succumb to the temptation to give any further hints that the degeneration of Leamas is always an act. After the end of chapter 2, when Control is about to explain how Leamas can "take a swing at Mundt" (27), Leamas's "decline" is described so objectively that it is easy to forget that it is all part of a carefully planned plot. Perhaps, after his interview with Control, Leamas really did go to pieces, land in jail, and then end up as a defector betraying secrets to the Abteilung, or whoever it is he is betraying secrets to, since that is also obscure.

One part of Leamas's behavior which turns out not to be an act is his affair with Liz Gold, and it raises an important question about *The Spy Who Came in from the Cold* which most commentators seem not to have noticed. This is the part that Liz plays in the elaborate scheme to discredit Mundt's pursuer, Fiedler, and thereby preserve Mundt as a valuable "mole" within the Deutschrepublik's Communist Party. Liz becomes the ultimate damning witness against Leamas at his trial in East Germany, and the prosecutor, Karden, puts her on the stand and elicits testimony from her which demonstrates that Leamas was a plant. But, presumably, Liz was not part of Control's original plot, and it is not clear just what sort of evidence the "Mundt forces" might have produced to implicate Leamas without Liz. Liz is clearly not knowingly complicitous in discrediting Leamas, and yet Control and Mundt could hardly count on her being attracted to him or he to her. Perhaps Liz and Leamas's affair was simply an accident—fortuitous for Control, who exploits it pragmatically, but unnecessary to his scheme in view of other implicating evidence. Leamas certainly believes this in the end, for he tells Liz in his final explanation, "They only had to put you and me in contact, even for a day, it didn't matter, then afterwards they could call on you, send you the money, make it look like an affair even if it wasn't" (243). Love, it seems, like other human weaknesses, plays into the bastards' hands.

The role Liz plays raises another disturbing question about the depth of Control's plot, and that is the degree to which Smiley is not only aware of it—and he clearly is—but actually involved in it. It is Smiley who goes to Liz after Leamas has been taken to the Continent and offers her consolation, leaving his card with her should she want to contact him. But it is just this contact, particularly with Smiley, which the defense counsel Karden uses to discredit Leamas and Fiedler at Mundt's trial. Yet Control claims, and it appears earlier in the book, that Smiley refused to have anything to do with the original apparent scheme to "get Mundt," although Smiley has every reason to loathe Mundt, who nearly had him killed during the investigation of the murder of Samuel Fennan in *Call for the Dead;* surely, Smiley would have disapproved even more of the deeper plot to discredit Fiedler and protect Mundt. On the other hand, Smiley is far too clever a field man not to know that visiting Liz would put Leamas in great danger. Also, it is Smiley who waits on the far side of the Berlin Wall to pull Leamas, and presumably Liz, after the trap has been sprung, which strongly suggests that Smiley is thoroughly implicated in Control's deception.

Whatever part Liz plays in the ultimate destruction of the disaffected strawman Leamas has created, her main role in the novel is to develop and modify the monolithic rock of Leamas's pedestrian psychology. At the beginning of *The Spy Who Came in from the Cold* Leamas seems professionally and personally burned out. The shooting of Riemeck marks the end for him not only as an effective agent but also as a feeling human being. Significantly, he attributes the death of Riemeck to "that damned woman," that is to Riemeck's falling in love and taking a mistress, whom Leamas now wishes were dead (as, indeed, she will be soon, at Mundt's bidding). More important, Leamas senses, he has been "slowing down" for a long time, losing the ability not only to react to life but to care about it. Liz has given him a new ability to care, he realizes, just before he is about to be shipped off to Germany for the "ultimate interrogation."

> He knew then what it was that Liz had given him; the thing he would have to go back and find if ever he got home to England; it was the caring about little things—the faith in ordinary life; that simplicity that made you break up a bit of bread into a paper bag, walk down to the beach and throw it to the gulls. It was this respect for triviality which he had never been allowed to possess; whether it was bread for the sea gulls or love, whatever it was he would go back and find it. (109)

He will not, of course, go back and find it, and that is primarily due to Control, the most controversial character in the novel. The man's eponymous title is only one aspect of his sinister anonymity. Actually, in all of le Carré's fiction there is not one other major character about whom so little is known to the reader. Leamas suggests that Control used to be an Oxford don and is married to a mousy little woman who thinks that her husband works for the Coal Board. A little more information is available in other novels, including continued mention of his addiction to foul lemon jasmine tea, but in *The Spy Who Came in from the Cold* he has all the personality of an administrative robot. Except that he gets Leamas killed, and the real question is whether it was done at his direction or at least with his tacit acceptance. Without any doubt he sends the man out as the bait in a highly dangerous operation about which Leamas is not only uninformed but misinformed. Control betrays Leamas to the media to force him to go to East Germany for interrogation, and there is no evidence that he intervenes to save his man. One very cynical interpretation of the end of *The Spy Who Came in from the Cold* is that Mundt, the Jew-baiting Nazi whose judgment on Liz is "She's trash, just like Fiedler," saves her out of some atavistic sense of obligation to Leamas, perhaps even despite Control's instructions to the contrary.

It is impossible to decide on the basis of the chaotic and violent ending of *The Spy Who Came in from the Cold* whether Control allows, or even orders, the death of Leamas or Liz, or both. Perhaps even a bizarre accident or lack of communication is responsible. Regardless, their deaths are the result of the profound disregard for not only human life but also human decency which characterizes Control throughout. This is the man who in his opening interview with Leamas justifies the wickedness that *good* men do (meaning himself) by saying: "We do disagreeable things so that ordinary people here and elsewhere can sleep safely in their beds at night. . . Of course, we occasionally do very wicked things" (23). This philosophy will be exactly repeated in slightly different words by the real target of Control's scheme, Jens Fiedler, the dedicated communist who is the head of East German counterintelligence. The "ordinary people" of whom Control speaks turn out to be Leamas, and we are not ever sure if Leamas finally condemns Control for the way he has been used and finally destroyed.

The foil for Control is Fiedler, not Mundt, who is simply Control's alter ego and a thinly sketched one at that. Fiedler, the brilliant ferret of the East German Abteilung, is honest where Mundt is corrupt. He is superficially an attractive character, for two powerful factors incline the reader to sympathize with him. First, as a Jew and an honest man, he is the target of the vicious hatred of the anti-Semitic Mundt, and, second, Leamas likes him because he thinks he recognizes in Fiedler a fellow professional and a kindred spirit. As Fiedler grills Leamas in a cushy holding facility deep in the Prussian forest, his intelligence and forthrightness impress his prisoner, and Leamas comes to see these interrogations as dialectical conversations between two honest brokers seeking the truth.

Fiedler, of course, has deliberately encouraged Leamas to think this way, but the command of dialectic is Fiedler's alone. It is at this point that le Carré most radically deviates from the standard spy discourse, in which a stupid and brutish thug trades one-line repartee with a quick-witted but temporarily captured agent. Leamas may not be truly stupid, but he is completely lost in abstract intellectual discussion. Fiedler, however, "loved to ask questions. Sometimes, because he was a lawyer, he asked them for his own pleasure alone, to demonstrate the discrepancy between evidence and perfective truth. He possessed, however, that persistent inquisitiveness which for journalists and lawyers is an end in itself" (142). Still, Leamas can do business with him, and the subsequent revelation of Mundt's corruption and personal ugliness incline him as well as the reader to see Fiedler as a victim, even something akin to a hero. The film version of *The Spy Who Came in from the Cold,* starring Richard Burton very effectively as Leamas, was generally letter faithful to the book. Shot in bleak black-and-white, it effectively replicated the grim, gray tone of the novel. One effect of this naturalistic leveling was to distort the character of Fiedler by giving the impression that he and Leamas are very much birds of a feather. The question of how Fiedler "ought" to be viewed is tricky, and director Martin Ritt's misapprehension is understandable. After all, Leamas is seduced into softening his attitude toward the man, despite knowing Fiedler's capacity for viciousness, and Liz describes him late in the novel as "kind and decent" (246).

To see Fiedler as anything but a ruthless ideologue is to misunderstand the character completely. Everything Leamas knows about the man is testimony to his brutality. This is the Fiedler le Carré's omniscient (and trustworthy) narrative persona describes as "remorseless in the destruction of others" and "animal-like." This is the Fiedler who tortured one of Peter Guillam's agents nearly to death and whom Leamas describes to Peters as "a savage little bastard." Most significantly, the real Fiedler is a self-professed Stalinist who clearly understands the viciousness not only of communism's means but also of its ends.

He is proud of his willingness to quote Stalin, although it is not "fashionable" even in Russia, and believes that "a movement which protects itself against counterrevolution can hardly stop at the exploitation—or the elimination, Leamas—of a few individuals" (143). His voice is really that of Karla (who virtually never speaks, despite his centrality to several le Carré novels), and to a lesser extent that of Dieter Frey of *Call for the Dead:* the first sends his wife to death for a cause; the second murders his lover Elsa Fennen for one. These men are neither "immoral" or "amoral," for they have all made inflexibility of morality the determining force in their lives. All have simply made the wrong moral choice—to place principles ahead not of personalities but ahead of people. They are all strong men, honest men, in many ways admirable men—and all are brilliant.

Not surprisingly, Fiedler runs rings around Leamas in debate, but the brutal ideologue keeps showing through, even when he sounds most rational. "I myself would have put a bomb in a restaurant if it brought us farther along the road. Afterwards I would draw the balance—so many women, so many children, and so far along the road" (144). Fiedler's apparent integrity in his dedication to theory, and indirectly to patriotism and his job, tends to obscure this willingness to destroy individuals in the name of a "higher" order. Nor is it entirely clear that Leamas himself can always see what is often veiled for the reader—Fiedler's savagery. True, Leamas is increasingly unable to forget that individuals come with faces, whether those of the child car crash victims in his nightmare or slaughtered refugees he has seen. But even to the end of the novel, when he has seen the true unfeeling soullessness of *all* political philosophies, he explains to

Liz what has happened in peculiarly ambivalent terms: "We're a tiny price to pay . . . but everywhere's the same, people cheated and misled, whole lives thrown away, people shot and in prison, whole groups and classes of men written off for nothing. And you, your Party—God knows it was built on the bodies of ordinary people. You've never seen men die as I have" (248). Is he excusing political belief by pointing out that all ideologies exact a price, or is he condemning all for their lack of humanity?

The possibility of Leamas's moral myopia—being unable to recognize the evil of Fiedler because of the man's skill and the greater evil of Mundt, whom Leamas thinks is the final target—is accentuated by the thematic tension in the center of the book of which the reader is likely unaware until the novel's end. As with the opening chapters, when the verisimilitude of Leamas's "deteriorating discard" obscures the truth that it is all a scam, in the same way much of the interview sections seem realistic enough to make it difficult to tell how much is simply Leamas blowing smoke to seduce Fiedler (and earlier Peters) into buying his story. But, when it is finally clear that Leamas himself has been deceived, it is evident that the Leamas who *thinks* he is fooling Fiedler is himself a dupe. Always, Leamas is a methodical professional, experienced and skilled in basic tradecraft, but he is not imaginative, perceptive, or even especially intelligent. He is hardly qualified to see through the complexities of a man like Fiedler. In short, he is not a very good judge of this sort of intellectual psychology, and so his judgment of Fiedler is suspect.

Leamas's intellectual limitations are enormously important to *The Spy Who Came in from the Cold* because they determine the progress of the vital secondary plot, which is that of Leamas's moral development. From his opening observation of the killing of Karl Riemeck to his last vision of the children about to be crushed by modern technology, *The Spy Who Came in from the Cold* is a study in observation, as befits a spy. Step by step, Leamas is exposed to examples of duplicity and moral ambiguity. Riemeck is betrayed and shot; Control calls on Leamas to humiliate himself and endure exile and prison; he is subjected to the venality of Ashe and Keever; Control betrays him to the media; the "savage" Fiedler seems a "better" person than might have been expected; just when Leamas is becoming comfortable with Fiedler, the rug is yanked out from under both of them by the treachery of Mundt, then Fiedler is temporarily restored, and the rug is yanked a second time. Leamas kills a man almost as an afterthought. Finally come the two great lessons in relativism: first, "suddenly, with the terrible clarity of a man too long deceived, Leamas understood the whole ghastly trick" (231); and, second, he and Liz are killed when it seems that they might escape.

Each of these shocks is a learning experience for Leamas, but it is not clear to him even at the end exactly *what* he has learned, for neither he nor any of the other characters in the novel—except perhaps the despicable puppeteers Mundt and Control—seem to be capable of coming to any kind of comprehensive overview of the meaning of such experiences. If he comes ultimately to any kind of vision, it is a vision of nihilism: "Christ Almighty! . . . What else have men done since the world began? I don't believe in anything, don't you see—not even destruction or anarchy. I'm sick, sick of killing but I don't see what else they can do. They don't proselytize, they don't stand in pulpits or on party platforms and tell us to fight for Peace or for God or whatever it is. They're the poor sods who try to keep the preachers from blowing each other sky high" (247). This is a pretty elemental and grim "lesson" to have gained from all these learning experiences, but it is as solid as Yossarian's epiphany in *Catch-22* when he finally understand's "Snowden's Secret," which explains the horror of war: "Man was matter, that was Snowden's secret. Drop him out a window and he'll fall. . . . The spirit gone, man is garbage. . . . Ripeness was all."[5]

Viewed this way, *The Spy Who Came in from the Cold* is simply an example of literary naturalism. The novel describes a series of pragmatic experiments, almost like Zola's *romans experimentals,* which place human beings in threatening environments and then observe behavior to deduce general theories that will explain how things operate. Everything fits such a reading. The grim, "chilly" atmosphere noted by so many reviewers of the novel is characteristic of prominent naturalists from Jack London to Hemingway. Human beings in such a world are helpless, crushable creatures who succumb either to monumental forces of history, politics, and society, or they claw themselves to pieces in a constant struggle for survival. The strong destroy the weak, and the weak are smashed by the strong and by forces they do not understand and which they cannot control. The "scientist" here is, of course, Leamas, and, by a cruel and ironic trick of fate typical of naturalist fiction, the objective observer is often also the victim dispassionately noting the progress of the forces that destroy him. The ultimate generalization about natural and human law cannot be far different from

Yossarian's, and Leamas's final wail is indicative of the moral nihilism that he has come to embrace: "for God's sake believe me. I hate it, I hate it all, I'm tired. But it's the world, it's mankind that's gone mad" (248).

Leamas's nihilism is simply a statement of intellectual bankruptcy, and it is a logical outgrowth of the spurious discussion that he and Fiedler have on the question of the end justifying the means. As a Marxist, Fiedler is dedicated to this proposition, and any humanity that he seems to show, particularly in contrast to Mundt—and almost *anybody* looks humane compared to Mundt—is a smokescreen covering the ruthless pragmatist beneath. For Fiedler this is not a "debate" at all, as he points out to Leamas when he mocks the Englishman's "Christian dogma." As a spy, an enforcer in the service of counterintelligence and the running dog for the ruthless Control in a plot to destroy Fiedler, Leamas is hardly the representative of Christian dogma which Fiedler claims he is. Leamas knows this and tries to justify to Fiedler the amoral code of expediency which he has lived by but doesn't believe. In the end he will still accept this code orally ("It's the world"), as his choice to die with Liz, who is sacrificed for "expediency," shows his rejection of it.

Leamas's death may prove that he has rejected the concept that people must do evil to do good, but he still closes his life paying lip service to the contrary. Le Carré was more explicit about what Leamas *should have* learned. In an open letter published in the journal *Encounter* in 1966 he replied hotly to a Russian journalist who had accused him of defending the Cold War. In the sarcastically titled "To Russia, with Greetings" (as opposed to Ian Fleming's Bond thriller *To Russia, with Love,* which was also the first Bond film) le Carré flatly rejected the proposition that the ends justify the means for democracies as well as communist dictatorships. "I sought to remove espionage from the sterile arguments of the cold war and concentrate the reader's eye on the cost to the West, in moral terms, of fighting the legitimized weapons of Communism . . . by methods of this kind, and still remain the kind of society that is worth defending."[6] The "To Russia" letter also clarified which side the novelist preferred and served as an unequivocal declaration of his anti-communism, if not a fire-breathing one. Critics who believe that le Carré damns both capitalist democracy and communism equally should look carefully at this first of several unequivocal statements of qualified preference for the former. He was to reiterate that preference repeatedly later, always maintaining the artist's right to reserve judgment: "If I knew exactly where I stood I wouldn't write. I do believe, reluctantly, that we must combat Communism. Very decisively."[7]

As for taking sides, another point needs to be made about *The Spy Who Came in from the Cold* within the context of le Carré's overall canon, and that is that Control's devious and morally questionable actions in this novel take place within the matrix of a limited and self-contained operation that, by its very definition, is covert and exceptional. The planting of Leamas as an infected information source to destroy one communist to save a worse one, because the worse one is useful, is a solipsistic renegade operation. Not only are Control's use of disinformation, deceit, and aggressive subversion not representative of "official" British intelligence policy; there is considerable suggestion that they are in defiance of them. Read within the context of all the "Circus novels," *The Spy Who Came in from the Cold* represents the beginning of a moral deterioration within British intelligence which approximates something like original sin. It is here, in furtively sanctioning a vicious personal strike upon a rival intelligence officer to protect his own corrupt "mole," that Control's controlling becomes egotistical pride and self-aggrandizement. Next will come the deliberate attempt to give a rival agency on his own side enough rope to hang itself (the encouragement of the abortive operation chronicled in *The Looking-Glass War*). Finally, having cut himself off from the people like Smiley who might have helped him, Control launches the betrayed "Operation Testify" to try and catch the mole within his own service, a paranoically secretive operation quite similar to the Fiedler-Mundt plot, except in reverse, with Control on the defensive. The fiasco of Operation Testify with Bill Haydon's betrayal of Jim Prideaux in Czechoslovakia leads to the fall of Control and lays the groundwork for George Smiley to purify the service. Control's using Leamas to destroy Fiedler is the first step in a progression of degeneration which must lead to Control's fall as surely as the murder of Duncan must lead Macbeth to Macduff's sword.

The reason the novel works so marvelously well, however, has little to do with esoteric moral questions of Control's soul. It works because it balances superb development of realistic detail with a perfectly executed tour-de-force ending in which the reader's sense of stability is violated just as Leamas's is. It is as if Ernest Hemingway had used all his gifts to establish a sense of reality and then borrowed an Ambrose Bierce reversal to produce a "zinger" conclusion. Despite *The Spy Who Came in from the*

Cold's repeated reminders that this is a world of espionage and perceptual relativism, the reader persists in trusting Leamas's understanding of that reality. By focusing obsessively on Leamas and effectively creating a dirty world of objective particulars about him, le Carré encourages the reader's acceptance of Leamas's perceptions as fact. As long as Leamas believes that Mundt is the real target of his subterfuge, the reader will believe it too. And for millions of readers the truth does not step out of its foul closet until the end of the penultimate chapter, when in a rage at his own gullibility, and disgust at what Control has tricked him into, Leamas screams the answer at Liz:

> I'll tell you. I'll tell you what you were never, never to know, neither you nor I. Listen: Mundt is London's man, their agent; they bought him when he was in England. We are witnessing the lousy end to a filthy, lousy operation to save Mundt's skin. To save him from a clever little Jew in his own Department who had begun to suspect the truth. They made us kill him, do you see, kill the Jew. Now you know, and God help us both. (241)

Although the actual plot is enormously complex, considering that *The Spy Who Came in from the Cold* is a relatively short novel, le Carré creates an illusion of simplicity by making Leamas the obsessive focus of the narrative. Except for a couple of brief cuts away from Leamas to Liz when he is being interrogated in Germany—both of which prepare for her being brought to him—Leamas is at the center of all the action. When he realizes that he has been fooled, so does the reader. The difference is that, as a professional spy, his job is not to be fooled; as the audience of a spy thriller, like the deceived "victims" watching a magic show, readers of *The Spy Who Came in from the Cold* are paying for just the opposite.

No discussion of the novel would be complete without a mention of setting. One reason that it has become, perhaps forever, *the* novel of the Cold War is its focus on that slippery interface between the communist world and the democracies, the schism between East Germany and West Germany. Germany itself has a symbolically gratifying appropriateness as an embodiment of the forces that both divide and unite the two worlds, for the Germans are a single people with a distinct cultural integrity, rent artificially but painfully by conflicting political forces; significantly, Germany has a long schizophrenic history along these lines dating back to the horrors of the Thirty Years' War. The symbol of that schism in the post–World War II world—one of the most mythically perfect and enduring symbols of political division in history, probably—is the Berlin Wall. More than twenty five years after writing the novel, le Carré wrote of the Wall as "perfect theatre as well as a perfect symbol of the monstrosity of ideology gone mad."[8] The framing action of the novel defines the theme, beginning as it does with a betrayal leading to the death of a character trying to cross the Wall and ending in the same place. As Leamas stands by the Wall, unable to help the fleeing Riemeck, so Smiley stands at the end reaching out to the doomed Leamas. For the generation of agents, and of ordinary citizens, fated to live in the divided world after World War II, the Wall was stronger than pitiful human efforts to cross it.

In terms of le Carré's work as a whole this linchpin novel begins and ends at the physical focal point that is symbolically both the fountainhead and center all his novels. *Flashpoint, interface, focus:* there are many terms to describe the centrality of the Berlin Wall to the Cold War and the entire history of the world in the second half of the twentieth century, but none of them sums up the literal and symbolic importance of this critical locus. Before the Wall was even built in August 1961, the border between East and West Berlin had been the critical site for the confrontation of the great powers, from V-J Day to the Potsdam Conference to the Berlin Airlift of 1948 and beyond. At that point the friction between the two mighty political blocs produces the greatest force, just as the epicenter of an earthquake is that point at which massive tectonic plates of the earth grind against one another until the forces explode. Le Carré is too good a writer to strain at a poor pun about "going to the wall," but it would be an appropriate, if not facile, phrase to describe the way the beginning and end of this novel spotlight the most symbolic image for all of the novelist's fiction—individual human beings in mortal danger.

CHAPTER FIVE

The Coldest War

The Looking-Glass War and *A Small Town in Germany*

Nothing John le Carré could have written could have matched the critical and popular triumph of *The Spy Who Came in from the Cold,* and it appeared for years that he was destined to be a literary one-trick pony. Even the most generous observers of his career admit that the decade after the novel's publication in 1963 marked a lull, if not an outright decline, in his literary powers and production. Unfortunately, even given the great success of his "Quest for Karla" trilogy, beginning in 1974 with the publication of *Tinker, Tailor, Soldier, Spy* and the acclaimed novels that followed, a sense of entropy and exhaustion hangs over the two spy novels of this slack period and leaves both underrated and underread. Unequivocally, both *The Looking-Glass War* (1965) and *A Small Town in Germany* (1968) are bleak, cheerless studies of the Cold War at its coldest, but in their very grimness lies their excellence. Together they may represent the truest picture in literature of the moral and spiritual wasteland of the international political world of the twentieth century.

The Looking-Glass War

Had *The Looking-Glass War* been as finely crafted and structured a novel as *The Spy Who Came in from the Cold,* it is still doubtful if it would be have been received as much more than a well-written letdown by the legions of le Carré fans who waited eagerly for it. So phenomenal was the success of the first book, and so severe and stylized a novel was it—so idiosyncratic, distinctive, and original—that it is doubtful whether *any* novel following it could have satisfied le Carré's demanding admirers. Any fiction resembling *The Spy Who Came in from the Cold* would have been declaimed by critics as imitative and anything very unlike seen as heresy. Since *The Looking-Glass War* was in many respects an intensification of the bleaker aspects of *The Spy Who Came in from the Cold,* it received the former rather than the latter reception. Not until le Carré tried something really different with *The Naive and Sentimental Lover,* in 1971, would he feel the sharper sting of critics who felt that a favorite author had betrayed them rather than simply left them unsatisfied. Still, le Carré felt that *The Looking-Glass War* "was received, in Britain, with such wholesale derision from the critical community that, had I taken it to heart, would have persuaded me to follow a different profession, such as window-cleaning, or literary journalism."[1]

The Looking-Glass War was still a very good novel, although certainly not as accomplished as a few of le Carré's critical admirers claim in comparison with its celebrated predecessor.[2] It suffers greatly, however, from a dramatic weakness, in that le Carré's central thesis in this book is that the Cold War is really a phony war and a dull one. Le Carré was determined to present the espionage "game" as even less appealing than in *The Spy Who Came in from the Cold:* "This time, cost what it will, I'll describe a Secret Service that is really not very good at all; that is eking out its wartime glory; that is feeding itself on Little England fantasies; is isolated, directionless, over-protected and destined ultimately to destroy itself."[3] Theoretically, such determination to paint the gray despair of the Cold War should enhance rather than detract from the novel's standing as a work of art, but certainly it greatly reduced reader appreciation. The "looking-glass war" of the title is a numbing and clumsy standoff, primarily waged by bureaucrats whose livelihood depends on perpetuating it; this Cold War is nasty, brutish, and much too long. Further, in such a struggle there is often no "war" to fight, so these bureaucrats must create one. Any novel attempting a portrait of such a leaden war runs the risk of becoming leaden itself, and le Carré rings the changes on the painfully awkward bungling of these Coldest Warriors by laboriously dragging the reader step by step through venal spy procedures that are not so much counterespionage as "non-spying"—the deliberate creation of an artificial war so that Cold Warriors will have an enemy.

To create *The Looking-Glass War* le Carré simply imagined the Circus of *The Spy Who Came in from the Cold* minus courage, integrity, and competence—the very qualities that morally justified its existence. At the core of this new novel le Carré created a fraud—a worthless British government intelligence service that neither shows nor traffics in intelligence. The director of this elderly dying remnant of World War II bureaucracy, called throughout this novel "the Department" (to distinguish it from the Circus), is Leclerc, an aging counterpart to the Circus's Control; le Carré despises clerks, namely Parker Wellow in *The Russia House,* and many others in his fiction. Leclerc shares all of Control's vices—pride, secretiveness, manipulation, willingness to appeal to ideals for selfish gain—and none of the Circus chief's virtues, including brilliance, patience, and basic honesty (except when sacred cows are endangered). Petty and fastidious, totally opaque as far as background or foreground beyond the Department, Leclerc is determined to protect his decaying service against rival intelligence groups like the Circus and against bad publicity that might result in cutting off its already meager funding. As with Control's obsession with finding the mole or Smiley's with Karla, Leclerc fixes on the idea of mounting some noble deed yet undone—an operation that will redeem his trivial agency and preserve his vanishing career. His efforts produce a series of fiascoes that eventually drive the Department into extinction but not before his bungling has killed several men. Pursuing will-o'-the-wisp hints from questionable information sources, Leclerc becomes intrigued by the idea that his agency may be able to verify the existence of East German missile emplacements, rumored to be under construction near the West German border. A first effort to "buy" photographs of the sites almost accidentally destroys a commercial reconnaissance flight— nearly costing the lives of twenty-five children aboard (very like Leamas's last horrible vision of the children about to be crushed in traffic). Leclerc then sends an untrained agency courier to collect film that may reveal the missiles. Making mistakes, the neophyte agent is killed and the film lost, although, significantly, it is not even entirely clear that his death may not be a genuine accident, as opposed to an assassination. Everything that seems suspicious in *The Looking-Glass War may* be an accident, except the grim consequences of the Department's incompetence.

Leclerc follows "Taylor's run," as the abortive mission of the dead courier is called, by "Avery's run," a more complex mission using John Avery, a spy-in-training of the younger generation who sees in Leclerc's stuffy, overt patriotism and stilted rhetoric echoes of the "great game" of espionage, of which spy manqué Avery dreams. Avery is a less levelheaded version of Smiley's protégé Peter Guillam, romantically worshiping a past he never knew and without the moral direction and balance of Smiley to correct him. Avery endures almost gladly a baroque rigmarole of rituals designed to bind him to the spiritual commitment of the Department as Leclerc sells it to him. Sent to retrieve the still missing film, Avery, too, fails, in part due to his own callow approach but largely because of the bad preparation and irrelevance of his mission. In returning to England, ashamed of his failure, he finds that the police, or someone posing as the police, have been asking his wife, Sarah, about Taylor's body, which has been discovered and linked to the Department. Avery flies at Sarah in a rage for letting the agency's secrets slip out, establishing again the incompatibility, in le Carré, of love and spying. Spies cannot afford the commitments of love, and often the tensions between conflicting loyalties will result in destroying or compromising personal relationships.[4] What Sarah realizes is that Avery can never admit that he cherishes the secrecy and the mumbo jumbo that separates the Department from his married life: "I think if you were allowed to tell me you wouldn't care about the job,"[5] she snaps at him bitterly late in the novel, when their marriage is wrecked. Meanwhile, Avery creeps back into the Department abjectly, his mission a failure, and the stage is set for the final abortive attempt to force reality and history to conform to the jaded myths of old men living out the legends of their own pasts.

Fred Leiser, an aging naturalized British citizen originally from Poland who once worked for the Department during World

The Coldest War

War II, is Leclerc's final choice to drop as a spy into East Germany and to check out the alleged missile sites, and Leiser must be the most pathetic spy le Carré ever created. In all the author's fourteen novels of intelligence work there is no less glamorous character. Smiley has the hidden glitter of his frightening competence throughout his career and the intensity of his focus on Karla late in it to magnify him in the reader's imagination. Even the saddest of other spies have hidden charisma—Connie Sachs her intimidating memory, Leamas his extraordinary courage and endurance and honesty, and Barley Blair of *The Russia House* a gruff independence. Leiser, however, is simply a shy, socially awkward man who "dresses like a bookie" and has no friends. On his last day in England before leaving on his dangerous mission he goes to a pornographic movie to fill his empty hours. Ten years before, during the war, he was an agent of some skill and much courage, but he has grown middle-aged and fat, and at first he wisely declines the Department's offer to reactivate him. Then he thinks of his meaningless life and accepts. Fred Leiser has nothing but his loneliness and his desperate need—more intense even than insecure, glory-seeking Avery—to belong. His emptiness and the smarmy way Leclerc and the Department fill it form the second half of the novel and cost Leiser his life.

Leiser accepts because he remembers the war, when he was young and strong and respected. In some sense all of le Carré's novels are about the legacy of World War II, both positively and negatively. That was a crusade in which the moral polarities were clear and the ambiguities of violent action minimized. In a positive sense that war gave Western battlers against the absolutism of communist ideology a sense of mission and the consciousness that there are rights and wrongs in political action, that there is a legitimacy in taking sides. Le Carré's characters are often called "Cold Warriors" by critics (although never by the author himself), but most of them would be more accurately described as men and women conditioned by a shooting war, now trying to apply the lessons and, more important, the codes of behavior of that conflict to the Cold War. The standards of manhood, loyalty, and absolute commitment are what young Avery craves in the Department and what Leiser readily accepts again, although those codes no longer apply; in a neat piece of linguistic punning and symbology (living by archaic codes) Leiser is caught by the East Germans because he is using out-of-date radio codes and decrypting switching techniques—predictably left over from the war. Ultimately, all the equipment that Leclerc gives him to train with, as well as to take behind the Iron Curtain, is obsolete World War II vintage, just as he is.

Leiser is doomed from the moment he signs on, and after a hurried training program he is sent sneaking under the wire into East Germany, monitored by Leclerc, Avery, and Department personnel from a farmhouse nearby in West Germany. His skills at deception rusty, Leiser unnecessarily kills a young and innocent border guard, and, if there is a temptation to see Leiser as a doomed hero romantically sacrificing himself for a lost cause, le Carré makes clear the lack of feeling with which he does the killing. Then Leiser ties himself down with the additional baggage of a sexual liaison with an East German farm girl, who is as lonely as he is. He never comes close to fulfilling his mission of gathering intelligence, and, as the East German "vopos" close in

on him, George Smiley arrives in the monitoring farmhouse to
tell Leclerc that Whitehall has intervened and ordered the operation shut down immediately to avoid embarrassing the government. As Avery weeps, realizing that seedy betrayal is the final
result of all this shoddy romantic game playing, Leclerc abandons Leiser to his death and flees back to England, planning to
deny any knowledge of the sacrificed agent should Leiser survive
inevitable capture. Leiser's death as the *vopos* close in saves
everyone a lot of embarrassment.

The intervention scene between Smiley and Leclerc and his
minions is one of the most cynical and powerful in le Carré's
condemnation of the intelligence establishment and the whole
psychology of espionage. Leclerc bristles in his pride against the
intrusion of the Circus on his territory, but Smiley swiftly
convinces him that the game is up. When Haldane, the
Department's donnish technocrat, who has preached emotional
detachment, reproaches Avery for crying, snarling, "We're technicians, not poets," Smiley finally turns on him bitterly: "Yes.
You're a very good technician, Adrian. There's no pain in you
anymore. You've made technique a way of life . . . like a whore
. . . technique replacing love. . . . Little flags . . . the old war piping
in the new. There was all that, wasn't there?" (310). Haldane,
truly immune to pain, is not stung, but Avery realizes that Leiser
is to be abandoned and screams an accusatory epitaph at Haldane,
claiming they must try to rescue Leiser—for love: "Love. Yes,
love! Not yours, Haldane, mine. Smiley's right! You made me do
it for you, made me love him! It wasn't in you anymore! I brought
him to you, I kept him in your house, made him dance to the music
of your bloody war! I piped for him, but now there's no breath in

me now. He's Peter Pan's last victim, the last one, the last love; the last music gone" (311).

If Avery's rhetoric waxes a bit unrealistically romantic at the last, the message is plain. Like a collection of Yeats's "outworn hearts in a time outworn," these defensive and egotistical men have nurtured a set of shopworn values for their own protection and profit, and the cost has been paid in other men's lives. The Cold War may be scarcely stirring in the greater world in which East and West face each other across walls of hatred, but it is coldest in the hearts of these withered leftovers of a war they understood, fought when they were young; then, perhaps, they were capable of compassion rather than just calculation.

The role of Smiley, Control, and the Circus in *The Looking-Glass War* is important in any consideration of the le Carré canon, and it is not an entirely admirable role, as admirers of Smiley as "Saint George" might expect. Of all the author's portraits of Smiley this one paints him in the most purely professional terms. Smiley and Control appear several times, as the novel crosscuts to the Circus personnel commenting on the pathetic misworkings of the Department and trying to decide whether to take a proactive or reactive stance toward Leclerc's mismanagement. There is almost no "human" information about the faithless Ann or the internal struggles besetting the Circus (in terms of absolute overall Circus chronology, Operation Mayfly, as the Leiser infiltration is called in the Department, takes place two or three years after the death of Leamas and during a rather slack time in the Circus). Smiley, and behind him Control, function in *The Looking-Glass War* as representatives of order and effectiveness juxtaposed to Leclerc's corrupted and dated romanticism. Even in the final scene, although Smiley certainly shows signs of compassion for the doomed agent, he is low-keyed and almost cool, except when he turns on Haldane. As always, his inherent professionalism and reserve keep him from the kind of emotional ventings of outrage and disgust which characterize others in his trade.

The bitter, self-destructive infighting between intelligence personnel at the core of *The Looking-Glass War* amplifies a leitmotif of *The Spy Who Came in from the Cold,* one that informs nearly all of le Carré's fiction to follow. Beginning with Control's rogue operation against Mundt in the latter novel, through Smiley's struggles with the obstructionist British agencies and destructive power grabs by American intelligence "cousins" in the "Karla trilogy," through the grotesque and often treasonable internecine conflicts of "friendly" intelligence personnel willing to sacrifice any lives, including those of their own agents, in *The Night Manager, Our Game,* and *The Tailor of Panama*—all published in the 1990s—the mind of the typical "pure intelligence" operative is neither pure nor, ultimately, intelligent. If Smiley looks more in sorrow than anger at the wreckage of Leclerc's selfish operation, it is because he knows that it represents less an aberration of Cold War espionage than a emblem of it.

Overall, the Circus looks good in *The Looking-Glass War,* but, then, it doesn't have much competition. Actually, Control seems to take a slightly sadistic satisfaction in the bumbling of Leclerc, and Smiley calls him to task for it. When Control complains that Leclerc "thinks I want to gobble him up," Smiley snaps, "Well, don't you?" Control's protestations of his dispassionate objectivity ring false: "Leclerc's so *vulgar.* I admit, I find him vulgar. He thinks we compete. What on earth would *I* do with his dreadful militia? Scouring Europe for mobile laundries" (282). If Control is above the self-seeking manipulation of Leclerc, we feel, it is only because the greater security of his position and of the Circus vis-à-vis lesser intelligence agencies allows him to be so. In *The Looking-Glass War* everyone is compromised, even Smiley. The business does that to people, Smiley suggests. When Control asks him how Haldane became the unfeeling person he has become, willing to go along with an operation so stupid and lacking in regard for its victims, Smiley replies: "He had a conscience once. He's like all of us. He's learnt to live with it" (293).

A Small Town in Germany

In *The Looking-Glass War* the ghosts of the past murder the hopes of the present; *A Small Town in Germany* is about the shadow of the past making the present murderous. Whereas in the former novel old men try to fight the Cold War with the morals, mores, and methods of World War II, *A Small Town in Germany* is about them *not* fighting the Cold War because the demons of that war are still not laid to rest. The men of *The Looking-Glass War* lie under the dead hand of the past, but in *A Small Town in Germany* it is not yet dead.

For the first and so far last time, among his political novels, le Carré abandons the Circus and the formal institutions of intelligence gathering (aside from a casual allusion to Smiley's Circus mentor Steed-Asprey). The Circus doesn't matter here, because the novelist is not just examining how history influences the present but showing how history *is* the present. In a sense *A Small Town in Germany* balances that preceding novel. *The Looking-Glass War* shows its Circus-like agency, the Department, as an empty shell because it clings to methods and traditions that are inapplicable in the complexities of the postwar world. But that past was not in itself corrupt. Although le Carré avoids maudlin chauvinism, within limits World War II was a moral one for the British, and they should bury the memories of it only because of the danger of good but stale custom corrupting the world. For the Germans, however, that war represented the culmination and fruition of everything that was depraved in the German soul and to use it as a pattern for current behavior would be to inflict upon the present values that were, and still are, inherently evil. In *A Small Town in Germany* that is exactly what is happening.

Thus, Bonn replaces London as the ossified setting of bureaucratic entropy, Germany replaces England as the nation and people rotting from their inability to cast off the past, and active Nazism replaces stagnant imperial romanticism as the disease that flares up to threaten the new generation. Bonn itself richly deserves the title of the novel, for it is a *small* town. "Bonn in the early 'sixties was a spooky place indeed," le Carré recalled. "Sometimes the very streets of the city felt like a perilously thin surface laid hastily upon the recent dreadful past, like one of those nicely mown grass mounds at Belsen concentration camp, covering the mute agony of the innocent dead."[6] Le Carré's Bonn is morally and creatively stunted in the same way Sinclair Lewis's Gopher Prairie of *Main Street* or Sherwood Anderson's Winesburg, Ohio, are *small* towns—provincial, paranoid, bigoted, and festering with repressed viciousness, hatred, and evil. As the administrative, rather than the natural, capital of the new Germany, Bonn is an artificial town of bureaucrats, which for le Carré makes it analogous to Dante's infernal City of Dis—the natural home only of hypocrites and demons but all dressed in tailored sheep's clothing. The novel's richly textured opening description of the city is indicative, comparable to Dickens's evocation of fog-shrouded London which opens *Bleak House.* The image of the twisted streets, the weird effects of light, and the surreal and disturbing urban images borrows, like the cityscapes of *The Cabinet of Dr. Caligari,* from the German expressionist painters and writers.[7] One thinks of Coleridge's invective against nearby Cologne ("a town of monks and bones, / and pavements fang'd with murderous stones"),[8] except that this Bonn is without soul, even a bad one.[9]

If the city itself in *A Small Town in Germany* is a grim Gothic stage set, it only complements the leaden cast. A quarter century after writing the novel, le Carré remembers, "The social atmosphere, in my recollection, was much as the book describes: neurotic and grudging under the soggy weight of the Nibelung mist."[10] The diplomats—German, British, and other—are appropriately cosmetic but soulless, like Peter de Lisle, who is "an elegant, willowy, almost beautiful person" yet substanceless. He is steeped along with his colleagues in a functionless British lethargy, utterly incapable of dealing with the dynamic evil of the rejuvenated Nazism of the new postwar Germans, led by the charismatic Karfield.

Juxtaposed to the well-bred ennui of de Lisle, his suave superior Bradfield, and the rest of the British diplomatic commu-

The Coldest War

nity is the disgruntled energy of Alan Turner, who is sent by the Foreign Office to investigate the inconvenient disappearance of Leo Hartung, a German by birth but now a naturalized British citizen attached to the British Embassy in Bonn. Hartung has vanished with crucial files, which may threaten the critical status of England vis-à-vis the European Economic Community. Turner is a crude, blunt man, much like Alec Leamas (although Turner is the more truly intelligent, as opposed to simply instinctive). Turner bulls his way through the embassy, asking embarrassing questions and treating the privileged and polished representatives of Britain's aristocracy with less than the respect to which they feel entitled. What is more disturbing, he moves closer and closer to the ugly truth that is buried at the bottom of this baroque edifice to Victorian and imperial pride. That bottom is more than symbolic in this case, for, in a sequestered room deep in the bowels of the embassy, Turner finds forgotten and squalid sanctuary, nicknamed "the glory hole" by the few who know of it. There the obsessed Hartung has hidden his secret. It is, not surprisingly, a ghost from Hartung's past as well as that of all Germany itself: Karfeld, the rising charismatic star of an intensely emotional nationalistic movement, was guilty of Nazi atrocities, and the reason Hartung knows this is from his own childhood experience as one of the man's Jewish victims. "Leo, you thief," mutters Turner to himself, "you came here to forage in your own dreadful childhood."[11] Again, le Carré's adults are haunted by their wretched pasts; is there a single one with a happy childhood?

Germany's vile twentieth-century history hangs over the whole novel, from the whisperings of Nazism in the early pages to the stunning "epilogue," which brings all the pieces together. In the final scene le Carré describes a Karfeld rally and speech as a cross between Grand Guignol and Leni Riefenstahl's Nazi propaganda film *Triumph of the Will* celebrating the Nuremberg rallies. Anyone who has seen a newsreel of Hitler whipping up a crowd will recognize the model for Karfeld, who moves seamlessly from a celebration of the German spirit to a virtual parody of Hitlerian rabble-rousing. Hartung finally appears for the first time, attempting to assassinate Karfeld, and is killed by the mob, although, as with the death of Taylor in *The Looking-Glass War,* the circumstances are ambiguous, and the English aristos may well have been involved. The novel ends with the cancerous emotional appeal of Karfeld alive and growing in a society already morally compromised by its own past but with Turner armed with the knowledge that presumably could bring the demagogue down if he chooses to use it.

Although the communist threat is replaced by the neo-Nazi threat and the Circus is absent in *A Small Town in Germany,* the central le Carré figure of the less-than-perfect spy/detective remains in the figure of Alan Turner. Tough and basic, totally cynical, and very bright underneath his deliberately stolid manner, Turner is lower class by birth and conviction, with understandable inherited resentments against and suspicions of the slick public school–educated men of the embassy. Turner is "clever, predatory and vulgar, with the hard, inhibited eye of the upstart," the brightest of them, Bradfield muses, and all the aristos of the novel recognize it. They also recognize that he is a danger to them, because his contempt for their snobbery makes him willing to offend them in getting at the truth, and his ability at "slumming" gives him accessibility to sources denied to them. Several times he makes useful contact with working-class people with whom he recognizes an affinity and who relate to him for the same reason.

The thing that Turner's roughness really makes him good at is interrogation. Interestingly, the other great interrogator in the le Carré cast is, of course, George Smiley, who is emotionally and procedurally the antithesis of Turner. Quiet, gentle, and reserved, if not actually aristocratic, Smiley impresses all the people he questions as a gentleman, and they are led to the truth by persuasion rather than by a projection of force. Turner comes on tougher, but he and Smiley share relentlessness and are honest with themselves, which are the most important qualities in a questioner seeking dark truths.

The overriding dark truth of *A Small Town in Germany* is that the Nazis are coming—again. If this sounds a trifle melodramatic, it is, and that is the chief weakness of the novel. Malcolm Muggeridge, a great admirer of le Carré's, complained of this book that "the Cold War setting, so acutely conveyed in *The Spy Who Came in from the Cold,* has become theatrical, stale and artificial."[12] He is right that le Carré seems less concerned here with creating the gritty "reality" that the earlier novel worked so fixedly to create, as with suggesting the horror of a potential reality if the Nazis or any political force like them achieved power again. The lurid black-and-blue tones in which the dismal scenes of the novel are painted are meant to evoke a sense of dread. This and *The Spy Who Came in from the Cold* are le Carré's darkest books. Nothing is more indicative of the nature of this novel than looking carefully at the prologue's eldritch portrait of Bonn and then the frenetic closing picture of the Karfeld rally, with its deliberate recreation of the tone and emotions of a Nazi torchlight rally. Until the dreadful accession of such a political party, le Carré wrote in the preface to the American edition of the novel, the German present is one of "disenchantment of the ruled, the sense of political dishonor and political stagnation, and alienation between government and people" (1).

Between the framing chapters, the first painting a sick "town" with a sick soul and the last a mass rally demonstrating that sickness, lies a classic novel of detection and the hunt; in fact, in the American edition of the book le Carré titled the first chapter "The Hunter and the Hunted." As is so often the case with le Carré, characters play both roles. Hartung, with his determination to sacrifice himself by killing Karfeld, is the hunter being tracked by Turner, who is himself threatened and beaten by anonymous forces, perhaps of the Karfeld camp, perhaps lackeys of the Bonn British society, which feels threatened by him.

No look at *A Small Town in Germany* would be complete without mention of the role of the British diplomats with regard to the revival of German right-wing fervor. They are, by nature, accommodating, as is the job of diplomats. Like much of the British diplomatic aristocracy—the pacifists, the Lady Astor crowd, the Chamberlain supporters—during Hitler's rise in the 1930s, the Bradfields in *A Small Town in Germany* "adapt" to the New Order, partly because it is expedient to do so, partly because it would require "bad manners" to resist. There is also political expediency. Not to mention the overall pattern of hypocrisy in postwar German society, for the British have no monopoly on willingness to sell out: Karfeld's "idea man" and main slogan

The Coldest War

writer is Praschko, a former friend of Hartung's and fellow refugee from the Nazis. The public profile of the British Foreign Office in Berlin, however, is based on accommodation with whoever is in power, no matter how filthy. As Rawley Bradfield, the brightest and most cynically honest of them, explains it in almost shocking frankness to Turner near the end of the novel:

> I am a hypocrite. . . . I'm a great believer in hypocrisy. It's the nearest thing we ever get to virtue. . . . I serve the appearance of things. It is the worst of systems; it is better than the others. That is my profession, and that is my philosophy. . . . I did not contract to serve a powerful nation, least of all a virtuous one. All power corrupts. The loss of power corrupts even more. (291)

It's hardly surprising that Turner is disgusted by the lot of them, and he blisters the English upper class in one of the most venomous attacks in le Carré's fiction:

> You make me puke. All of you. The whole sodding circus. You didn't give a twopenny damn for Leo, any of you, while he was here. Common as dirt, wasn't he? No background, no childhood, no nothing. Shove him the other side of the river where he won't be noticed! Tuck him away in the catacombs with the German staff! (133)

Only the German staff is no longer willing to be confined to the catacombs by the condescending British. They're out there in the final scene at the Karfeld rally laying the groundwork for another New Order. Le Carré set *A Small Town in Germany* in the "immediate future," perhaps a couple of years after its publication in 1968. As it happens, le Carré's apocalyptic vision of a new rough beast slouching toward Bonn to be born didn't materialize then and hasn't, for the most part, yet. One interesting aspect of the neo-Nazi group in the novel is its willingness not only to compromise with communism but positively to conspire with the Russians to put the democracies down. The particulars of *A Small Town in Germany*'s ugly European dystopia did not materialize anymore than did Orwell's *1984* come to pass by that date. The vision of both novels, however, is still chilling, and their image of postwar European society, if not exactly prescient, is hardly encouraging.

CHAPTER SIX

Interlude

The Naive and Sentimental Lover

The ugly critical reception that *The Naive and Sentimental Lover* received when it was published in 1971 does not need extensive examination, and neither does the novel, although it is the product of a fascinating midlife crisis that le Carré, like many writers, attempted to convert into literature. Most critics have simply ignored this novel; Tony Barley's book-length study of le Carré, for example, mentions *The Naive and Sentimental Lover* only once in passing as the novelist's "sabbatical excursion . . . involving a small cast of non-political characters."[1] Like many reviewers, Barley felt that le Carré's turn toward personal psychology and romance was disastrous, but even, if the work were without artistic merit—and it is not—it would still be fascinating for any reader interested in the life of the author or in the architectonics of his canon.[2]

The true companion piece to *The Naive and Sentimental Lover* is *A Perfect Spy* (1986), although few critics have noticed the connection. Taken together, *The Naive and Sentimental Lover* and *A Perfect Spy* are by far the most autobiographical and personal of le Carré's novels, and their publications—fifteen years apart—bracket the author's successful and respected work, the three "Smiley novels" of the Karla trilogy, beginning with *Tinker, Tailor, Soldier, Spy* along with *The Little Drummer Girl* (1983). In *A Perfect Spy* le Carré would explore within the espionage genre many of the themes that he posited in *The Naive and Sentimental Lover,* which is a study of the mutually destructive interaction between compromised conventionality and the corrupt Dionysian psychology of an uninhibited artist. Like Aldo Cassidy, the "naive and sentimental lover," Magnus Pym, the title character of *A Perfect Spy,* is a "people pleaser," an insecure and unfulfilled person who searches for an identity by a chameleon adaptation to the behavior of other people.

Cassidy is an eminently conventional businessman and, significantly, a graduate of Sherborne, that very real boarding school where le Carré himself struggled with his own identity in the crucible of British class prejudice. As with le Carré, Cassidy's mother abandoned him in childhood, and he was left in the care of a slick social-climbing father who pointed his son toward a career as a gentleman, since he had not been born one himself. Like the young le Carré, Cassidy graduated from a "minor" Oxford College and launched himself upon a respectable career, but, unlike le Carré, Cassidy never broke with the bourgeois objectives that shaped his youth. In early middle age Cassidy finds himself at the beginning of the novel professionally successful as a prosperous businessman and staunch British clubman—the model of conservative public propriety. His private life, however, is a mess. He is married to a dull, bovine woman, is obviously failing as a father to his two boys, and is miserably frustrated by a career that offers him no artistic sustenance, no matter how much money he makes. For Cassidy wants more. A failed first novelist, he is an artistic dilettante who moons over Sinatra records and pines for spiritual fulfillment.

Aldo's one area of success is business, although le Carré does little in the novel to validate the assertion of this character's expertise. The one invention that made Cassidy's fortune—a safety brake for prams, baby carriages—was really an accidental application that happened to make him rich. He feels trapped by the materialism of his commercial career, although, again, there is little in *The Naive and Sentimental Lover* in terms of a convincing picture of the Philistine wasteland of commerce which Cassidy must endure: British fiction, like American, has great difficulty dealing sympathetically with business.[3]

On one of his periodic fantasy flights from his job and family Cassidy meets Shamus, the embodiment of what he would like to think of as his alter ego. A thief, a wastrel, a cynic, and a debauchee, Shamus is a failed writer who beats his women, betrays his friends, and steals from everyone; his specialty is breaking into empty houses and living in them a while, leaving them in ruins. Shamus's rootless anarchism, symbolized by his lack of a surname, seems to Cassidy an antidote to the bourgeois plodding of his own life. Naturally, when Cassidy takes an interest in him, this English version of an aging hippie is delighted to attach himself to the businessman like a remora to a shark, and Cassidy begins supporting the vagabond artist and his lover, Helen. The writer's reckless, destructive irreverence sucks Cassidy into the Rabelaisian maelstrom that is Shamus and Helen's life. Cassidy is particularly charmed by the writer's contempt for conventional family life and for Cassidy's wife, Sandra, in particular, whom Shamus—and Cassidy after him— begin calling "Bosscow." Predictably, Cassidy, Shamus, and Helen conclude their confused relationship in an extended, and very messy, Walpurgis Night that ends with Shamus and Helen vanishing into the mist and Cassidy presumably returning to his family a sadder but wiser man. Le Carré's obvious model for Shamus was the alcoholic Welsh poet Dylan Thomas (whom Shamus quotes several times), and Shamus's long-suffering lover, Helen, is at least in part patterned on Thomas's wife, Caitlin (although, unlike Helen, Caitlin gave as good as she got in the Thomas family brawls). There are many other ways in which Shamus and Helen are poor copies of the Thomases, but the most important difference is that, whatever his defects of character, Dylan Thomas produced great poetry, whereas Shamus's art is far more simply sullen ranting than craft.

At the heart of *The Naive and Sentimental Lover* lies the essential social conflict between destructive creativity and sustaining conventional values. Le Carré, who knew German philosophers, is exploring the ground that Nietzsche laid out, particularly in *Thus Spake Zarathustra,* in which he defined the world as divided between the creator/destroyers and the nurturers, who maintain and protect that which the creators have made. The problem with this novel is that Shamus is a failed creator, and Cassidy is a failed nurturer, regardless of his success in commerce. Neither of these men is a fit representative of their mythic archetypes, and therefore their salvation or destruction in romantic terms is not of great consequence. When Shamus and Helen revert to their vagabond ways there is no sense that a great artist has been lost, and when Cassidy returns to his role as the stereotypical Proustian bourgeois a little man may be sadder but wiser, but there is no sense that a noble soul has tasted the heady wine of the creative life and then rejected it out of conscience, as with Isabel Archer in James's *Portrait of a Lady.* With Shamus and Cassidy whatever happens to these two burnt-out cases simply doesn't matter very much.

Interlude

The fact that Cassidy is a manufacturer of prams who becomes infatuated with the lifestyle of a man who beats women and dances on tables should be an indication that *The Naive and Sentimental Lover* is *potentially* a comic novel. It is not clear, however, that the author saw it that way. Le Carré would eventually show a talent for self-mockery in *A Perfect Spy,* and much of his other writing that draws upon his life evidences a keenly observant honesty about both his own limitations and those of the worlds in which he has lived. Certainly, there are bits of him in the lonely boy Roach in *Tinker, Tailor, Soldier, Spy* and the orphan youth of Jonathan Pine in *The Night Manager* and even the puppy dog gruffness of that "honourable" schoolboy Jerry Westerby. In *The Tailor of Panama* le Carré would create in Harry Pendel a virtual parody of the artist as a creator of fictitious spy stories. But the relationship between Cassidy and Shamus is so unlikely as to strain our credulity, unless it is designed to do so as an exercise in the grotesque, which le Carré seems unwilling or unable to do. The author seems determined to take these two poseurs—the one pretending to be a solid citizen, the other pretending to be an artist—seriously.

Some of le Carré's problem may be his reverential treatment toward love. Even some of his most ardent admirers have suggested that Smiley's adoration of the feckless and faithless Ann—"the last illusion of the illusionless man," Karla calls it—is more fatuous than need be. *The Naive and Sentimental Lover* explores far more completely than any of the Smiley books le Carré's attitudes toward love and, particularly, the cruel and destructive aspects of the emotion. Throughout most of le Carré's celebrated spy novels love has simply been the opposite of hate and indifference, and le Carré does not really differentiate between the latter two states. Actually, of the two indifference, or its concomitant, inability to love, is by far the more common in his fiction. The great villains of the spy novels are not so much haters as people who have either never had or have lost the ability to love, particularly to love individual people. Karla has misplaced his ability to love by giving it to ideology, Bill Haydon probably never really had it, and Magnus Pym cannot find a place for his. But here in *The Naive and Sentimental Lover* are three people who appear during much of the novel to be capable of deeply loving each other, and the results are disastrous. Perhaps the reason is that their capacity for love is really only apparent, and the catastrophic coming together of their egotisms and their neuroses makes any real love between them impossible. Whatever the reason, all three of them—Cassidy, Shamus, and Helen—are simply too self-centered to carry the burden of representing the deep and serious emotional forces that a successful story of love implies.

This shallowness of character coupled with seriousness of plot is complicated by the rhetorical sophistication of the novel. One serious problem with *The Naive and Sentimental Lover* is stylistic. Le Carré had not yet developed the reputation for stylistic complexity which he gained with *Tinker, Tailor, Soldier, Spy,* a novel that many readers found heavy sledding, notwithstanding its commercial success. Still, most of that novel's readers seem to have recognized that the abrupt shifts of psychology, scene, and rhetoric were all directly a function of the labyrinthine nature of the problem that Smiley was unraveling. And in *Tinker, Tailor, Soldier, Spy* le Carré did not suddenly shift narrative perspective in the middle of a paragraph or splatter the page with stream-of-consciousness expressionism that the reader had to stop and sort before moving on. Some of *The Naive and Sentimental Lover* seems to imitate Ruskin, some Samuel Beckett, and the lusher sections not surprisingly show the influence of the German romantics. But the real stylistic and structural godfather of much of it seems to be Joyce.[4] Here's a representative passage:

> Cheeribye, the porter had said, seeing them to their room, mind you get your money's worth.

> Do stations never sleep? he wondered. Clang-clang, clang. You must dance but I must sleep.
> Got to be a lion tonight over; mouse-time again soon.
> "Cassidy."
> "Yes."
> "I love you"
> "I love you"
> "Really?"
> "Really."
> "I could make you the happiest man on earth."
> "I am already." (370)

This could be straight out of *Ulysses*. Pound's *Cantos* may have had a small part, too, and it is sure that surrealism, either in art or poetry or both, had some share in producing the shifting miasma of impressions that make up much of the novel. It would not be surprising to find out that le Carré had been studying the satirist art of George Grosz or Kafka's shorter sketches. Anthony Burgess or Vladimir Nabokov may be able to dabble in such sophisticated tap-dancing with the language, but in le Carré it has a forced and fragile quality.

Anyway, neither the public nor the critics bought it, and *The Naive and Sentimental Lover* has stood for a quarter of a century as le Carré's only failure. Undoubtedly, much of the unfriendly reception of the novel was due to the author's entrenched reputation as a writer of thrillers. As Owen Dudley Edwards wrote, in one of the few sympathetic studies of *The Naive and Sentimental Lover:* "The Establishment does not like it when the butcher-boy instead of his normal delivery arrives with a somewhat thorny rose-bush—it insists these must be spurious roses. Mr. le Carré if he is to be tolerated, must be pigeon-holed."[5] It is hardly surprising. Just as his fling with the Kennaways marked his only real deviation from bourgeois culture and morality, this novel marks the novelist's only real aberration into the unrestrained and undisciplined. Just as his affair with the Kennaways was his major adventure with bohemian, free-form creativity, so much of the novel resembles stream-of-consciousness poetry—or an attempt at it. Le Carré is not a poet, however, and vivid and challenging as much of the novel is, the overall effect is one of confusion. Fortunately, it was only a prelude to a triumphal return to known fields and pastures old.

CHAPTER SEVEN

Tinker, Tailor, Soldier, Spy

Tinker, Tailor, Soldier, Spy (1974) is the quintessential Smiley novel. It defined the most important political theme of the postwar world, the Cold War, and it established George Smiley—perhaps one of the most memorable characters of modern Western literature—in the public mind. Millions of readers think of all or most of le Carré's novels as featuring Smiley. Actually, he is important in only five of le Carré's fifteen Cold War, and now "post–Cold War," novels. Of those five *Call for the Dead* and *A Murder of Quality* are novellas, and Smiley's role as the detached puppet master who pulls Jerry Westerby's strings in *The Honourable Schoolboy* makes him more part of the framing action in that novel than part of the core plot, which describes the actual execution of "Operation Dolphin." Considering, then, the limited role Smiley occupies in the overall sweep of le Carré's fiction, the popular conception of Smiley's lifelong battle with the KGB as le Carré's controlling motif is deceptive: that struggle is really only the subject of a brilliant but brief "prologue" novella *(Call for the Dead)* and the two "bookends" of the "Quest for Karla" trilogy, *Tinker, Tailor, Soldier, Spy* and *Smiley's People.* Except for these, Smiley is ancillary—often even a vestigial "character" in the colorful Circus collection. He hangs on the fringes of *The Spy Who Came in from the Cold* like a reproachful conscience hinting at the moral and practical lunacy of the action; he appears deus ex machina to mop up the sad remains in *The Looking-Glass War;* and, as a retired éminence gris and raconteur, he initiates Ned's recollections in *The Secret Pilgrim.* The rest is silence, and the author has indicated that he has no intention of resurrecting his most famous spy in any future works.

The success of these "Smiley novels" in establishing the character in the reading public's imagination testifies to their power of myth-making. Even though the phenomenal sales of *The Spy Who Came in from the Cold* make it the most popular serious example of its genre ever written in English, or any language, Smiley is entrenched as *the* character of le Carré's creation and probably his most enduring contribution to literary history. Despite the distinction of le Carré's later "non-Smiley" works—and several are very distinguished—it is likely that the novelist's place in literary and popular history will rest primarily on Smiley's sloping shoulders. This pudgy, befuddled, beleaguered intellectual with the Jesuitic mind of an investigator of the Spanish Inquisition and the field instincts of a professional soldier is not only the most fully realized character in spy fiction but is subtly crafted by the artistic standards of any literature.

So widely accepted today is the quality of *Tinker, Tailor, Soldier, Spy* and its importance in the le Carré canon that it is hard to remember that a generation ago the book received mixed reviews at best. Richard Locke roasted it in the *New York Times Book Review* ("melodramatic and sentimental")[1] and Roger Sale's *Hudson Review* comment was worse ("really dull and really pretentious").[2] Pearl K. Bell's remarks in the *New Leader* were perhaps most revealing of the reaction of critics used to thinking of "quality" spy novels as Eric Ambler as opposed to Ian Fleming: "It is myopic and unjust to link le Carré with high art: The criteria for judging literary fiction are simply irrelevant to his superb entertainments and can only muddle a reader's pleasure."[3]

Le Carré tried writing *Tinker, Tailor, Soldier, Spy* without Smiley, focusing at first on the story of the betrayed friendship between Jim Prideaux and Bill Haydon,[4] but found that only through Smiley's donnish, intensely intellectual psychology could the story's complexity be focused.[5] The key to the work is that its opacity—the murky, subjective process of arriving at truth through the dogged application of intelligence to complex and ambiguous objective particulars—is perfectly suited to George Smiley's mentality. Smiley is, by inclination and emotion, more professorial than conspiratorial, more scholar than spy. His intellectual curiosity, ruminative temperament, and academic training are more suited to the Oxford don he would have been had not history in the form of the threat of fascism intervened. The treasured volume of Grimmelshausen's *Simplicissimus,* an arcane classic of eighteenth-century German neoclassicism which Smiley leaves at his club early in *Tinker, Tailor, Soldier, Spy,* and which he remembers is still uncollected on his last page of the novel, is the symbol of his true self, endlessly put on hold by the pragmatic pull of realpolitik.

Although in *Tinker, Tailor, Soldier, Spy* he complains angrily that he was "forced out" of the Circus prematurely (and there is no doubt he was forced out, whether prematurely or not), Smiley is in his mid-sixties by the time he exposes Bill Haydon. Despite his uncompromising intellect, which is still razor sharp, he has the body, behavior, and psychology of an old man whom life has passed by. He is in most respects elderly, outhustled by young women hailing taxis, forgetting things at his club and frequently showing signs of exhaustion at the demands of this complex case, with its potentially compromising and psychologically draining personal aspects. He tires even reading files in his hotel room, and his reaction to the climax of his quest is almost lethargic. In victory he seems to lose focus, with an elderly man's inability to concentrate. In their final meeting, after listening to Haydon making excuses for his treason, Smiley wants to reply, "but there seemed no point" (349). The bittersweet entropy that marks the end of the novel is drawn directly from Smiley's psychology.

In literary history Smiley is the descendant of a distinguished line of cerebral detectives whose mental powers are dramatically juxtaposed with lack of strength—often weakness—of physique and personality. These include the turn-of-the-century French detective writer Jacques Futrelle's "Thinking Machine," Agatha Christie's effete Hercule Poirot, and Rex Stout's ponderous Nero Wolfe, who acknowledges his inability to function in the real world by never leaving his apartment. Behind them all is Sherlock Holmes, who, Arthur Conan Doyle makes clear, may have surprising physical prowess but is obstinately lacking in social graces. Another significant analogue is Holmes's alter ego and brother, Mycroft Holmes, who solves all his problems from the intellectual sanctum sanctorum of the Diogenes Club; Smiley, too, is a member of unfashionable clubs, but he is not a "clubman."

Thinking of Holmes, it is difficult not to read all the Karla novels in the light of Arthur Conan Doyle's account of Holmes's extended duel with the "Napoleon of Crime," Professor Moriarty, who, like Karla, was a "genius, a philosopher, and abstract thinker," with the demeanor of a schoolmaster and the focused will of the mad scientist he truly was. John le Carré, like every British schoolboy, read avidly of the Holmes-Moriarty struggle, particularly the dramatic account of its apotheosis in "The Final

Problem," when both of the geniuses plunge into the Reichenbach
Falls, apparently to their deaths, locked in battle in each other's
arms. Like Holmes, Smiley, who comes back at least three times
from retirement, shows a talent for resurrection.

What distinguishes Smiley from all his fictional forebears,
and from virtually every other important character in detective
and spy fiction, is his ability to love. Although the flamboyance
and melodrama of Ian Fleming's novels give James Bond the
appearance of being a romantic, the swashbuckling 007's con-
quests are purely sexual and purely one-sided—all eros without
agape. Despite his superficial credentials as a clotheshorse and
discriminating palate in food and liquor, Bond's ethic is based
clearly on the moral equivalency of "kill and/or be killed."
Smiley's, on the other hand, is rooted in an ambivalent version of
"love thy enemy" (or, at least, "try to relate to him"). While
Bond's reputation as a womanizer thinly disguises an inability to
commit to or understand any woman (except, perhaps, in *On Her
Majesty's Secret Service*), at Smiley's core lies his devotion to his
unfaithful wife, Ann. Further, he is highly sensitive to love in
others, particularly his enemies. It is he who understands and
respects the attraction of Else Fennan to Dieter Frey, sympathizes
with and helps Liz Gold when she is grieving for the lost Leamas,
and feels that Bill Haydon's "unforgivable" crime is hurting Ann.
In this, and every other respect, he is an "anti-Bond."

Nothing is more revealing of Smiley's character than the
closing paragraph of the second of *Tinker, Tailor, Soldier, Spy*'s
three sections. At this moment, just when Smiley has essentially
"cracked the case," he falls asleep dreaming "of Ann, and in his
tiredness cherished her profoundly, longing to protect her frailty

with his own. Like a young man, he whispered her name aloud, and imagined her beautiful face bowing over him in the half-light" (256). Smiley's reveries—many of them primarily concerned with bringing his keen intellect to bear on the unmasking and destroying of treason—often close thus, as he slips back into that secret sanctuary of adoration which contrasts so touchingly with his trade. There is not another major character in espionage or detective fiction who is so romantic, so emotionally vulnerable—so human.[6] Smiley's love for Ann is not simply a sentimental Achilles heel, either, for his humanity extends beyond her. His bitter regret over his ability to kill Dieter Frey in *Call for the Dead* (and his reflection that Frey was a better friend for not killing him first), his solicitude for Leamas and Leiser in earlier novels, and his empathy with Stella Rode in *A Murder of Quality* all testify to his compassion. In *Tinker, Tailor, Soldier, Spy* this empathy informs his entire tracking of Bill Haydon, and it is the quality in him that Karla expects will cloud Smiley's judgment, because Bill is Ann's lover—"the last illusion of the illusionless man" (350). It is not so much that Karla overestimates Smiley's humanity—indeed, Smiley is profoundly wary of pursuing Bill for a personal agenda—as that the quality of Smiley's mind is so keen and his integrity so great that he cannot deny the truth regardless of extraneous concerns such as his own feelings.

Characteristically, though, when Bill is actually trapped, Smiley's humanity makes it impossible for him to exalt either. As soon as the actual trap is sprung and Haydon is caught, Smiley becomes virtually dysfunctional, leaving the scene, apparently too embarrassed and chagrined to face the man who has so wronged him and whom he has finally nailed (337). Later, during an interrogation, when Haydon, who still doesn't "get it," has the audacity to say he hopes that Smiley will "remember him with affection," Smiley is simply unable to tell him that "he would not remember him in those terms at all" (349). True hatred, it seems, is not part of his formidable equipment. That equipment is completely disguised by everything about Smiley taken at first glance. He is introduced, or reintroduced, to the reader in the second chapter of *Tinker, Tailor, Soldier, Spy,* and it must be the most unprepossessing portrait of a hero in espionage literature:

Unlike Jim Prideaux, Mr. George Smiley was not naturally equipped for hurrying in the rain, least of all at dead of night. Indeed, he might have been the final form for which Bill Roach was the prototype. Small, pudgy, and at best middle-aged, he was by appearance one of London's meek who do not inherit the earth. His legs were short, his gait anything but agile, his dress costly, ill-fitting, and extremely wet. (18)

Smiley's lineage is conspicuous by its absence. Whereas le Carré gives at least thumbnail sketches in *Tinker, Tailor, Soldier, Spy* of all other characters, major and minor, virtually nothing is revealed of the youth of this most important one. Smiley's parentage and ancestry, education, and even the year of his birth are unknown(divergent projections from different books suggest sometime between 1905 and the outbreak of World War I).[7] In a later book, *The Secret Pilgrim,* Smiley casually remarks that he was prepared for confirmation by a retired bishop and that he went to an undistinguished public school; admittedly, both details suggest at least the fringes of the upper middle class. Still, little is known about him before his recruitment for the service by Steed-Aspery at Oxford.

Smiley is clearly a gentleman, at least in manners and speech. Politeness, unwillingness (or inability) to display emotion, and a characteristic English reserve mark his behavior. This is not unimportant, for, within the British class system as le Carré presents it, it is not possible to be "classless," and everything about Smiley suggests good breeding. Still, in contrast to his colleagues and enemies, all of whom are clearly pigeonholed in terms of class origin and affiliation, Smiley is peculiarly amorphous. Married to an aristocrat, he often relates best to working-class psychologies like Inspector Mendel and Sam Collins or renegade and rebellious rejectors of their upper-class roots like disreputable Connie Sachs. An administrator and government functionary himself—at least by the time of the main action of *Tinker, Tailor, Soldier, Spy*—Smiley loathes politicians like Ann's cousin Miles Sercomb, administrators like Percy Alliline, and even relatively benign bureaucrats like the cabinet officer Oliver Lacon (Smiley clearly agrees with his friend Sam Collins, who sneers: "Power corrupts, but some must govern. Brother Lacon will scramble to the top of the heap" (235). The aristocratic clubman Roddy Martindale, who presses for toady gossip of the Circus, clearly disgusts Smiley.

One key to Smiley's character is its suggestion of social insecurity, and in this he is surprisingly existential, almost diffidently alienated. Often, this manifests itself as a neurotic inferiority complex, characterized (since Smiley's appropriate mode as a spy is inquisitorial and critical) by catechism and self-flagellation. "Sheer lack of will-power," he accuses himself, in this case for failing to break with the Circus, his wife, and London (24). Parallel to his constant investigation of Bill, of the Circus, of treason, is an inner inquisition of himself—which must always lead to self-reproach. When he recalls for Guillam his interrogation of the captured Karla in India, he remembers it as grilling himself (205). Often his insecurity seems exhibited in a self-deprecating humility that sometimes borders on self-abuse, and, despite his talents, he seems incapable of pride; when he starts to feel it, his nagging conscience pulls him up. "'It was sheer vanity in him to believe that one fat middleaged spy is the only thing capable of holding the world together,' he would tell himself" (73).

Smiley's psychology resembles that of a lapsed Catholic theologian, and in this le Carré is very much the descendant of James Joyce, who clearly influenced him. Compare Smiley's interrogations of Tarr, Max, Jim—even the supportive Connie Sachs—with the catechismal method of Stephen Dedalus's Jesuitic conversations with Lynch, Cranly, and other religion students in *A Portrait of the Artist as a Young Man* or the "Ithaca" chapter in *Ulysses,* the rhetorical mode of which is catechism. The cautious, defining rhetoric, the rigorous rationality, and the tremulous underpinnings of a shaken moral and spiritual faith mark the trembling intellectuals who haunt the pages of modern psychological and political literature from Kafka to Camus.

Smiley's self-effacement in *Tinker, Tailor, Soldier, Spy* is almost perverse. On the one hand, like the "Hound of Heaven," he pursues the truth with surgical intelligence and a frightening personal courage in his willingness to confront the awful implications of his inquiry. Several times it is he who must frame for his discreet interlocutors the statement of Ann's adultery. Smiley reads Haydon's steps in the footprints of other people. On the other hand, Smiley takes every step himself with an almost sheepish humility that, were it less well-bred, might suggest Uriah Heep. From the opening description of him as "one of London's meek who do not inherit the Earth" to his last thought in the novel, seeing his wife, Ann, as "essentially another man's woman" (54), Smiley is the antithesis of the confident, aggressive, sexually successful agent radiating machismo like James Bond.

Juxtaposed to this Milquetoast exterior is Smiley's profound professionalism. He is the epitome of subtle tradecraft to his colleagues. When Jim Prideaux notices the unchanged shoes of the Czech counterintelligence agents following him, "he didn't suspect, he knew, as Smiley would have known" (275). Even when distracted, Smiley is instinctively watchful, counting the steps in his house and shops on the way to the British Museum to keep his mind sharp (26) or checking the darkened streets repeatedly when he senses more than actually sees Jim Prideaux following him. Often the innocuousness and the professionalism merge: Guillam lets Smiley out in traffic, has a last-minute thought, turns to call to him, "but Smiley was gone. He had never known anyone who could disappear so quickly in a crowd" (208).

Perhaps the hardest thing to remember reading *Tinker, Tailor, Soldier, Spy* is that Smiley is not only the hero of the novel—and he clearly is, despite the book's profound cynicism about his trade—but he is a highly successful hero. If discovering and trapping Haydon is a Pyrrhic victory in its emotional cost to Smiley, it is plainly a triumph. In fact, of the fifteen novels in the espionage canon it is only the four Smiley novels that are unambiguously stories of successful operations directed by a heroic intelligence—Smiley's. For all his exhaustion and disillusionment at the close of the chase, for all his humanist reservations about the morality of doing unto Bill Haydon as Bill has done unto everyone, for all his recognition that Bill is only a symptom rather than the disease—still, Smiley has clearly *won* and won big. If le Carré closes *Smiley's People,* the novel that concludes Smiley's "Quest for Karla," with Guillam doggedly insisting that Smiley accept his victory over his archenemy, so, too, might *Tinker, Tailor, Soldier, Spy* have closed with a similar reminder. But the mood of this novel is understatement (as it is the mood of its hero), and the consciousness of victory must rest in the mind of the reader.

If Smiley is St. George or the Red Cross Knight of *Tinker, Tailor, Soldier, Spy,* then Bill Haydon is unequivocally the dragon, the villain, the Antichrist, and Archimago. He is Smiley's foil in every way. The epitome of the dashing and colorful agent, Bill is both a genuine romantic and a romantic manqué, "dashing Bill Haydon, our latter-day Lawrence of Arabia," as Peter Guillam bitterly reflects. *Tinker, Tailor, Soldier, Spy,* however, is ultimately about the failure and hypocrisy of such romanticism in the real world. Guillam's anger when Bill is caught, when Smiley has to caution him not to kill Haydon in his rage, derives from Guillam's long admiration for Bill as "the torch-bearer for a certain kind of antiquated romanticism" (334).

Perhaps the only weakness in *Tinker, Tailor, Soldier, Spy* is the unmitigated villainy of Haydon. Affected, prideful, bigoted, and personally disloyal—as his character unravels at the close of the novel he is unveiled as a poseur, a seducer, a debauchee, and ultimately an opportunist. He lacks the conviction and courage of Karla, the cynical depth of Magnus Pym in *A Perfect Spy,* or the ideological purity of Khalil in *The Little Drummer Girl.* The most apology that can be made for him is framed by Connie Sachs, who lumps Haydon's plight with that of Smiley and the whole British upper class: "Poor loves. Trained to Empire, trained to rule the waves. All gone. All taken away" (109). "All taken away." In a sense *Tinker, Tailor, Soldier, Spy* is a study of how two types of well-bred people respond to loss, or to a world suffering a dying fall. Smiley adapts with a bittersweet grace, because he has enough self-respect to know that he is something more than a "British gentleman." Haydon, though, is something less, as Smiley well knows, meditating on Bill's treatment of his friends: "Bill's real trick was to use them, to live through them to complete himself, here a piece, there a piece, from their passive identities, thus disguising the fact that he was less, far less, than the sum of his apparent qualities . . . and finally submerging this dependence beneath an artist's arrogance, calling them creatures of his mind" (151).

The several comparisons of Haydon to Lawrence of Arabia are particularly significant. T. E. Lawrence, a British intelligence officer during World War I, "went Arab" and led a ragtag army of Bedouin soldiers against the Turks. Highly publicized, he went into hiding after the war and produced a massive poetic memoir, *The Seven Pillars of Wisdom,* which became a cherished guide-book for a cult of idealistic young men drawn to the intellectual soldier of fortune as a role model. One version of this mythological British adventurer is the flamboyant spy, in fiction and in life.

Tinker, Tailor, Soldier, Spy

This was the model for Bill Haydon, as Smiley realizes. He senses that Haydon's treachery derives not from mendacity or venality or even from a sense of commitment to any morality or ideology but, rather, from an egotistical love of theatrics and self-promotion: "Bill had loved it, too, Smiley didn't doubt that for a moment. Standing at the middle of a secret stage, playing world against world, hero and playwright in one: oh, Bill had loved that, all right" (353). They are all self-promoting idols, le Carré suggests, and often, as with Bill Haydon, with feet of worse than clay.

Bill Haydon is a composite of four men—Kim Philby, Guy Burgess, Donald Maclean, and Anthony Blunt—of whom Philby is the most important in providing the prototype for le Carré. It is useful with any roman à clef to understand what the key represents, and it is particularly so with this novel. American novelists tend to create characters and situations that are sui generis, for Americans are less a people than a gathering of peoples. Whereas American writers probe the condition of individual Americans, often without regard to any particularly *American* qualities about them, British literature since long before Matthew Arnold has been concerned with "the state of England," and *Tinker, Tailor, Soldier, Spy* is no exception.

The novel is based on a series of sensational spy exposures that embarrassed the British Secret Service in the quarter century after World War II. In 1951 two Cambridge-educated long-term members of British intelligence, Guy Burgess and Donald Maclean, made international headlines by defecting to Russia when it was about to be revealed that they had been spying for Russia since long before the war. For a decade rumors persisted that more "moles" (although le Carré had not yet popularized the word) lurked deep in British intelligence. Then, in 1963, an even better-known aristocrat within the service, Kim Philby, fled to Moscow as independent investigators within and without MI5 were about to reveal his complicity with Burgess and Maclean. Still, there were whispers of a "fourth man." A decade later this even more securely buried mole came out of the closet and proved to be Sir Anthony Blunt, a distinguished art historian and the official art advisor to the queen.[8] The defections were highly publicized international scandals; within Britain they were the subjects of fascination and horror. Only the Profumo scandal of 1963—also reeking of espionage but with generous dollops of sex as well—gripped the attention of the English public as strongly.

As it happened, the publication of *Tinker, Tailor, Soldier, Spy* in 1974 coincided with Blunt's unmasking, but it was Philby with whom, understandably, most critics and nearly all the public quickly identified the character of Bill Haydon. Some commentary has treated the novel simply as a thinly disguised roman à clef, for obvious reasons. Philby—named Kim by his father after Rudyard Kipling's fictional portrait of a British boy training to be a spy—was the son of St. John Philby, a famous soldier of fortune and self-promoting Arabist of the T. E. Lawrence stripe whom *Newsweek* described as "an explorer, eccentric, Muslim convert, liar, con man, voluptuary, spy."[9] Like Haydon, whose father Ann Smiley calls "the monster," St. John Philby was an unloving father. He was also a vain man who was a family tyrant and a terrible parent; comparisons with le Carré's father and Ricky Pym of *A Perfect Spy* are obvious. Much else about Haydon invites identification with Philby. His sexual predatoriness, easy-going noblesse oblige charm, aristocratic access to bureaucratic power in a class-conscious society, and self-justification through mouthing agitprop jargon all correspond with Kim Philby's character.

If Philby among the "Cambridge Four" is the strongest model for Haydon, the other three—Guy Burgess, Donald Maclean, and Anthony Blunt—certainly contributed to le Carré's portrait. Haydon is clearly bisexual—rather sordidly so, for le Carré usually staidly identifies homosexuality in men with immorality; only Philby, of the Cambridge traitors, was purely heterosexual. Even in a world noted for the intellectual chic of homosexuality, Burgess was notorious, particularly for his penchant for "lowering" affairs (like Bill Haydon's sailor boy). Further, it was Blunt, like Haydon, who was "arty," and Burgess seems more the model for Haydon's hauteur.

Le Carré's own attitude toward Philby also invites identifying the notorious defector as the particular model for Haydon, for the novelist has been outspoken about his contempt for Philby's character and morals. In 1968 le Carré's widely discussed introduction to *The Philby Conspiracy* stung the shrinking ranks of Philby loyalists[10] (which still included the influential Graham Greene, who continued to defend Philby long after his defection and in 1969 himself wrote a laudatory introduction to Philby's apologia in his memoirs, which Philby had written in Moscow).[11] Le Carré said: "I had a difference of opinion with Graham Greene over Philby; we take different views. I'm obliged to say that I feel Philby was essentially dead wrong all the way through and all the time . . . his consistent objective was to get rid of the values I hold

to be all right, and I don't go along with it." Le Carré's attitude
had hardly changed nearly twenty years later when he visited
Moscow following the Cold War thaw and refused to meet the
ailing Philby, citing "a profound loathing" for the man.[12] He is
still adamant. "He was a traitor and a murderer," he told an
interviewer recently, "he did betray people who died horribly in
consequence of that."[13] Le Carré wrote his definitive statement
on Philby in his introduction to the Lamplighter Edition of
Tinker, Tailor, Soldier, Spy in 1991:

> I always had a quite particular dislike for Philby. . . . The
> reasons, I fear, have much to do with the inverted snobbery
> of my class and generation. I disliked Philby because he
> had so many of my attributes. He was public-school
> educated, the son of a wayward and dictatorial father—the
> explorer and adventurer, St. John Philby—he drew people
> easily to him and he was adept at hiding his feelings—in
> particular his seething distaste for the bigotries and preju-
> dices of the English ruling classes. I'm afraid that all of
> these characteristics have at one time or another been mine.
> . . . I knew what it was like, as he did, to be brought up by
> a man so oversized that your only resort as a child was to
> subterfuge and deceit. And I knew, or thought I knew, how
> easily the anger and inwardness thus born could turn
> themselves into a love-hate relationship with the father
> images of society, and finally with society itself.[14]

The persistent sympathy of Greene and other critics of the
British intelligence establishment may account for the perverse

obtuseness of some critics in believing that *Tinker, Tailor, Soldier, Spy*'s portrait of Haydon is not only ambiguous but almost admirable. Some of this may simply derive from confusing Smiley's confession of his total inability to understand Haydon with excusing him (353). Deciding that "treason is very much a matter of habit," however, does not condone it. Tony Barley claims that, "with Haydon, le Carré eschews completely his moral venom for the real-life spy and gives instead a character whose motives and determinations alike, though ultimately intangible, are worthy of balanced appreciation."[15] This may well be one of the most dramatic misreadings of character in modern British criticism, and it is difficult to understand how any reader can find Haydon sympathetic.

Smiley and Haydon stand at opposite ends within le Carré's fascinating portrait of the British intelligence establishment, the Circus. In *Tinker, Tailor, Soldier, Spy* le Carré paints the organization as a richly detailed portrait comparable to the social profiles of the great British novelists of manners—Dickens, Trollope, Thackeray, Austen, and Fielding. The texture of the London underworld of *Oliver Twist* or of the rural parsonage circle of *Barchester Towers* are no more skillfully drawn. Here fully developed are all the mechanical details of "tradecraft": the elaborate ritualistic rules cover all agent activity from observing even passersby's shoes to checking in and out of the file room. Here in its totality is the famous jargon that defines the Circus as a demimonde complete with its own arcane language. Guards are "babysitters," assassins "scalphunters," and U.S. intelligence (the CIA) is "the Cousins." Agent technique is "tradecraft," codes are "unbuttoned," agents are "blown" if discovered, and so on. At the center of the novel, in every way, lurks a "mole," the word for a deeply buried spy which has found its way so thoroughly into popular vocabulary that, if le Carré did not invent it, he made it a commonplace of general usage in the English language.[16] With loving realistic fidelity le Carré compiles the accretion of objective particulars that make *Tinker, Tailor, Soldier, Spy* a masterpiece of realism.

The world of the Circus, for the first time in le Carré's fiction, completely subsumes that of the novel (and, considering that for much of the novel the Circus is dominated by Bill Haydon, it has become a corrupt mansion of realistic detail—perversely a "Hotel de la Mole"). All the major characters are not only spies; they are Circus spies. Even the Enemy is represented not by Karla and Moscow Centre but by Bill Haydon, a thoroughly English communist and one who, through his background and training, represents the "old Circus" of the venerable Oxford dons Fanshawe and Jebedee rather than the eclectic, polyglot "new Circus" of Hungarian émigré Toby Esterhaze, red-brick and working-class Roy Bland, and mercantile Scot Percy Alleline (whom Haydon sneers at as a "Caledonian ragpicker," even as he rides Alleline's gullibility to the heights of deception). Life in the new Circus is a far cry from the elegance of James Bond and "M" lunching at "Blades." Even on the purely physical level it is often just short of sordid, as are Smiley's breakfasts of undercooked sausage and overcooked tomato in the seedy "safe" Hotel Islay or the depressing apartment of Bill's sordid love life with his floozy mistress and baby which Smiley uncovers after the capture (343–44).

The implications are clear: the true enemy is within. From the deceptively simple children's rhyme of the title (identifying a traitor who kills his friends as "one of us") to the neat twist by which Smiley and his allies must subvert the institution to which they belong for its own good, *Tinker, Tailor, Soldier, Spy* is about the familiar corrupted into the alien, the vicious and deceitful masquerading as the innocent and decent.

Counterpointed to the solipsistic world of the Circus, and parallel to it, is the world of Thursgood's school, where Jim Prideaux goes to ground. All the major themes of *Tinker, Tailor, Soldier, Spy* are neatly reproduced in the subplot of Jim, his tremulous protégé Bill Roach and the savage mini-society of a British public school. Wounded in body and spirit, Jim seeks refuge here from the system that has so damaged and betrayed him (and from the friend, Bill Haydon, whom he still trusts). Ironically, he finds in the British public school a microcosm of the systems that he flees—both the Circus and British society. Traditionally in English literature, for good and for bad, the public school is portrayed as a paradigm of British society and, particularly, the class system, writ small, from *Tom Brown's School Days* to *Good Bye, Mr. Chips.* (Matthew Arnold's father was the headmaster of Rugby, preserved in the encomium of his son and the acerbity of Lytton Strachey's description of Thomas Arnold in *Eminent Victorians.*) The snobbery, the insularity, the smug conviction of the righteousness of the "haves," the alien-ation of the "have-nots," and the assertion of the rightness of fundamental "Englishness"—all are embodied in the conception of the privileged boys' boarding school. Here the secret machi-nations that Jim has tried to escape in the world of espionage reappear in the form of the strict social machinery of the school.[17]

In one sense Jim—the most "English" character in le Carré's novels before Jerry Westerby in *The Honourable Schoolboy* — fits right in at Thursgood's. His arrival in his beloved Alvis (a notoriously rickety English car that he patriotically calls "the best car in the world, now out of production thanks to Socialism" [117]) is a fine comic set piece. Jim's lumbering athleticism, gruff good humor, and shameless Tory chauvinism are matched by his muscular dealing with even the effete French language that he teaches ("*Mon cher Berger,* if you do not very soon summon one lucid sentence of French, *je te mettrai tout de suite à la porte, tu comprends,* you beastly toad?"). Thursgood's would seem to be a logical home for him, but there are serpents in this English Eden too. Jim's instinctive sense of his own precarious inability to detach from the dangers of his past is soon echoed in the quaking insecurity of the worshipful Roach, who both spies for Jim and on him. All these school sections of *Tinker, Tailor, Soldier, Spy* are suffused by an atmosphere of paranoid watchfulness. For the first two-thirds of the novel the perspective cuts back and forth from Smiley's team of "mole trackers" to Jim at Thursgood's. Gradually, the world of Circus violence and conspiracy reaches into the school, and Jim, aware of the noose of the political world closing again about him, prepares to defend himself and to go back into action. Knowing that he is monitored by Smiley and his lieutenant, Mendel, Jim abandons the "safe house" of the school and tracks his trackers through the last third of the novel to take revenge on his traitorous friend Haydon.

   Thursgood's, therefore, is a miniature of English society—a boy's world that mocks, in several senses of the word, the greater "game" that these schoolboys will play as men.[18] The title of *Tinker, Tailor, Soldier, Spy,* le Carré's most brilliant, is an indication of the role that games, both of boys and men, play in the development of the novel. "Tinker, Tailor, Soldier, Sailor" is a children's counting game as well as a mnemonic device used by children to distance themselves from the uncomfortable task of making emotional value commitments. Children count off by numbers to leave "choosing" to fate—not to accept the responsibility for potentially wounding decisions. The Circus, with its elaborate jargon, its extensive panoply of gamesmanship and tradecraft (often le Carré makes the Cold War seem like big boys playing "Dungeons and Dragons"), and its formalized ritualizing of conflict is mirrored in the elaborate games children play. And, just as the unexpected and ugly adult word *spy* leaps out at the reader from the midst of innocuous trades in the title, so does the brutal reality of violence, betrayal, and death abruptly intrude into the formalized games these grown men play—games patterned after their childhood entertainments.

Boys and men are interchangeable in *Tinker, Tailor, Soldier, Spy.* As Bill Roach is a "little old man" carrying the weight of the world, the "men" of the Circus are in many respects the Lost Boys of *Peter Pan* who never grew up. Bill Haydon wields adolescent slogans, delights in being puckishly a "bad boy," and finds his sexuality most expressively in escape with a girl-child mistress and a gay sailor boy. Toby Esterhaze, physically no larger than a child, primps like a teenager and tries on lifestyles like one too. Peter Guillam—morally, at least, on the side of the angels—is a forty-year-old boy who hero-worships the older generation at the Circus (as young Avery fawns on the senior men in *The Looking-Glass War*) and frets over his inability to commit to women or love. Ricky Tarr—who is characterized as constantly playing with sticks, cards, and other games—giggles over the elaborate foofaraw of Circus tradecraft and has a perverse conception of family life out of "Under the Yum-Yum Tree." Significantly, the novel offers virtually not a man or woman with a successful family life except the dismal, gray cabinet minister Lacon, whose insipid children swarm like Mrs. Jelleby's in *Bleak House*. There is not a successful marriage in the Circus nor any fulfilling relationship between men and women, except perhaps between Smiley and Connie Sachs, a pairing with aberrant psychological overtones.

On the subject of gamesmanship and family there is le Carré's longest-running inside joke in *Tinker, Tailor, Soldier, Spy*—the analogy of this book to Rudyard Kipling's *Kim. Kim* is the only really successful full-length novel written by the single most popular British writer in the first half of the twentieth century and the one who defined the English male's self-conception. It is the story of a boy who is adopted by the British Secret Service in India (or adopts it) and is then elaborately tutored in espionage by mentors who train him for "The Great Game" (*Kim*'s euphemism for spying) through games and apparently childish role-playing. Kim is, of course, the name of the man after whom *Tinker, Tailor, Soldier, Spy*'s traitor is most closely patterned—Kim Philby, who was named by his father after Kipling's hero.

Thursgood's is also representative of another aspect of *Tinker, Tailor, Soldier, Spy* which is critical not only to the novel but to all of le Carré's work: the deadly and corrupting importance of class in British society. If the social satire of the school scenes seem to smack more of Evelyn Waugh, Angus Wilson, and Kingsley Amis than of "hard-boiled" international espionage, it is only because we think of le Carré less than those writers

as a master of the novel of manners.[19] The social engine that
drives the Circus is jockeying within the "old-boy network," and
the novel is redolent of scathing shots at "Anglo-Saxon attitudes," from the sketch of the restaurant where Smiley and
Guillam meet and endure wretched service to Ann's description
of her cousin's gauche Rolls-Royce, "the black bedpan."

Considering the snobbery and hypocrisy of Haydon, Miles
Sercomb, Roddy Martingale, and the sycophants like Toby
Esterhaze who are toff "wannabes," it would be tempting to read
Tinker, Tailor, Soldier, Spy as a nasty satiric swipe at the upper
classes, if the lower classes did not come off just as badly. Any
proletarian critic who thinks le Carré is a Marxist admirer of the
working class need only look at the character of Roy Bland.
Crude, graceless, and ultimately self-serving, he is interrogated
by Smiley in his natural environment, a pub, where he declares
his true colors: "As a good Socialist, I'm going for the money"
(147). Bland has spent his life in the peculiar position of being a
working-class ideologue pretending to be a working-class idea-
logue. He can mouth all the neo-Marxist generalizations about
class warfare which he learned from his brutal trade union father,
but he uses the role of resentful "bloke" as a front for spying. And
as the deskman of the service in charge of East Europe and
communist satellites, he must of necessity do most of his spying
on friends whose true class affiliation is his own. The supreme
irony of *Tinker, Tailor, Soldier, Spy*'s commentary on class is
that the aristocratic, racist Bill is a mole for the proletariat. "Bill
was a romantic and a snob," Smiley concludes finally. "He
wanted to join an elitist vanguard and lead the mass out of
darkness" (353). It is this "greenery-yallery, Grosvenor gallery,

foot-in-the-grave young man" who calls Percy Alleline a "Caledonian rag merchant" and sneers at the Jews (150) and who justifies his sordid betrayals by the cliché "vox populi, vox dei" (the voice of the people is the voice of God).

At all levels—Thursgood's, the Circus, the great game of society—*Tinker, Tailor, Soldier, Spy* balances appearance against reality. In all the "winners"—those with birth and breeding, beauty and manners—are often *not* what they seem. Although they dominate the style and structure of all three institutions, it is often the Roaches and the Smileys who end up not only morally but effectively victorious. The standard medieval moralist's metaphor of outward beauty concealing inward rot applies to Bill as surely as it applies to Oscar Wilde's Dorian Gray, to whom Smiley compares Bill. If on one level *Tinker, Tailor, Soldier, Spy* is a social satire, on another it is something quite different, a love story, although one deeply hidden in the murk of espionage. Both the intensity of the love theme and the circumspection with which le Carré hides it are surprising, considering that this novel followed the critical and popular crushing of his more overt love story, *The Naive and Sentimental Lover.*

Smiley the cuckold is manifestly a failure as a lover at the beginning of *Tinker, Tailor, Soldier, Spy*. But, then, he looks like a failure as a spy at first too; if appearances count, he may seem a failure in love at the end of the novel as well, when he spies on Ann as "essentially another man's woman" (354). We must not leap too quickly, though, to accept Smiley's self-deprecating assessment (at the moment we might remember that she is coming to him and he has just defeated his rival in love as well as war). It is typical of Smiley that "he wondered whether there was any love between human beings that did not rest upon some sort of self-delusion," but it does not reduce the value of his love to insignificance. It is the measure of Haydon's treachery—and the cardinal sin for which Smiley cannot forgive him—that he betrays both love and friendship to distract Smiley from pursuing his (Smiley's) suspicions during Testify.

In the world of *Tinker, Tailor, Soldier, Spy* all love, like all human values, is qualified and imperfect. Even Smiley, who seems capable of a seemingly limitless, saintly, almost fatuous love for Ann, realizes that people are only capable of so much. In one of his most revealing comments he says to Guillam: "I have a theory, which I suspect is rather immoral. . . . Each of us has only a quantum of compassion. That if we lavish our concern on every stray cat, we never get to the centre of things" (196). The line is a key to Smiley's value system. Limited or not, love—and its nonerotic form, humanity—is Smiley's ultimate value but not in the abstract. Theory for Smiley is nothing. As he tries to tell Karla when he interrogates the Russian, "political generality was meaningless . . . only the particular in life had value" (204). This is what separates him not only from Haydon but from many of Smiley's nominal allies such as Roy Bland, who embarrasses Smiley by spouting anticommunist claptrap (145). In the final analysis only humanity exercised one-on-one has meaning, and this is why at the moment that he is about to close the trap on Bill, who has destroyed so many, Smiley hesitates, because, even with a moral atrocity like Haydon, "nothing is worth the destruction of another human being" (33).

There has been some tendency in later le Carré criticism to read *Tinker, Tailor, Soldier, Spy* largely as part of the "Quest for

Karla" package—that is, as simply one chapter in Smiley's (and ultimately England's) epic struggle with international communism.[20] Le Carré had probably not projected the novel as the start of a trilogy when he began writing it, and the story stands very much by itself, structurally and thematically. It is likely that, in the writing, le Carré underwent a change in the direction of his canon, for *Tinker, Tailor, Soldier, Spy* obviously began as a counterpoint to *The Spy Who Came in from the Cold, The Looking-Glass War,* and *A Small Town in Germany.* For all the steadfast "Englishness" of characters such as Leamas, those were distinctly *foreign* novels, and in all three the focus was steadily on targets and topics away from England: Leamas and Control manipulate Fiedler and Mundt; Leclerc and other non-Circus intelligence personnel focus on East German rocket secrets; Turner meditates the grimy mysteries of Hartung's German past. Significantly, all of those early full-length novels are about operations that can only be considered failures, even fiascoes, certainly from a human point of view. All three begin as studies of British intelligence attempting to control the Cold War; all end in betrayal, death, dissolution, and disillusion. But, for all the apparent moral ambiguity of its resolution, *Tinker, Tailor, Soldier, Spy* is about a success. In fact, inside all the multiple dolls of its intricate plot lies a classic Sherlockian story of detection carried through to the discovery and defeat of the enemy.[21] In this it is in the line of classic British espionage fiction—that of John Buchan and Graham Greene.

Little of *Tinker, Tailor, Soldier, Spy* is really Karla's. Karla may be the "Prime Mover" here, but he only pulls strings in the most distant sense. Only twice does his presence become more important. The first is in Smiley's lengthy account of the Russian's strengths (and weaknesses) when interrogated in India and the other at the very end of the novel when, in Smiley's imagination, "the unyielding face of Karla replaced Bill's crooked death mask." The second instance is obviously a linkage into future novels.

It is indicative that the opening words of *Tinker, Tailor, Soldier, Spy* are "The truth is . . ." and the last are ". . . a dream," for much of what the novel has to say is that in the devious and shifting world of espionage the search for truth is ultimately ephemeral and loses itself in a mist of generalization, insinuation, approximation, and deceit. A standard, and politically correct, contemporary critical reading of *Tinker, Tailor, Soldier, Spy* is that the novel balances Western espionage—notably, of course, British—against Russian and cries, "A plague on both your houses!" Certainly, there is much that is critical in the final picture of both systems, and, since *Tinker, Tailor, Soldier, Spy* is focused on the British system, it is naturally that which the reader sees—"warts and all," in a favorite phrase of the novel.

Ironically, much of the novel's apparent disillusion with the "spying game" comes to the reader through the disillusion of Smiley and is therefore, in itself, an affirmation of the superiority of the Western system. For all his jaded recognition of the weaknesses of the service, and for all the exhausted distaste that the ferreting out of the mole Gerald produces, Smiley's disdain is itself testimony to his morality. Despite reservations Smiley *is* a British spy —and remains one after the action of this novel. (In fact, to carry the narrative momentum forward, it is as a result of the action of this novel that Smiley becomes, for a time, the head of the service, the "top spy.") Conversely, it is simply impossible to imagine in John le Carré's world a comparable Russian spy, one filled with compassion, reservation, and fundamental human decency. In fact, Smiley's greatest "error," as he recounts it in *Tinker, Tailor, Soldier, Spy,* is in assuming, even temporarily, that his Russian counterpart, Karla, may have even a modicum of humanity. As Smiley tells Guillam, when he interrogated Karla in Delhi, he fell into a kind of asexual "honey trap" in responding to Karla as if he, the Russian, were motivated by the same human concerns as Smiley himself. Since Karla seems in many ways comparable to Smiley—in humility, integrity, professionalism—Smiley tries to speak to his humanity (in this case the Russian's presumed capacity for love of a woman, Karla's "Ann"). But Smiley finds that he is "interviewing himself" (320), because Karla is truly a fanatic and, as such, "fireproof," at least in as far as humanitarian appeal is concerned.

Further, there is simply no equivalency between the viciousness and depravity of the two systems. The "sins" of the British in *Tinker, Tailor, Soldier, Spy* are represented by the stupidity of Toby Esterhaze, the smugness of Miles Sercomb, the narrowness of Jim Prideaux, and the greedy ambition of Percy Alliline. These are surely character flaws, and these men are not—except for Jim— attractive characters, but they are not even remotely akin to the savagery and moral obtuseness of the opposition. It is the communists who torture Jim, shoot Irina and Boris, and periodically purge horribly the best people on their own side. If Smiley's virtue is unappreciated, and he is ill used by those he has served so well, he is at no time in danger of being shot *because* he is virtuous, as Karla is. Doubtless, le Carré spells out the atrocities

of communism even more thoroughly in other novels—*The Spy
Who Came in from the Cold,* for example—but any reader who
sees *Tinker, Tailor, Soldier, Spy* as damning the East and the
West equally "simply isn't paying attention," as Robert Penn
Warren said of critics who thought *All the King's Men* glorified
Huey Long.

Nor does communist ideology look any better when awkwardly adopted by Englishmen than it does when practiced by
Russian zealots. If Karla is a flinty fanatic, devoid of compassion,
he has a kind of myopic integrity which makes him superior to
Bill Haydon, who has only a collection of agitprop slogans and
chic leftist jargon to offer when he finally tries to explain his
empty "ideology" to Smiley (346–49). When Bill is finished
mouthing his ill-digested party line, he has so thoroughly lost
track of his muddle of half-truths that he can no longer tell what
he believes, and perhaps he has even deceived himself into
believing that Smiley can find him anything but distasteful, more
likely disgusting. That he can hope "that Smiley would remember
him with affection" after the corrupt obscenity of his behavior is
incredible only by misunderstanding (as some critics have) the
totality of Haydon's mental and moral corruption. Smiley is
unimpressed and "wanted at that point to tell him that he would
not remember him in those terms at all, and a good deal more
besides" (349).

Finally, discussion of *Tinker, Tailor, Soldier, Spy* would be
incomplete without considering the novel's complexity and
subtlety of structure and style. If le Carré's first four novels of
espionage were complex, they were also concise, and they
delivered their labyrinthine plots with a focused narrative per-

sona that sorted out the complexities for the reader. The fixed point of view—of Smiley in *Call for the Dead* and *A Murder of Quality,* of Leamas in *The Spy Who Came in from the Cold,* and of the three doomed protagonists (Taylor, Avery, and Leiser) in *The Looking-Glass War*—did much to keep the murky atmosphere and chain of ambiguous and suspicious events from disturbing, if not confusing, the reader. When Taylor is run down by a sinister car in an airport early in *The Looking-Glass War,* it isn't clear who killed him or why or even, for certain, that he has been murdered, but it is quite clear that the tone is that of danger and doom. But *Tinker, Tailor, Soldier, Spy,* like Browning's "The Ring and the Book," unfolds in a series of perspectives in which a great crime—Bill Haydon's betrayal of his country, his friends, and himself—is exposed through a series of vignettes, each representing the squalid effects of that crime on human beings.

The opening chapter, which might be called "The Coming of Jim Prideaux," presents in the battered wreckage of the body and mind of the betrayed agent the human effects of Haydon's treachery, but the reader has no real conception for fully half the novel of Jim's role in the case at hand. Part of the complexity derives from le Carré's trick of filtering the perception of Jim through the mind of a little boy, the naive Roach, like Henry James's brilliant description of evil through the sensibility of a child in *What Maisie Knew.* Bill is the most important of a group of "watchers" in the novel—apparently detached observers with a stake in the action but who, for a variety of reasons, are like Conrad's *desengagées;* they "look on, make no sound." The most obvious of these is the pathetic Roach, whom Jim Prideaux actually appoints as a "watcher," although at first Roach has no idea of the seriousness of what Jim is "watching for." He is one of several who note, and often describe, behavior they misunderstand or understand incompletely. All of Smiley's allies fall into this category: Connie Sachs, Ricky Tarr, Peter Guillam, Mendel. These are all passive characters, taking their cue from their leader, Smiley, a watcher himself.

The technique of building the novel through a large number of suggestive vignettes, often observed or "watched" by characters with partial knowledge of their significance, is paralleled by le Carré's presenting the many threads of the plot to the reader in the same way. Seldom is the significance of any particular scene immediately clear, and the final panorama of treachery, pursuit, and resolution is assembled rather as bytes are spread around a computer disk—here and there, often apparently at random, but coming together ultimately when the informing intelligence is applied to them.

Tinker, Tailor, Soldier, Spy operates symbolically in much the same way, establishing suggestive details, the meaning of which only becomes evident as the novel unfolds. Le Carré is not a symbolist in the overt Melvillian sense, didactically wringing from significant objects all conceivable metaphysical interpretation. Often, however, his choice of detail in *Tinker, Tailor, Soldier, Spy* has a wry irony that borders on the sardonic. Take, for example, Jim Prideaux's "planting" of his revolver in the Thursgood vegetable patch, where, by the haunting light of the moon, he digs it up under the spying eyes of Bill Roach, who watches the gun and its bullets metamorphose from innocence into deadly significance as the boy recognizes them for what they are. The gun lies underground, yet violently potent, through the first half of the novel, like the fruit of William Blake's poisoned tree, waiting to be needed for "germination." Then the image of the gun festers in Bill's mind, breeding fear, almost madness, until he is finally able to dismiss it as a dream. Similarly no reader who remembered Jim's wringing the owl's neck wonders who killed Bill Haydon.

As for styles, *Tinker, Tailor, Soldier, Spy* is the first of le Carré's books to exhibit the extraordinary verbal flexibility that makes the author a master observer of the idiosyncrasies of character as well as a deadly social satirist. Some of his neatest tricks are subtly recondite, like the use of Elizabeth Barrett Browning's dog Flush for Connie Sach's spaniel or the even more obscure use of Ellis for Jim Prideaux's work name— borrowed from a code name that the gaudy and indiscreet Guy Burgess bandied about as a communist spy before he defected to Moscow in 1950. Most of the author's stylistic legerdemain is more obvious. Le Carré can shift styles in a paragraph. A Faulknerian quality echoes in some of the meditative rhetoric in many stream-of-consciousness passages, particularly in sentence structure and rambling sentence development (209), whereas Hemingwayesque bluntness or enumeration of objective particulars in the style of John O'Hara characterizes others. He is best, though, in setting up characters and making them talk, like a good show business master of impersonation. Thus, Bill Haydon's precious style writing a note to a "dear" homosexual Oxford don, recommending his friend Jim Prideaux as "the young gentleman whose name is in the attached fragment of human skin" and describing his own slumming as "my custom to put on Arab costume and go among the 'Great Unwashed'" (283). This is the same Jim who is mocked by a sarcastic literary review of Bill's paintings, which Jim helped set up, as "Dobbin to the Arts."

"Dobbin to the Arts"? The critic was unkind but accurate, for Jim has indeed thought of himself as Caliban to Jim's Prospero. Smiley knows Jim's limitations, but he is too gentle to point them out, even when Jim tries to defend Bill to him as warranting dispensation for minor aberrations in lifestyle, because "artists are different." Of course, what Smiley also doesn't point out to Jim is that Haydon isn't much of an artist, and treason isn't a minor aberration, particularly when it's your best friend whom you betray. But Jim figures that out for himself, with a bit of help from Smiley.

CHAPTER EIGHT

Cold War in the Wings
The Honourable Schoolboy

Sandwiched between two "Smiley" novels that are clearly more artistically successful—*Tinker, Tailor, Soldier, Spy* and *Smiley's People*—and having a far more tenuous claim to being about Smiley than either of them, *The Honourable Schoolboy*'s critical reputation has been on the decline ever since its publication in 1977. It seems hard even now to remember that the novel appeared with much fanfare, including an extensive cover story in *Time* hailing le Carré as the premier spy novelist of all time and praising *The Honourable Schoolboy* for its "luminous intelligence."[1] The novel won several literary prizes and broke all sales records for its genre, including the benchmark established by *The Spy Who Came in from the Cold.* But there were, even then, dissenting voices. Anthony Burgess, while acknowledging "a dozen set pieces . . . that are awesomely fine," roasted the novel in the *New York Times Book Review,*[2] and in the years since, as the critical reputation of the other two "Quest for Karla" novels has risen steadily, that of *The Honourable Schoolboy* has slipped.

Perhaps some of the muted critical reaction to the novel has derived from its almost tangential role in the Quest for Karla trilogy. The immediate action of both *Tinker, Tailor, Soldier, Spy* and *Smiley's People* (which followed *The Honourable Schoolboy,* in 1980) focuses intensely on a life-and-death struggle between George Smiley's forces of good and Karla's forces of evil. That le Carré, to his credit as an artist, explores the moral ambiguities of defining both "good" and "evil" does not detract from the intensity of either struggle. *The Honourable Schoolboy,* on the other hand, traces the development of a dazzling but chaotic sideshow far from le Carré's familiar European turf. The plot is as intricate as the author's complex collage method of building it through accretion of obscurely interrelated vignettes. Essentially, it is the story of a Circus "sting" operation, an attempt to reach Karla by striking at his Southeast Asian network and, particularly, his area mole, Nelson Ko. The Circus, now temporarily led by Smiley, after the exposure of Haydon recounted in *Tinker, Tailor, Soldier, Spy* (always called "The Fall" in post-Haydon Circus novels), finds Ko by tracing and then closing a "gold-seam," which is Circus jargon for a route for laundering money through banks. The imperfect implement that Smiley uses to get Ko, and through him Karla, is Jerry Westerby, the "Honourable Schoolboy" of the title.

The book has been particularly criticized for unwieldy size, slow pace, and ponderous accumulation of detail. Even le Carré himself is acutely aware of the novel's weaknesses, apologizing that it was "written on the hoof, in a climate so altered that I for one would not know how to recapture any part of it if I were to try to tell you the same story in recollection today."[3] The novel does not have the tight orchestration of *The Spy Who Came in from the Cold* or *Call for the Dead.* Its predecessor, *Tinker, Tailor, Soldier, Spy,* although extremely complex, had the structural integrity of a fine watch, with all the parts complementing one another neatly and coming together in a perfectly orchestrated resolution. *The Honourable Schoolboy,* however, is very much a novel of accumulation and spends pages building atmosphere and establishing the texture of the worlds through which the characters move. The book opens with ten pages recording the gossip of drunken journalists at the Foreign Correspondents' Club in Hong Kong and devotes substantial chunks of its final third to descriptions of the flora and fauna of Cambodia and Thailand, as the "hero," Jerry Westerby, takes a sort of perilous Cook's tour for spies before coming to his violent end. There's no doubt that there *is* a lot of scene setting and that the book *could* be a lot shorter. It is clumsy in actual plot and top-heavy with description of landscape, historical background, and dialogue, but then so is nearly all of Dickens, and it is to Dickens and other novelists of "accretion" that le Carré looks for models in this novel.

Le Carré gives a pretty good idea of what he had in mind for *The Honourable Schoolboy* in a conversation that the books's title character, novelist manqué Jerry Westerby, has with his literary agent, the redoubtable "Ming," who tells Jerry:

> Nobody's brought off the Eastern novel recently, my view. Greene managed it, if you can take Greene, which I can't— too much popery. Malraux, if you like philosophy, which I don't. Maugham you can have, and before that it's back to Conrad. . . . Go easy on the Hemingway stuff. All that grace under pressure, love with your balls shot off. . . . It's been said. . . . Longer sentences. Moment you journalist chappies turn your hand to novels, you write too short. Short paragraphs, short sentences, short chapters. You see the stuff in column inches, 'stead of across the page. Hemingway was just the same. Always trying to write novels on the back of a matchbook. Spread yourself, my view.[4] (96)

Cold War in the Wings

Le Carré's, too, at least in *The Honourable Schoolboy.* The novelist had proved elsewhere he could do the "matchbook" writing, and now he wanted to create the "big" picture. This book *is* big, and ambitious, deliberately sprawling across countries and cultures, steeping the reader in a rich brew of atmospheric texture designed to capture the essence of a multifarious society of enormous variety and complexity. If the novel is a failure, it is an honorable failure of a writer who, in this one case, perhaps wrote not wisely but too much. The book's epitaph might be that of Icarus: "Greatly did he fail, but greatly did he dare." *The Honourable Schoolboy* may go down as one of those well-meaning and fascinating literary attempts to shoot the moon which fall short, like Steinbeck's *East of Eden,* Styron's *Set This House on Fire,* or Faulkner's *A Fable.* Even then readers who complain that there is too much in it, or that it moves too slowly, might be asked if they level the same criticism against *Our Mutual Friend, Anna Karenina,* or *Middlemarch.*

Part of the novel's bulk derives from its subject matter, foreign to le Carré, whose intimate familiarity with the culture and politics of Central Europe made it possible for him to write his earlier novels out of his head. For *The Honourable Schoolboy,* however, he had to research his material through several trips to Hong Kong and the related Orient and through interviews and some purely academic research. He wanted to get it right, and he "worked up" his subject. Le Carré preceded the novel with a foreword in which he thanked sources as disparate as "the staff at the *Far Eastern Economic Review,* Major General Penfold and his team at the Royal Hong Kong Jockey Club" and "certain Hong Kong Chinese friends who, I believe, prefer to remain anonymous." Some of the material he lifted from these sources may be artistically extraneous, but they make of the book, if nothing else, a fascinating Baedeker of the region.

Some of the novel's problems are inherent in its subject, which is Southeast Asian politics in the 1970s, which were chaotic and defied definition. At the tail end of the Vietnam War, as communist China was sinking into a paranoid identity search, as Hong Kong faced the certainty of its apocalyptic cession to the Red Dragon, and as nascent nationalism was suffering growing pains everywhere in the region, Southeast Asia was beyond concise comprehension. Le Carré had been lucky with the topicality of his earlier books: *The Spy Who Came in from the Cold* had been boosted by the Cuban missile crisis, *A Small Town in Germany* by the Berlin Wall, and *Tinker, Tailor, Soldier, Spy* by Kim Philby's defection. The attempt, however, to give an overall portrait of the Southeast Asian political quagmire in the wake of the fall of Saigon was probably beyond the skills of any novelist. Some of that confusion doubtless derives from le Carré's moral limbo vis-à-vis the Americans and especially "the Cousins," members of the United States CIA, who can scarcely be counted as "one of ours" in this novel, particularly since they betray Smiley at the end. In previous books le Carré took well-deserved jabs at American vulgarity, arrogance, and syntax, but in the main the Americans were fellow soldiers on the right side. Yet the ten-year spectacle of the United States napalming peasant villages and playing "kneesies" at the bargaining table with Vietnamese political scum like Key and Thieu was a far cry from tracking cold-blooded killers like Karla. Thus, by setting *The Honourable Schoolboy* in Vietnam's backyard, le Carré creates an environment of heightened moral ambivalence. All in all the novel stands justly accused of unnecessary heft and confusion.

Still, the richness of the book surpasses anything in the author's previous fiction. Sections are worth reading just as examples of rolling prose or for the chorus of voices which le Carré catches with the skill of a gifted impersonator. The varieties of speech are stunning, and the keen car of a writer who took an Oxford First in languages is apparent everywhere. From the clipped almost pigeon patois of the drug runner Ricardo to the formal jargonese of American bureaucrats, each ethnic and cultural voice is a tour de force of mimicry. Anthony Burgess, known for his own linguistic virtuosity, wrote of the dialogue in *The Honourable Schoolboy:* "His Hong Kong Chinese sound like the real thing, as do his Americans . . . and the horrible Bolshies and the Yellow Perils of the Circus."[5] The cast of characters is a dramatis personae of all the sorts and conditions of men and women. Like Kipling's portrait of the "great garden" of Indian life in *Kim* (perhaps the single most important influence on all le Carré's work), le Carré's collage of traders, whores, spies, imperialists, and every racial and psychological type from the Chinese gangster with a heart of gold to his Eurasian concubine is a virtuoso panorama of a melting pot that doesn't melt.

The peripheral characters themselves are as good a collection as any in le Carré's canon, and it is hardly surprising that le Carré felt that in this book that his "minor characters are always getting out of scale."[6] Considering how exotic several of them are, they avoid the kind of cartoon grotesquerie so easy for an author to slip into when working with ethnic types that have often been stereotyped. Take the Chinese gangster Drake Ko. A mobster, drug trader, smuggler, and dealer in the protection business, he could degenerate into a squalid version of Ming the Merciless, yet for all his corruption he is a human being and is painted without patronizing. In one sense his love for his family is the hallmark of the strongest moral code in the story, and the closest thing the novel comes to tragedy is the image of him enraged and brokenhearted after the Cousins have snatched his brother Nelson from both him and Smiley. He is also the purest representative in the novel of genuine love. It is he who not only loves Lizzie Worthington but respects her and treats her like a lady out of that love—like Don Quixote's myopic denial of Dulcinea's profession, perhaps, but with the same decency that true chivalry should exhibit. Lizzie, too, is an extraordinary complex of conflicting forces: a whore who lives for love, a bourgeois manqué who prostitutes herself, a cynical courtesan with the sentimental heart of a child. The rest of the cast also avoids being a collection of cartoons, ranging from the detestable Tony Ricardo, a Mexican drug runner and petty criminal who "talked about his big soul, his great sexual potency, and the horrors of war," to "Old Craw," a larger-than-life Australian correspondent who "intones like the voice of God" and is based on legendary British newsman Richard Hughes.

At the center is Jerry Westerby, "a fool who tried to hustle the East," in Kipling's memorable phrase, which le Carré used as a section epigraph in *The Looking-Glass War.* Jerry is another of le Carré's divided personalities out of failed father figures, all based on Ronnie Cornwell; they include Haydon, Smiley, and ultimately—and most thoroughly—Magnus Pym in *A Perfect Spy.* Jerry's father, Sir "Sambo" Westerby, was a British press lord and, in addition to neglecting his son, passed on to him noblesse oblige delusions of grandeur. Fifty years of mediocre scrambling as a jack-of-all-trades have not withered nor custom staled the infinite variety of Jerry's personality, or, rather, "personalities," for he trims his sails to fit the social weather. The psychological opposite of Leamas and the plodding true professionals (even flashy Bill Haydon had the "patient care of a true agent runner"), Westerby is a thorough dilettante—a bit of a novelist, a bit of a journalist, a bit of a businessman, a bit of a spy. Physically, he resembles the Jim Prideaux model: big, bumptious, and muscular, full of vitality like an excited puppy. The enthusiasm masks his father's legacy, a deep-seated insecurity. He is bluff about women, jumps to win friends by buying drinks at the bar, and talks the ingratiating flattery of the inveterate people pleaser. "Point me and I'll march!" he says to Smiley when approached about reaching Karla through the Kos.

There's one other thing about Jerry: his appalling sentimentality. Le Carré has more than a soft spot for sentimentality, but he's also aware of it as a weakness, and in Jerry it is a mortal one. Being the kind of man who gravitates to young women to bolster his ego, Jerry abandons his Italian mistress by telling himself he's leaving her for "honour" and "the Service" then finally ends up betraying both because he's in love with Lizzie Worthington, whom he perceives as needing rescue from the moral degradation of the Kos or the communists or anybody. Jerry needs somebody to save and has convinced himself that he has finally found love with this woman. Perhaps he has, but he dies before he or the reader find out.

At first glance Jerry makes an odd "Our Man in Hong Kong" for the cautious Smiley to choose for Operation Dolphin, the attempted penetration of Karla's Southeast Asian network to uncover a mole working for the Russians in mainland China. Naturally, le Carré explains carefully why an amateur part-time spy like Jerry, an "occasional" in Circus jargon, should be selected for such an important assignment (Bill Haydon apparently hadn't gotten around to betraying the occasionals). But it does seem to indicate the degree to which Karla is becoming an obsession with Smiley. Not incidentally, Smiley's psychotic factotum, Fawn, is really acting out his mentor's anger and frustration when he kills Westerby after the no-longer-honourable "schoolboy" betrays his mission for love. Surely the strangest of Smiley's followers at the Circus, Fawn's very presence as part of the little band of brothers seems to be a sign of Smiley's willingness to use any weapon in his search for Karla's destruction, which Ann now calls Smiley's "black grail." Ann herself, once nonnegotiable in Smiley's formidable collection of values, is now also sacrificed to the Karla hunt, for Smiley has more and more trouble even thinking of her as his mind fixes more and more on his bête noire. Smiley is no longer able to see, as he would have earlier in his career, that his diversionary strike at Karla through China has a lot in common with Control's disastrous uses of Leamas and Prideaux—both dangerous, overly complex operations run at great risk to the operative agents.

The complexity and the low chance of success lend a desperate quality to the small task force that Smiley assembles for this heroic gesture. One of the points to the entire body of le Carré's espionage fiction is that spies are an unlikely bunch at best, often a motley collection of unglamorous folk and frequently the also-rans and losers of the more visible world. The ad hoc Circus that launches Jerry Westerby is far from operating "at best." Connie Sachs is here again, glad to be back in harness but somewhat degenerated even from the cast-off semi-invalid she was becoming in *Tinker, Tailor, Soldier, Spy* although still the possessor of an almost supernatural memory. Sam Collins also returns with the slightly underworld bookie aura of casino management about him, and the seedy China hand Doc di Salis is back, and—worst of all, by far—the sinister Fawn, the muscle of the group, with his horrible velvety manners and his willingness to inflict pain. Added to these are the ragtag personnel of the Circus's Southeast Asian Network, although the only one of these whom we see in focus is Bill Craw, the Australian Buddha-like oracle of bibulous wisdom who presides over the press club bar. The single truly "normal" member of the group seems to be Peter Guillam, although much of Peter's sarcastic bad temper continues from *Tinker, Tailor, Soldier, Spy,* and his love life, as always, is an adolescent mess.

The chaos of Vietnam-era Asia is paralleled by the chaos in the Circus. Funds have been cut, threats of further purges in the wake of the Haydon fiasco have been made, and Smiley has been informed that he is a purely stopgap leader of the organization. The Westerby operation will end with a new crowd of amoral incompetents taking over the Circus—Saul Enderby and his cadre of Whitehall-pleasing yes-men, all wearing custom-tailored suits and spouting the public relations jargon of politicians. All in all it is a much diminished service, consisting of a group of frazzled survivors, none of them capable of imposing the discipline necessary to make Operation Dolphin the kind of focused effort that other Circus operations have been. What Operation Dolphin lacks is the relentless single-mindedness that Control's

Fiedler-Mundt conspiracy had. That was an operation, however, that destroyed several people, some of them innocent, to save a swine, but the description of its internal integrity gave *The Spy Who Came in from the Cold* the tightness for which it is famous.

Everything about Operation Dolphin smacks of looseness, including the structuring of the novel that describes it. It is an ill-defined operation, indeed, drawing the attention of the Circus almost artificially away from the familiar territory of Europe. Hong Kong, the initial setting and base of the operation, is the frenetic last outpost of a fragmented British Empire that has been dissolving for more than a half-century. The fantastic, polyglot nature of the Crown colony, apprehensive and uncertain under the threat of eminent union with communist China, provides a fit setting for an operation that rides off in all directions at once. The elusive "gold seam" that begins as a glint in Smiley's eye in London leads the superspy to reach into the Tuscan hills for the improbable Westerby and ship him off to Hong Kong and a frantic odyssey among everybody from the rich and famous to the wretched of the earth. It's a picaresque parody of espionage written by an acid-penned social satirist with a genius for thumb-nail sketches as well as five- and ten-page vignettes that could stand alone as short stories. Whether the seething cornucopia of character and incident is a "good" novel is another matter.

The "special relations" between the Circus and the Americans are more strained in *The Honourable Schoolboy* than they are in any other le Carré novel, including even *A Perfect Spy*— a novel in which the British protagonist commits treason and actively spies upon the CIA. Perhaps it is the inflamed sensitivities of the Vietnam War period that lend[5] to *The Honourable Schoolboy* a sense of ill will and competitiveness between the

Cold War in the Wings

Circus and its U.S. counterpart which foreshadows the American betrayal of the British. It is a betrayal that Guillam foresees, but, when he warns Smiley not to trust the Americans, Smiley tells Guillam not to be "paranoid" and so stumbles into the Cousin's trap. Smiley, the spider of the novel, is not so much caught in his own web as has his fly snatched from it. Virtually everyone ends up losing. Westerby finds what he thinks is true love late and throws his life away for it, as did Alec Leamas. Drake Ko loses his brother, Lizzie Worthington her lover, the Americans their decency (and Smiley's trust), Smiley the valuable prisoner who should have been his reward, and many minor characters their lives. There is little evidence that Karla has even been wounded, although his "mole," Drake Ko's communist brother Nelson, has been blown and captured. The conclusion of *The Honourable Schoolboy* leaves less resolution than ongoing ferment. And a terrific pastiche of life in compelling places during compelling times.

The sprawl and scope of *The Honourable Schoolboy* creates an interesting balance when considered within the matrix of the Quest for Karla trilogy. Both *Tinker, Tailor, Soldier, Spy* and *Smiley's People* are in every respect novels of confinement, introspective and inward looking. Both are complex, sometimes to the point of obfuscation; *Tinker, Tailor, Soldier, Spy* in particular is one of the most complex spy novels ever written, rivaled in le Carré's canon only by *A Perfect Spy* (1986), which isn't really a spy novel at all. Both *Tinker, Tailor, Soldier, Spy* and *Smiley's People* are spatially almost claustrophobic, focusing on Smiley squirreled away in small rooms hatching plots and brooding over papers. For all their structural shifting in time and in and out of psychologies, both of these framing novels of the

Karla trilogy are ruthless about extraneous material; the "quest for Karla" really is their only subject, and the novels move toward it with no detours or distractions. Wedging the expansive *The Honourable Schoolboy* between such focused, almost constipated novels of introspection is like boxing a raucous circus between two intense Edward Albee monologues. The trilogy begins in a profound concentration on the problem of Karla, sprawls in the middle into a gaudy sound-and-light show in which both Smiley and Karla are lost, and then zeroes in on the Karla problem again for the close.

The Honourable Schoolboy does not, of course, stand entirely outside the trilogy. Smiley is still onstage, although in a most subordinate role, and there is a good deal of detail about the decline of the Circus after "the fall," the Circus term for the unmasking of Bill Haydon and the subsequent purge of his admirers and dupes. With crosscutting from Westerby's adventures to Smiley and his loyalists back at the Circus, it is impossible to forget that the attempt to get Nelson Ko is a Circus operation and that the gray figure of Karla, always staring fixedly from the picture on Smiley's wall, is the ultimate object of it. In the latter part of the novel Smiley himself comes to Asia, accompanied by his cupbearer, Peter Guillam, and their part in the final stages of the operation is considerable, including Smiley's disastrous negotiation with the Cousins, who snatch Ko from him when the elusive Chinese is finally caught. Still, *The Honourable Schoolboy* is in no way George Smiley's novel, nor is its central focus Smiley's quest for Karla, and, if the principle critical criterion for judging it is the question of how thoroughly it advances the story of Smiley's *mano a mano* with his Russian counterpart, *The Honourable Schoolboy* must be judged insubstantial and flawed. Perhaps, however, it is mainly the excellence, particularly in terms of controlled structure, of the le Carré novels that bracket *The Honourable Schoolboy* which highlights the novel's weaknesses. Certainly, it does not focus coherently on the compelling psychology of George Smiley, as do the other two.

Even so, secondary as he is to the overall plot, the novel does seem to trace another step in the moral and professional decline of George Smiley. This is certainly not to imply that le Carré is moving toward anything like a "depraved" or degenerate Smiley. Such a character is difficult to imagine, but within limits Smiley is the closest thing in le Carré to a "parfit, gentil knyght." The standard of both professional and personal behavior which he sets for himself in *Call for the Dead, Tinker, Tailor, Soldier, Spy,* and other early novels stands morally tall against the less admirable codes of ideologues like Dieter Frey and Karla, degenerate intellectuals like Haydon, or self-serving opportunists like almost everybody else in those works. Smiley in *The Honourable Schoolboy,* however, is bordering on disorganization on the one hand and obsession on the other; he is certainly a principal figure in the bureaucratic machine that indirectly kills Jerry Westerby.[7] In Smiley's next book, *Smiley's People,* in which he finally defeats Karla, he will conquer the disorganization, partly by the expedient of being limited by circumstances: being no longer head of the Circus in *Smiley's People,* he cannot squander his energies on activities such as Operation Dolphin which don't lead directly to Karla. Mainly, however, he will intensify the obsession until only Karla's picture fills his moral horizon, and he will seem to have decided that it is worth losing at least some of his soul to bring down his adversary.

CHAPTER NINE

Last Illusions
Smiley's People

There was little reason for critics to expect *Smiley's People* to be much of an addition to the canon of le Carré's work before the novel was published. *The Honourable Schoolboy,* regardless of its enormous popular and financial success, had not been among the author's finest works, and the difficulty of writing a follow-up to a book as brilliantly self-contained as *Tinker, Tailor, Soldier, Spy* suggested the probability of an opportunistic sequel, confusingly plotted and awkwardly executed. Certainly the catch-all "generic" title promised little. Surprisingly, *Smiley's People* more than fulfilled the promise of *Tinker, Tailor, Soldier, Spy*'s open-ended conclusion (with its deliberate lack of closure of the Karla plot). The new book genuinely resolved Smiley's "Quest for Karla," and most critical commentary recognized that it was a better novel than *The Honourable Schoolboy.*[1] The apparently modest, generic title itself proved to be another example of le Carré's often extraordinarily clever but unobtrusive technique, like the multiple significance of *Simplicissimus* in *Tinker, Tailor, Soldier, Spy.* Who *are* "Smiley's people"? The main point about them is that they have an amorphous quality that defies definition. One subset of them, of course, is the collection of ragtag castoffs and hangers-on of the Circus whom Smiley uses as he did in *Tinker, Tailor, Soldier, Spy:* Connie Sachs, Peter Guillam, and retired Inspector Mendel. Beyond them are the motley international flotsam and jetsam who are alternately Karla's victims and

Last Illusions

his bane: the murdered General Vladimir, his emissary Leipzig, his pathetic petitioner Maria Ostrakova, and, beyond these declared allies, finally even the loveless diplomat Grigoriev, whom Smiley coerces. Ironically, the ultimate member of Smiley's people is Karla's mentally ill daughter, Tatiana, who provides Smiley with the human chink in the fanatic's armor. Beyond these, even, ultimately Smiley's people are all those who choose humanity over ideology and individuals over institutions. They are plural: "people," as opposed to "the Circus," "England," "Moscow Centre," "communism," and all the other philosophical monoliths that deceitfully attract loyalty with the chimerical promise of a "higher" morality.[2]

Smiley's People is more than simply a logical continuation and conclusion of the incomplete action of *Tinker, Tailor, Soldier, Spy*— "further adventures of Smiley and Karla." There is a temptation, though, to read the novel this way, as little more than a coda to the previous Karla story in which the ace spy catcher gets his man. *Smiley's People* seems to grow out of two key sections of *Tinker, Tailor, Soldier, Spy,* one obviously the last linking scene in which the face of Karla replaces that of Bill Haydon in Smiley's meditation on the ultimate nature of treason and evil. The other is Smiley's recounting to Peter Guillam at dinner his interrogation of Karla in an Indian prison. In that grim cell he laid before Karla his own humanitarian philosophy of life and probed the Russian in vain for some response. Finally, Smiley tells Guillam that he has concluded that he was only "interviewing himself," and he declares Karla a "fanatic" and almost "fireproof" but predicts that his Russian nemesis will eventually fall because he "lacks moderation." In the opening chapters of *Smiley's People* it may seem at first that le Carré is simply reentering Smiley's world as he left it at the close of the previous Karla novels, with the Smiley/Karla stalemate largely unchanged and the implication that Karla will *never* be caught— that he and Smiley may duel mythologically forever as if they were an eternal constellation of spy fiction. Actually, there has been a shift in the precarious balance of power, and not the least important aspect of it is an alteration in Smiley himself.

If Smiley and his covert profession are essentially un- changed in *Smiley's People,* then the book is only a natural ending to *Tinker, Tailor, Soldier, Spy* and the other episodes in Smiley's long struggle with Karla. After all, it is not unreasonable to expect that Smiley might eventually trap his enemy, even given the handicap of Karla's mole and the subverting element of Smiley's Achilles' heel, the faithless Ann. Even so, Smiley was always, by his own account, a bit "better" than Karla (as he told Ann in *Tinker, Tailor, Soldier, Spy*), and it was only a matter of time before he would overcome the incompetence of British bureaucracy and the hobbles of his own humanity to beat the Russian superspy in their brutal game. Further, much in the opening of *Smiley's People* suggests that little has changed. As with *Tinker, Tailor, Soldier, Spy,* Smiley begins the novel as a forcibly retired failure, for the third time created inquisitor- without-portfolio by the bureaucratic Oliver Lacon, who of all the government pooh-bahs seems to be the least obstructive of effective intelligence work. Once more Smiley's allies are shop- worn and shabby at best, and the handicaps of cowardice, egotism, self-interest, and stupidity still hinder all of them but Smiley himself. Ann and her lovers still flit about as a distraction in the wings, the pompous bureaucracy of Whitehall and the Circus (Saul Enderby and the resilient Toby Esterhase now in ascendance) impede the search for truth, and Smiley's "black-dog" of depression and self-doubt mocks the instinctive professionalism that will bring him victory.

In *Smiley's People* the game *has* changed, however, and early in the novel apparently for the worse. *Tinker, Tailor, Soldier, Spy* was primarily a quest of the mind, and Smiley was the spider drawing the threads together. The process of detection in *Smiley's People* is more physically complex, if more cognitively simple. There is no dual plot, as in *The Honourable Schoolboy,* nor is there a shadow plot like that of Jim Prideaux and Thursgood's as in *Tinker, Tailor, Soldier, Spy.* As that novel bore relentlessly in toward the heart of the corrupt Circus and Haydon perverting it from within, this novel throws its arms out—to greater London, Paris, Moscow, Switzerland, and, finally, Berlin. There Karla's defection neatly closes the framing action of pure Cold War confrontation begun with the opening scene of *The Spy Who Came in from the Cold* in which Leamas's agent is shot crossing in the same place.

At first it is hard to see how the balance of power between Smiley and Karla may have shifted except to the aged Smiley's disadvantage. It has, though, and in a way that previous followers of Karla's brutality could not anticipate, for Smiley finally traps the incorruptible ideologue by finding Karla's one human Achilles' heel, his illegitimate, psychotic daughter. In using Karla's "crimes" in the eyes of communist bureaucracy to protect the daughter, Smiley reverses the process of emotional coercion that Karla used in *Tinker, Tailor, Soldier, Spy* when he tried to cloud

Smiley's judgment through Bill Haydon's seduction of Ann. Now, in *Smiley's People,* Smiley's willingness to manipulate Karla through the otherwise incorruptible Russian's affections tips the balance of power in Smiley's favor. It also indicates a subtle change in his character in ways that the casual reader may not notice.

A quiet and almost unnoticeable key to *Smiley's People* is that in this novel Smiley gets rid of Ann—that "last illusion of the illusionless man"—at the same time that he ferrets out his adversary's own "last illusion," the pathetic daughter. Now it is Karla who has acquired the deadly handicap of emotional baggage, and both he and Smiley know that you can give hostages to fortune without marrying to do it.[3] And, as Karla has weakened, Smiley has grown stronger, at least in terms of effectiveness, if not character. Unobtrusively, Smiley has changed, has become professionally tougher and less prey to the sort of existential guilt which plagued him during his interrogation of Karla (when he let the Russian take Ann's gift lighter as described in *Tinker, Tailor, Soldier, Spy*). A new, harder Smiley is manifest not only in his willingness to use Karla's love for his daughter to track and trap him but also in the totality of his focus on his mission to destroy Karla.

In this book alone le Carré approaches making the kind of antiwoman statement which some critics have accused him of making before. In *Smiley's People* women become not only distracting excess baggage but also impediments to success.[4] Karla is destroyed because he cannot bring himself to dispose completely of a woman (who is also, of course, the product of his weakness for another woman), and Smiley conditions his psy-

Last Illusions

chology for unconditional battle by removing its greatest distraction: Karla will not lay another "honey trap" for him, no matter how subtle.

Smiley is not merely tougher; there is a new aspect of his character. Often literary sequels establish character in an initial story then simply recycle it through following ones. Sherlock Holmes doesn't change one iota from *The Sign of the Four* to *The Hound of the Baskervilles.* Remarkably, in *Smiley's People* le Carré manages to amplify the character of his hero in the process of showing the spy's evolution. As the inertia of the pursuit carries him relentlessly toward confrontation with Karla and victory, defeat, or mutual destruction, Smiley's character deepens. If Smiley was not merely a functionary in *Tinker, Tailor, Soldier, Spy,* as Gregory Stokes in an otherwise perceptive article on that novel obtusely claims,[5] he was surely the instrument of a mechanistic and bureaucratic process of assemblage. Whether we see Bill Haydon or Karla or even evil itself as the target of Smiley's investigation in that novel, Smiley in the main gives himself over to the process of uncovering, moving on "automatic pilot" toward his victory and Bill's destruction. In *The Honourable Schoolboy,* of course, Smiley is hardly in evidence enough to notice whether his character changes, nor whether it is markedly different from that in *Tinker, Tailor, Soldier, Spy.*

Part of le Carré's deepening of Smiley's character in this novel is a result of deeper exploration of the doppelgänger motif in *Smiley's People.* As several critics have noticed, the world of *Smiley's People* is a world of doubles, even beyond the normal thematic preoccupation of spy fiction with alter egos, secret sharers, and multiple identities.[6] Not since *Call for the Dead* has

Smiley so combined in himself the passive, scholarly deskman and the activist field agent (nor does Smiley travel so much in any other fiction). Smiley and Karla, of course, complement each other, and together they form a composite of the image of the modern spy—as Connie Sachs says, "twin cities . . . two halves of the same apple," in the same scene in which she speaks of his vengeful "Karla look" over the killing of Vladimir (205).[7] Just as *Tinker, Tailor, Soldier, Spy* ended with Smiley brooding on the image of Karla's face which replaces Bill Haydon's, so in *Smiley's People* he broods on Karla's photograph, trying to merge his foe's consciousness into his own. In that merging the dualities that have informed all of the Smiley fiction—between East and West, philosopher and activist, good and bad, institution and individual—all come together in a Götterdämmerung of fusion as le Carré draws the curtain on the long struggle that has been at the center of his canon.

It is not only George Smiley to whom le Carré seems to be saying good-bye in this novel but perhaps the Cold War as well, which is remarkable considering that *Smiley's People* was published in 1980 and planned several years before that—a good half-decade before even as prescient a critic of communism as le Carré could read Gorbachev's handwriting on the Kremlin wall (in fact, 1980 was a grim time politically, when the Cold War actually appeared to be intensifying).[8] Future le Carré novels, including particularly *A Perfect Spy, The Russia House,* and *A Secret Pilgrim,* would rehash stories from the heroic battle but in retrospect only. *Smiley's People* is the Ragnarok of le Carré's epic. Understandably, by this point Smiley's people, and their enemies too, are old—all tired and suckled in creeds outworn.

Last Illusions

The past rises up for a final time here and lays its ghosts to rest in a present that hangs on the brink of perestroika, although none of the characters are prescient enough to know it. There is no young blood among these worn-out survivors. Even the perennial boy/man "young Peter Guillam" (as Percy Alliline and others contemptuously called him in *Tinker, Tailor, Soldier, Spy*) is pushing fifty (and a baby carriage), and the ageless Inspector Mendel is now "old Mendel" to Smiley. The rest of the cast is elderly.[9] Maria Ostrakova, that most battered of displaced persons, responds to an image from her past—that of her own daughter—so distant and buried that she literally can't recognize whether a photograph is of her own child. The septuagenarian general Vladimir, whose real cause is the forgotten one of Estonian independence, tries to get in touch with Smiley under the old pseudonym of "Max," reaching out to a Smiley who no longer exists. Connie Sachs, sick and exhausted in body and mind, lapses into fantasies, finally provoking even the chivalric Smiley to turn on her, angrily trying to drag facts from her through rambling, abstract games, but she is unable to duplicate her virtuoso memory journey in *Tinker, Tailor, Soldier, Spy*. The final human image of the novel is that of the defeated Karla as he defects: "One little man . . . aged and weary and travelled, the short hair turned to white by a sprinkling of snow. He wore a grimy shirt and a black tie: he looked like a poor man going to the funeral of a friend. The cold had nipped his cheeks low down, adding to his age" (372). It is truly the end for all of them.

Smiley is the focus of the novel—more than he has been in any le Carré novel since *Call for the Dead* nearly twenty years before. But this is no longer the Smiley who agonized over killing

Dieter Frey as Dieter wouldn't kill him. Nowhere is the change more dramatic than in Smiley's rejection of Connie in the exact middle of *Smiley's People,* a scene that is the key to characterization in the novel. Here, in chapter 14, Smiley again unlocks Connie's "wordhoard," flattering, coaxing, wheedling, the information buried in her prodigious memory. This is a seduction scene, parallel to the one in *Tinker, Tailor, Soldier, Spy,* in which he does the same. But there Smiley was kinder, less calculating, and less defensive. The Connie/George scene in *Tinker, Tailor, Soldier, Spy* was a sentimental set piece between old friends, but this is an ugly exploitation of a sick woman. As the depressed, shaky Connie flirts with him, Smiley finally loses patience and yells angrily at her. The ugliness is emblematic of the sad deterioration of this generation of Cold Warriors. Connie, whose brilliant memory and gruff honesty once nailed Bill Haydon, has rotted into a diseased hulk whose mind comes and goes and who coyly plays little-girl fantasy games with her "lover," George, while her half-crazy real lover, "Hillary," flits about the margins. The formerly saintly George who comforted Connie in their exile in *Tinker, Tailor, Soldier, Spy* now "works" the sick old woman as he might interrogate a suspect.

Indeed, the saintly Smiley—as much a symbol of Christian humanity as Faulkner's Ike McCaslin—has not only aged but hardened. It is not only Connie he rejects but the faithless Ann. In previous novels Ann was the final nonnegotiable bedrock of Smiley's humanity. His endless willingness to forgive her infidelities made her the symbol of a charity that rendered Smiley sometimes fatuous but also demonstrated his essential decency, with a willingness to forgive and turn the other cheek which sometimes bordered on the grotesque. In *Tinker, Tailor, Soldier,*

Last Illusions

Spy to Smiley Bill Haydon's ultimate sin was not deceit, treason, betrayal of friendship, or even murder; it was hurting Ann, for loving her is Smiley's last remaining romantic fantasy left from the young, idealistic scholar of German who he once was. But here, in *Smiley's People,* the worm has apparently finally turned, for Ann repeatedly begs for reconciliation and forgiveness, and repeatedly he refuses.

Memory has always been essential to the character of Smiley and the Smiley novels and to all le Carré's works (as it was to be central to *A Perfect Spy* and *The Secret Pilgrim*) in novels following the Karla trilogy. Usually, however, Smiley would range in his mind over the sins and secrets of the past—his own and others'—with a sense of wistful resignation. Now he has hardened:

> To forget the hurts, the list of lovers; to forget Bill Haydon, the Circus traitor, whose shadow still fell across her face each time he reached for her, whose memory he carried in him like a constant pain. Bill his friend, Bill the flower of their generation, the jester, the enchanter, the iconoclastic conformer; Bill the born deceiver, whose quest for the ultimate betrayal led him to the Russians' bed, and Ann's. To stage yet another honeymoon, fly away to the South of France, eat the meals, buy the clothes, all the let's pretend lovers play. And for how long? . . . In a single surge of memory, he reconstructed all the things that had hinted and whispered to him throughout the endless days; he heard the drum-beats of his own past, summoning him to one last effort to externalize and resolve the conflict he had lived by; and he wanted her nowhere near him. (143)

This is a new Smiley, one capable of anger, indifference, opportunism—even perhaps, in his own genteel way, revenge and cruelty. This "new" Smiley is capable not only of browbeating Connie but also of blackmailing the pathetic Grigoriev. This Smiley cuts away the human attachments that handicapped him in the past but also kept him from the amoral coldness and brutality of his profession. It is this detachment that makes it possible for him to go for the only jugular Karla has—*his* remnant of humanity. This hardening in Smiley's character is perhaps the greatest accomplishment of *Smiley's People*. It must have been tempting for le Carré to let Smiley exit, tired and battered, with his ideals unrealized but with his purity intact. But how much more convincing is the admission that, no matter how initially humane a person may be, a compromising trade like espionage and counterespionage compromises even its most decent: Men wash their hands, in blood, as best they can. So *Smiley's People* concludes le Carré's extended epic of the battle between the good man of the West and the evil man of the East, and they merge into each other as they walk offstage. Karla has fallen because his humanity made him vulnerable; Smiley drags him down by a willingness to exploit that. It is tempting to hear, as some readers do, only sarcasm in Smiley's closing "acceptance" of his "victory," when Guillam says, "You won": "Did I? . . . Yes. Yes, well I suppose I did"[10] (374). Certainly, if *Smiley's People* is considered outside its place in the spectrum of Smiley fiction encompassing twenty years of le Carré's writing, and more of Smiley's professional career—that is, if *Smiley's People* stands alone—then it is the story of the inevitability of good and evil adulterating each other and of moral struggles resolving themselves in moral nullity.

Last Illusions

But it is not nullity, nor is the adulteration so balanced that Karla and Smiley are somehow morally equal at the end. Readers who have followed Smiley in earlier books may err too far here in being aware that Smiley's morality has suffered a depreciation. Remembering him as the impassioned voice of individual humanism in previous encounters with Karla, it is distressing that he compromises those values now. This should not, however, be interpreted to mean that a Smiley less than simon-pure is capable of accepting the atrocities that Karla takes for granted: the shameless manipulation of Maria Ostrakova (who would surely be assassinated by the brutal Kirov, "the Ginger Pig," as Connie calls him); the brutal slaughter of Vladimir; the matter-of-fact disposal of Tatiana's mother because she was "inconvenient"; and the whole panoply of terroristic mechanics which characterizes the grim world of Moscow Centre. If Karla seems sympathetic simply because he has come afoul through his minimal humanity of the savagery that he himself has done so much to perpetuate, his last spiteful act reveals that his venom remains even though his ability to strike is crippled. At the very moment that he is capitulating to Smiley in defecting, he casts away Ann's love gift to her husband, the engraved lighter that he stole from Smiley twenty years before. It is simply impossible to imagine Smiley in similar circumstances doing the same.

Another emblem of the disparity of Karla's inhumanity with Smiley's blunted humanity is the character of Tatiana, who seems to represent the most humane side of Karla. But her schizophrenia is the embodiment of the divided nature of the self in the Cold War world as well as the impossibility of Karla's genuinely mellowing. As she is aware in her more lucid moments, as a direct result of her father's actions, her mother has been killed and she herself driven to mental illness. She is simply one more of the many people Karla has destroyed. As Smiley observed in *Tinker, Tailor, Soldier, Spy,* Karla "lacks moderation," and the human wreckage in the wake of a genuinely dedicated communist ideologue precludes the possibility of atonement and forgiveness. The Karla of *Smiley's People* seems softer, and, correspondingly, his new "work name" for British intelligence is "The Sandman." Le Carré, however, with his depth in German literature, undoubtedly borrowed the character not from Hans Christian Anderson's fairy tale of a life-affirming, child-loving sandman but, rather, from a well-known one of Hoffmann's *Tales* in which the Sandman brings sleep and its *semblable* death; also, as Sigmund Freud explicated it in his 1919 essay "The Uncanny," the Sandman tore out children's eyes and was a key figure in exemplifying the psychological phenomenon of "doubling" so central to *Smiley's People.*[11]

No follower of le Carré can read *Smiley's People* in a vacuum, and everything about the author's handling of the novel (including the rather strained forcing of *The Honourable Schoolboy* between it and *Tinker, Tailor, Soldier, Spy*) compels seeing this story as the final act of an extended cycle stretching across the breadth of the Cold War and examining the development of one good man who represents the strengths—and some of the weaknesses—of one side in that war. In the overall view *Smiley's People* is both George Smiley's dying fall and his victorious apotheosis.

CHAPTER TEN

"The Theatre of the Real"
The Little Drummer Girl

Le Carré, who had been known to be evasive if not actually dissembling in interviews, claimed that he abandoned George Smiley after his famous detective/agent finally beat Karla at the end of *Smiley's People* because the perfection of Alec Guinness's television portrayal had frozen the character for all time: le Carré could not imagine Smiley in any other way, and therefore the character had no room to grow in his imagination.[1] What is more likely is that he sensed that the rumblings of glasnost, already felt by perceptive observers of Soviet Europe, were foreshadowing an end to two generations of Cold War confrontation, at least in terms of the bipolar, monolithic "us-them" terms that character-ized it during the third of a century after World War II. In a *Newsweek* interview just before *The Little Drummer Girl* was published, le Carré claimed that he wanted, "the opportunity to write about the new generation, younger people, modern prob-lems."[2] Whatever the reason, his new horizons turned out to be in the Middle East—an area by then arguably more volatile and a greater threat to world peace than Europe.

"Younger people" meant particularly Charlie, le Carré's first successful romantic heroine, really his first effectively drawn female, discounting the androgynous Connie Sachs.[3] The folksy, masculine, and slightly aggressive nickname (for Charmian) is a tip-off to her character: "known to everyone as 'Charlie' and often as 'Charlie the Red' in deference to the colour of her hair and to her somewhat crazy radical stances, which were her way of caring for the world and coming to grips with its injustices."[4] And that's what *The Little Drummer Girl* is about: Charlie, and through her the reader, "caring for the world and coming to grips with its injustices," which nearly costs her her sanity, if not her life. Le Carré dedicated the book to Alec Guinness, who had become a friend, but as a novelist he had left Smiley's Cold War behind.

The critics were almost unanimous in feeling that the author's choice of both Charlie and the setting were fortunate.[5] *The Little Drummer Girl* received the greatest encomium on publication of any le Carré novel before or since. "It becomes instantly apparent that we are in the hands of a writer of great powers," wrote William Buckley on the front page of the *New York Times Book Review.*[6] Harold Bloom believed that *The Little Drummer Girl* was "le Carré's best book so far," mainly because it lacked the pretension and "ambitions" of the novel that followed it, *A Perfect Spy.*[7] A few critics who had complained that le Carré's treatment of the Cold War had reached a murky philosophical cul-de-sac with the Karla Trilogy hailed *The Little Drummer Girl*'s apparent return to a world of moral "rights" and "wrongs."[8]

What was most significant about the plaudits was that in many respects *The Little Drummer Girl* was the most politically unfashionable statement yet by an author who, without producing neochauvinist propaganda of a Bondian or Tom Clancy variety, had repeatedly irritated leftist critics by suggesting that the communists were not only equally responsible for the Cold War but even a bit more reprehensible than their counterparts in the West. Now came *The Little Drummer Girl,* which again pilloried both sides in an international conflict and charged both with wicked behavior.[9] While researching the book, le Carré met with Yassir Arafat, the chairman of the Palestine Liberation Organization and leader of its "activist" branch, Al Fatah, who asked the novelist what he wanted. "Mr. Chairman," said le Carré, "I want to put my hand on the Palestinian heart." Arafat pulled le Carré's hand to his chest and said, "Sir, it is here, it is here."[10] To Israeli loyalists such contact with "the enemy" implied betrayal of the Israeli cause. Certainly, when it was published *The Little Drummer Girl* dared to suggest that the Arab/Israeli war—hot and cold—which had scarred the Middle East since World War II, not only had two sides but that the Israelis were often nearly as culpable as the Arab terrorists, sometimes even more so. This bordered on heresy, for many of the liberal critics who welcomed fiction condemning both East and West in Europe had far more partisan agendas when it came to taking sides in the Middle East. Predictably, some critics were aghast at le Carré's temerity in attributing something like genocide to the Israelis. In a blistering review in the *New Republic* David Pryce-Jones acknowledged the power of the novel (in fact, felt that its artistry made it particularly dangerous) but reflected the extreme horror of reviewers politically committed to Israel: "But now an author of renown and standing comes to inform the Palestinians that they . . . have been selected for premeditated assault by a people too powerful to be defended [*sic*], but so inherently evil that peace cannot be made with them . . . whatever they do in these frightening circumstances, the Jews will still be the death of them. Real enemies are not so harmful and demoralizing as friends [le Carré] like these."[11]

This castigation was not surprising, for genuine sympathy for the Arab cause among liberal intellectuals had generally been confined to ethnic Arabs such as Edward Said and an irresponsible radical fringe figureheaded by actress Vanessa Redgrave (who certainly bore a resemblance to *The Little Drummer Girl*'s portrait of Charlie, although le Carré says his sister Charlotte was the most important model).[12] To have as popular a writer as le Carré, and particularly a *serious* popular writer, weighing in for understanding for the Arabs was disturbing to many intellectuals, who had taken support of Zionism as much for granted as loathing for the swastika. The idea of presenting genuine sympathy not only for the Palestinian cause as a political movement but even for the Palestinians as suffering human beings was anathema both to pro-Zionist commentators and to most liberals and many conservatives as well. It is often forgotten by liberals that unequivocal support for Israel is an article of faith for many fundamentalist Christian sects. Nothing was surer to provoke howls of outrage from both the extreme Right and the extreme Left than a novel condemning Israeli treatment of the Arabs. *The Little Drummer Girl* may suggest that both the Israeli and the Arab houses are inviting plague, but Israel's treatment of the Arabs is clearly condemned in its pages. Still, the book is hardly unequivocally "pro-Arab," although le Carré was certainly concerned with presenting the Palestinian dilemma sympathetically, because, he said, "We all have that [positive] image of Israel in different forms, but, as it happens, I don't think anybody's written with anything like compassion about the Palestinians."[13] There is unquestionably much in the novel that presents them compassionately: the images of the bombed refugee camps, the dreadful poverty, the impossibility of getting anyone (except scheming communist agitators) to take their plight seriously, the smoldering wrath of young men and women raised with a heritage of dispossession. And, of course, there are the Palestinian virtues, so totally neglected in the Western press and literature: the dedication, courage, loyalty to one another, sensitivity, and capacity for love—that very capacity that gets them killed—of Michel and Khalil and Khalil's family, and the anonymous suffering masses of the Palestinian people. Most of all, in the Palestinians le Carré pictures a passionate sincerity that unquestionably predisposes the reader to accept even some of their most blatant hyperboles and generalizations, such as Khalil's gross simplification of the moral polarity as he sees it: "The Zionists kill for fear and for hate . . . Palestinians for love and justice" (399).

Further, since most of le Carré's novels are in some sense bildungsromans, in that they present a protagonist to some degree naive who learns by bitter observation the limitations of his or her moral position, the "learning experience" in *The Little Drummer Girl* is obviously Charlie's, and what she learns is that the Palestinians are human too. To betray them and kill them and behave as if they had no cause is not only ignorant but wrong. Still, suggesting, or even demonstrating, that the Israelis in particular and the West in general have committed great injustices in Palestine does not make the novel subversive, and in this, as in all John le Carré's novels, there is a balance of evil. Palestinian atrocities figure almost as vividly as do Israeli injustices. The novel opens with a Palestinian terrorist bombing that slaughters innocent victims (the only Jew killed being a child) and closes in a coda chapter with a reminder that Arab terrorist organizations continue waging war against guiltless people to gain attention. Michel is willing to send his lover to die planting a bomb on a plane which will kill dozens of innocent people, and overall the picture of the Arab treatment of women is one of primitive behavior at best.

As in nearly all his other fiction, for le Carré there is no innocence possible for those who unilaterally choose either side in this bitter struggle. Such a position obviously outrages many who feel indicted by the novel's implication that preferring one side does not entail an oath of silence never to acknowledge the legitimacy of the other. One way le Carré frames the social and political questions of the Middle East is by detaching them from religious questions. The reader is allowed to consider the issues of the novel from all points of view but never from the point of view of justification by faith. Removing the religious issue has the virtue of forcing the reader to look at them "naked," without the smoke and mirrors that religious rhetoric often uses to hinder objectivity and avoid treating atrocities as atrocities and human claims as valid appeals to humanity. On the other hand, to write a serious novel about a war that both sides tend to regard as a religious war, without dealing with religion except as part of the scenery, leaves relevant material withheld. This is, incidentally, the very area in which le Carré's only serious contemporaneous competitor in the area of making espionage into literature, Graham Greene, is strongest, although Greene's specialty is individual crisis of faith rather than balanced consideration of religious positions.

Everything *The Little Drummer Girl* has to say is wrapped up in the character of Charlie, and the most significant thing about her is that she is neither Arab nor Israeli, which automatically puts her outside the basic struggle of the novel. Of all the characters only she really has the option of choosing. She, presumably, can take sides on the basis of conviction rather than inheritance, personal loyalty, inherent bias, or blood debt. She finds, however, that "her" choice is not her choice—that she is influenced and manipulated by forces, many of which are beyond her control or comprehension. As a European, Charlie represents the West, and one of le Carré's points is that the West is *not* uninvolved in the Middle East. *The Little Drummer Girl* is shot full of a lot of history, most of it designed to fill in the background of the Arab/Israeli problem, and various characters repeatedly inform Charlie, and the reader, of the complicity, particularly of the British, for the theft of Palestine from its indigenous people. It was the British who forced the Jewish refugees from the Holocaust to seek a homeland in the Middle East, the British who encouraged a United Nations settlement that divided the Palestinians and failed to provide any real autonomy for them in the new state of Israel, and, of course, the British—along with their allies, the Americans—who had promoted the prosperity of that state, armed it, and stood by without complaint as it pursued a policy that, according to Palestinians, amounted to genocide. Khalil's last words, as he realizes that Charlie has betrayed him are, "And you are the same English who gave away my country."

It is important that Charlie is English but, more important, that she is in a sense a whore, which is hardly an unmitigated condemnation. Some of the strongest characters in literary history could be, and often are, called "whores": Moll Flanders, Becky Sharpe, Carrie Meeber, Brett Ashley, and a host of other gritty survivors whose compromises are harder earned than the

pale virtues of simpering Pamelas. The regretful sinner, re-
deemed and saved, has been at the heart of much great fiction, and
the image of the fallen women who repents, is forgiven, and goes
and sins no more has been compelling since the story of Mary
Magdalene. Le Carré surely uses this time-honored literary motif
but with new subtleties. *The Little Drummer Girl* genuinely
explores what it means to be a whore and, particularly, what it
means to realize what you have become and what the consequences of that fall are, both to yourself and to others. As it
happens, in *The Little Drummer Girl,* the consequences to
"others" are far more traumatic than they are for the victims of,
say, Brett Ashley's whoring (but, then, we suspect that Brett may
revert to "being a bitch" more easily than Charlie, who has
watched the victims of her whoring die before her). Charlie
begins the novel as a "loose" woman, and because of her
promiscuity she is used as the bait in a "honey trap" to lure Michel
and Khalil to their deaths.

Charlie is a true gem in the pantheon of le Carré's characters,
for the novelist displayed comparatively little gift for real creation of romantic heroines, sullied or not, either before or since
writing *The Little Drummer Girl.* Yet here is a fully realized
woman, deep and subtle, believable in her virtues and her defects
and, most important, fascinating. That she is an actress is critical,
for acting is the hallmark of all spies, certainly of all le Carré's
spies.[14] To be an actor, or an actress, is to be both a liar and a
creator, and the tension between the two roles produces in the
character an endemic anxiety that charges the personality like
psychological electricity. A "dedicated" actor without a role to
play is like a loaded gun (perhaps the famous one that George

"The Theatre of the Real"

Bernard Shaw said must be fired in a play if mounted over the mantle in the first act). Charlie, who is *au fond* (a term she might use), a serious person, yearns for a role in what Kurtz, the stern godfather of Israeli intelligence, calls the "theatre of the real." Filled with energy and a desire to "do good," she lacks direction. As le Carré put it, "She has loyalty in her pocket like loose change and they [the Israelis] show her how to spend it, how to invest it, who to be."[15] Like all people, and particularly, le Carré implies, dabblers in political causes, Charlie wants a free lunch. She yearns for some "pure" receptacle for her slightly radical leanings, some cause to which she can commit herself and still be a good person. She is also, in her own way, a practitioner of the theme of the artist as the creator of fiction—a theme that le Carré would develop even more thoroughly in *The Tailor of Panama* more than a decade later.

This sense of incompleteness makes Charlie susceptible to becoming what all le Carré's spies are to a greater or lesser degree—double agents. With some characters these Janus-faced roles are overt, at least to the reader, as with Leamas, Haydon, or Magnus Pym in le Carré's next novel, *A Perfect Spy;* others are less obvious—Smiley investigating his own people secretly in *Tinker, Tailor, Soldier, Spy* or Elsa Fennen spying on her agent husband in *Call for the Dead.* In Charlie's case this duality is particularly complex. She is a radical actress acting as a radical to effect a "good" that an important part of her is increasingly seeing in terms of the evil it effects. To do this she becomes a lover of a man (Joseph) whom she must betray by becoming the lover of another man (Khalil) whom she also must betray to be true to the first lover, at the very time that part of her is genuinely feeling not just sympathy but love for him (Khalil). The flow chart of psychic selves divided against psychic selves boggles the organizational skills of the average reviewer.

Charlie is also seeking, in rather conventional terms, a man, or at least a masculine figure. Le Carré is no radical feminist in terms of psychological characterization, and men in his fiction traditionally represent direction and leadership. Charlie needs a combination of mentor and lover. Being an intrinsically sexual and social creature, she functions best in highly interactive relationships, and one way of seeing her behavior in *The Little Drummer Girl* is as an odyssey in search of a mate who will make it possible for her to find herself by fitting into a relationship with a strong man. Nor surprisingly, that mate turns out to be a father figure, Charlie's "agent-runner," Joseph (or Gadi Becker, his real name). Older, battle scarred, world-weary and worldly wise, he is the epitome of the kind of patriarchal authority and direction which Charlie is lacking and seeking. Significantly, however, he is a humane patriarch. Le Carré provides, as he so often does, a darker alter ego for Joseph, and that is Kurtz, the director of the murderous operation to kill Khalil, who embodies all Joseph's strength without any of his introspective doubts and reservations about the morality of their task.

It is Kurtz who provides the first and most destructive of Charlie's father figure/lovers (although without a sexual rela-tionship) in terms of manipulation of the malleable Charlie. At this early stage of the novel she is far more the product of a man's molding than her own person, which she will be struggling to be by the end. In his lengthy exploration and preparation of her— another one of le Carré's tour-de-force interrogation scenes

"The Theatre of the Real"

(101–40)—Kurtz works her like a hostile detainee, acting both"good cop" and "bad cop" and playing on her multiple neurosis until he has reformed her into the agent that he needs to attract and kill his prey. This extended scene, in which the brilliant Kurtz artfully reels Charlie in and out like a fish on a line, finally "landing" her as a prize catch, recalls brilliant interrogation scenes in which Smiley in particular plays the same role with hapless pigeons from Ricky Tarr to Jim Prideaux (although both Karla and Bill Haydon defeat his questioning, the one through strength of character, the other through lack of it). Some critics have called Kurtz "a sort of Israeli Smiley,"[16] largely because of the similarities in interrogation and psychological sensitivity to the subjects of inquisition. But Kurtz is no Smiley, although the Smiley of the final stages of the hunt for Karla shows signs of developing the kind of ruthless obsession with a goal which brooks no intrusion of disruptive ethics. It's also hard to imagine Smiley, who is so chivalrous, so forgiving of Ann, and so solicitous of Connie Sachs, warping a "trainee" for the kind of mission Kurtz intends for Charlie. Kurtz is a kind of pimp—and, in the sense that he is a father figure, a father who pimps his own daughter—for part of what he offers Charlie is a lover, who turns out to be Joseph.

It is Joseph's humanity that makes him emotionally and eventually romantically open to Charlie. Of course, he initially seduces Charlie to bind her to him and so does a little whoring himself. Yet he does develop a real love for and with her, and in this he is morally much superior to Kurtz, who is a fanatic willing to prostitute all other values to that of destroying the enemy, which in his case is a difficult motive to separate from revenge.

Joseph, however, like Charlie, is a person of many personalities and one capable of change. He is a consummate Mossad professional, a mythic and romantic soldier of fortune nicknamed "the Steppenwolf" in popular gossip, after a romantic German "superman" hero. But he is also a meditative, almost mystical, introspective brooder whose commitment, unlike Kurtz's, has gone through a cynical evolution. As a young man, he fought for glory then for "peace" and finally for "Israel," which for him is a far more pragmatic concept than for Zionist zealots.

The central part of *The Little Drummer Girl,* in which Joseph trains Charlie to spring her elaborate "honey trap," is one of the most complex and technically sophisticated in modern British literature.[17] It involves psychological reconditioning with personality changes that would have confused a Pirandello audience. (And there is no figure in the modern theater with more significance for Charlie's roles in this novel than Pirandello; in many ways *The Little Drummer Girl* is "alternate Charlies in search of an author"). To condition Charlie to seduce a Palestinian, Joseph dips into the Stanislavsky school of method acting by playing the role of a Palestinian lover himself, a "part" that has dangerous and unsettling effects on him, for his own war weariness and natural tendency to self-critical introspection make him an unstable personality subject to wrenching insecurities about both his own identity and the value of his commitment to counterterrorism.

The effect on Charlie of this "method" training is equally disturbing, for, in learning to act like a Palestinian, she exposes herself to the ultimate danger for any blind ideologue steeling him- or herself to violence: she comes to know, and thus respect, her enemy. To get inside Khalil's defenses, and to assimilate Palestinian thinking, she penetrates the Palestinian refugee community as a whole and Khalil's family in particular, seducing his terrorist brother, Michel and snuggling up to his family, and especially his sister Fatmeh. She is successful in persuading all of them—except perhaps Khalil's terrorist compatriot, Tayeh—that she is not only a fellow traveler but also a potential soldier in their "holy war," and she betrays Michel to the Israelis and is in a position to seduce Khalil and set him up for an Israeli kill. By this time, however, the complexity of her multiple role-playing is straining Charlie's tenuous conception of her "real" self, and in the novel's climactic scene she cracks. As Khalil lets down his guard in Charlie's embrace, she seems to have lost all sense of reality. The lines between Kurtz's "theatre of the real" and the theater of herself—and perhaps many other psychological "theaters"—have dissolved. Just before Joseph ambushes the defenseless Khalil, she has become totally disoriented. Thinking over the whole complex charade, she thinks: "It was the worst play she had ever been in. . . . Her urge to smash the tension was the same as the urge to smash herself" (415). As Joseph is about to spring the trap, it is Charlie who has confusedly become paranoid about the noises around the house, although she seems not so much to be trying to warn him of his danger as simply unsure about which role she is supposed to play. Finally, in the confusion of her despair, unable to figure out *who* she is, she falls back on her default role throughout: "'Darling,' she whispered. 'Khalil. Oh Christ. Oh, darling. Please.' And whatever else whores say" (417).

More than a decade has passed since the publication of *The*

Understanding John le Carré

Little Drummer Girl, and, although the novel still arouses resentment from pro-Israeli critics and accusations of Arab bashing from the other side, overall the novel has fared well in the judgment of time. Despite voices to the contrary, most critics concurred with Harold Bloom's praise. Few, however, agreed with Bloom that *The Little Drummer Girl* lacked ambition, for it is one of le Carré's most complex novels. The novel is usually included in lists of the author's finest works of art, along with *The Spy Who Came in from the Cold; Tinker, Tailor, Soldier, Spy;* and perhaps *A Perfect Spy.* In terms of plot and theme *The Little Drummer Girl* harks back to le Carré's first great success twenty years before, *The Spy Who Came in from the Cold.* In that novel the forces of democracy compromise themselves by adopting the enemy's brutal philosophy of ends justifying means. Using a wicked subterfuge, British counterintelligence penetrates the enemy's defenses and destroys him from the inside, subverting his best instincts and using them to get inside his guard for the kill. Again, in *The Little Drummer Girl,* the central plot involves a complex conspiracy by which the hunter becomes the hunted. Charlie, the ironically labeled "little drummer girl," is both bait and executioner, and she, like Leamas, studies her prey, learns to accommodate herself to his lifestyle, and pays a bitter price for the destruction of a human being. If Charlie's price is not as high or the cost to her humanity as great or the ultimate authorial judgment about the corruption of both sides not as ambiguous, the basic thematic pattern is the same. To get close to her target Charlie must learn about him and his values, and, in doing that, she loses not only the will but also much of the justification for her killing. As Adlai Stevenson suggested that anyone who could win the U.S. presidency must disqualify himself for the job, so any effective antiterrorist in the murky Arab-Israeli conflict must lose her humanity or have it seriously compromised.

In Charlie's case what is compromised is her sanity too. The novel's devastating last chapter describes the Israeli invasion of Lebanon in June 1982 and the subsequent destruction of the Palestinian communities in which Charlie had found a surrogate home among Khalil's people while practicing her surrogate personality. The brutality of the invasion sends the normally unflappable Kurtz into a deep depression but only "for a month or more." For Charlie recovery takes longer and is more qualified. She is under the intense care of a psychiatrist, who recommends that the news of the destruction be kept from her. "It could unhinge her, the psychiatrist said; with her imagination and self-absorption, she could perfectly easily hold herself responsible for the entire invasion" (425). After all, as a result of her experiment in the theater of the real "the divide between her inner and outer world had been a flimsy affair at the best of times, but these days it had virtually ceased to exist" (429).

She does seem to recover, though—partially—by declaring one of those separate peaces by which le Carré characters go AWOL from an immoral world; if Leamas had done the same, he would have survived. Charlie goes back to England and back to the actual theater in which the footlights mark the division between the actors and the audience. She is inclined, when Joseph suddenly shows up to renew their relationship without the corrupting fudge factor of espionage directives, to tell him that she has been too badly damaged to find love in the "real world." "She wanted to add something about the theatre of the real, how the bodies didn't get up and walk away. But she lost it somehow" (430). So she and Joseph, since they were not the ones dead, turned to their affairs and presumably make something of a real life instead of brooding on the shattered fragments of the multiple lives that have cost them so much. Charlie, having tried to find herself by being *engagé,* now turns, as so many of le Carré's moral characters try to do, and finds herself within an individual human commitment. No longer folding her tents like, or with, the Arabs, she silently steals away.

CHAPTER ELEVEN

Whose Name Was Writ in Water
A Perfect Spy

The name Magnus Pym is a good place to begin consideration of *A Perfect Spy*. Everything in this highly autobiographical novel, including its title, is a kind of Joycean inside joke. (The *truly* perfect spy is one who not only is disguised as but *is* a perfectly respectable observer, like a novelist perhaps.) *Magnus* is, of course, the royal, Latinate form of *great* as in "Charlemagne" (Carolus Magnus), whereas plain-speaking John Pym was the bluntest and most English of the Roundheads who overthrew Charles the First. The very name Magnus Pym is a complex oxymoron embodying irreconcilable contradictions that end in self-destruction. The Everyman who would be king, the Englishman who sells his country and his soul to foreign gods, will by his inability to resolve the conflicts within himself become a failure not only as a spy but as a person as well. Those conflicts between eclectic elements which would suggest that they *might* make him a perfect spy make him incapable of the commitment necessary to know who he is a spy for. Magnus spies *on* and *for* everyone, most of all himself.

Ironically (and this is by far the most ironic book of a highly ironic writer), Magnus doesn't come even close to perfection in spying on anything but his own life, and that only when he is in the process of finally relieving himself of the burden of his wretched, divided mortality on the last page of the novel. His introspection and his comprehension of his own twisted values, his gently sarcastic perception of the idiosyncrasies and frailties of Rick, Axel, Jack, and the whole spectrum of humanity from ambassador-level foreign service officers down to lowly land-lady Miss Dubber—all are little short of prescient. If Magnus is any good at being a spy, his career primarily demonstrates it in respect to his analysis of himself. As for genuine espionage, the reader will never know from the novel whether Magnus was even a competent spy. The book might well have been titled "The Education of a Spy," for the principal subject of it is the under-mining of Magnus's morality as it develops. There is probably less about espionage in the novel than in any other major modern spy novel. Magnus presumably is a double agent, betraying British secrets to the Czechs, and thus also to the Russians, while feeding worthless doctored information back to the British. But at no time is it clear who is doing what to whom. There are some vague references to Soviet bloc military movements and mention of Magnus photographing nuclear fa-cilities, but there is no *operation* here. As a deskman for British intelligence in the United States, it is suggested, he copies and transmits to the Soviets classified material. But what? At the bottom of the labyrinthine tangles of *The Spy Who Came in from the Cold* or *Tinker, Tailor, Soldier, Spy,* for example, there was a hard core of covert activity which could be clearly identified once all the threads were revealed. In short, in those novels there were *sides,* and they interacted in ways that made it possible to tell which was which.

Even Magnus's final "operation," his own abrupt disappear-ance with which *A Perfect Spy* opens, is murky. At the end of the novel it is plain that he is probably "blown." British intelligence, suspecting through close computer analysis of his record that he is a double agent, is closing in. Still, through much of the novel le Carré suggests that the fugitive Magnus, hiding as Mr. Canterbury in Miss Dubber's "safe house" in Devon, is sitting on some explosive secret. Perhaps the "burnbox," which he has stolen only for the gun with which he will take his life, contains a secret akin to the information betrayed in *The Russia House* that Soviet technology is worthless or the undelivered code word, *Tinker,* which would have unmasked Haydon during Operation Testify.

If there are secrets, they are unimportant to *A Perfect Spy.* Here there are no sides. There is only Magnus and his father, and their biography is basically the story of how a bent twig turns into a twisted tree. Abandoned early in life by a distant and fragile mother, who gives evidence of being psychotic long before that abandonment, Magnus is raised by a father who is a charismatic and energetic fraud. The would-be spy's youth is a continual roller coaster of fraudulent pyrotechnics. Rick Pym fills his son's childhood with the "business deals" of phony paper corporations ("Rick T. Pym, Prop."), a bevy of flashy women collectively called "the lovelies," a collection of petty criminals who resemble nothing so much as the cast of a British *Guys and Dolls* (Syd Lemon would be perfect as Nathan Detroit), and a parade of half-owned racehorses ("neverwozzers") who, like Rick himself, promise big payoffs and finish out of the money. "You always loved fireworks, old son," he often tells his boy, and it is true.[1]

So dominant is the character of Rick Pym, particularly in the first two-thirds of *A Perfect Spy,* that it is tempting to see him as the true protagonist of the novel, which is then really a son's story of his father.[2] Le Carré's portrait of Rick is surely one of the finest in his fiction. Glittering and fascinating, Rick is the miles gloriosus and the Artful Dodger, Falstaff and Fluellen, John Bull played by W. C. Fields. Through all his long life Rick frantically attempts, often with a precarious modicum of success, to substitute appearance for reality, gesture for act. He speaks, without realizing the irony, of his life as a "struggle for liquidity," which really only means that someday he may be able to pay his bills. He is absolutely incapable of real "liquidity" in the sense of having genuinely valuable assets as opposed to spurious, apparent ones. Indeed, as the subtle Magnus writing his memoir is well aware, Rick's liquidity is that of water—indefinable, ephemeral, and flowing away when needed. Were he a pure fake, callously and deliberately misrepresenting himself for profit, he would be a petty monster. But the key to Rick, as later to his son, is his capacity to manipulate love—not only others' love for him but also his own for them. As a good salesman can convince himself of the worth of the shoddy goods he sells, so can Rick convince himself and his victims that he cares for them. And none of his tangled relationships has more of the appearance of genuine selfless feeling than that with his son, Magnus. Rick is really convinced that he is the "best pal" of Magnus, whom he always calls "old son." Certainly, his final effect on the boy is to instill in him the insecurities and moral relativity that will finally lead to Magnus's suicide.[3] Certainly, too, Rick shamelessly exploits his son, often using the boy's rapidly dwindling innocence to cloak his own schemes. There is also, however, a genuine affection between the two. Somehow Rick manages to find the money to pay the school bills, manages to find the time to visit the boy and play with him, manages to convince the lonely boy that his father cares. What is most damaging is that he offers his son an ambiguous role model, that of a loving and attractive fraud. Whether Rick is capable of caring is ultimately a mystery, as it will be with his son. Both, like Smiley's image of the Russian dolls, are psychologies so layered that the "last doll" will never be revealed.

Particularly significant is the matter of Magnus's education, in part because it is derived directly from le Carré's own legacy from Ronnie Cornwell. Education, as Kenneth Rexroth once observed, is the business of developing a lifestyle, "whether it's that of an Oxford don or a German socialist tool and die maker." For Rick education, like any other asset, is valuable only in terms of dividends. Significantly, he picked up the idea of improving his lot in life by educating Magnus to be a gentleman from Cherry, one of his mistresses. It is this determination, gradually adopted by Magnus, which makes the differences between father and son more apparent and the similarities less so.

If Rick Pym were a more obvious and less devious bounder, it would be easier for Magnus simply to break with him (or perhaps accept the man's villainy), but the father's constant patter of deception extends to his relationship with his son, whom he flatters, bribes, and cajoles, although when crossed, even by Magnus, a "flick knife" in his voice betrays a brutality his silken personality conceals. And for those caught in his seductive web Rick Pym is a mightily persuasive personality. All of his "court" of hangers-on stay loyal despite suffering from his schemes, and one of them, Syd Lemon (a sort of criminal Sam Weller to Rick Pym's criminal Pickwick), actually does prison time to protect Rick. Hardly surprisingly, Rick's adaptable son, like a chameleon, learns to change shades to fit his father's shifting demands and, predictably, too, usually wants only to please the compelling father, whose mercurial personality he can never really define. "All Rick demanded was the totality of your love, and all you could do was give it to him blindly." And Magnus "believed it all. He was the most willing child laborer in the world, so long as there was approval waiting for him around the corner" (42).[4] Magnus's longing for that approval, however, can be as mercurial as his father's willingness to give it, and his desire to please is undercut from an early age by a concealed resentment of Rick's paternal tyranny; it is Magnus who, still a boy, destroys Rick's chances of election to Parliament by leaking information about his father's criminality to the public.

Muddling through to adulthood by learning to adjust to Rick's slippery dishonesty, Magnus verges on breaking away from his father's corrupt paternity when he finds two more flawed father figures in the Czech refugee and communist agent Axel, whom he meets in Vienna, and British intelligence officer Jack Brotherhood. These two represent another of le Carré's exercises in doubling, for they divide between them the character flaws of Rick Pym. Magnus's pet name (and code word) for Axel is "Poppy," supposedly for the poetic World War I poppies of Flanders Field but also because he becomes Magnus's surrogate father. "Sir Magnus," he always calls Pym, in gentle mockery of his young protégé's aristocratic pretensions. Axel's genuine bitterness against establishment false fathers, the "aristos" of the world, as he calls them— the capitalists, class snobs, robber barons, and nabobs of the military/industrial complex—not only blinds him to the evils of the communist system but makes him masochistically willing to accept the monstrous injustices that the system inflicts on him. He cannot recognize that communist "gray men" are even worse than their capitalist counterparts. Axel's intellectual disability is counterbalanced by genuine emotional commitment and great courage (for he is repeatedly imprisoned and tortured by his own colleagues). Magnus's other surrogate father, Jack Brotherhood, on the other hand, seems pragmatically honest in a cynical sort of way but is totally lacking emotionality. His life is a series of sterile relationships with both women and men, and his most powerful personal feeling has been for his Labrador bitch, whom he has the satisfaction of giving a "good death" when she gets too old to hunt (160). He cannot do the same for himself or Magnus. In no le Carré novel are names so blatantly symbolic, and none is more ironic than that of Jack, who theoretically offers the lonely emotional orphan Magnus membership in the "brotherhood" of the Circus, but his own cold, diffident life makes it clear that there is no more a true family there than anywhere else.

For all of his adult life Magnus oscillates between these two men, desperately eager to please either of them, ultimately willing to betray both. While still a student in the first flush of his friendship with the beleaguered Axel, he deliberately turns the refugee in to the authorities for punishment and possible death, apparently to win the approval of Brotherhood. When the resurrected Axel, now openly a communist agent, contacts him years later, Magnus offers himself to him as a double agent betraying the British, evidently out of guilt for his perfidy before.

With the possible exception of his son, Tom, and his father's old friend Syd Lemon, there is literally no one in the novel whom

Magnus does not deceive. He cuts his teeth in duplicity by betraying his prep school mates and then gratuitously sabotages his own father (however undeserving of filial loyalty he may be), by publicly exposing Rick's police record when he runs for political office. Once established with "the Firm" (this novel's inhouse euphemism for the British intelligence agency) and seduced by Axel, Magnus plays for decades as a double agent while working with the West Germans, the Austrians, and particularly the Americans. He cuckolds and abandons his first wife, Belinda, and does the same with his second, Mary, whom he married to get ahead in the Firm, since she is Brotherhood's secretary (and mistress) and from a family of career intelligence officers. It is Mary who finds in Magnus's papers the cryptic notes "Duplicity is when you please one person at the expense of another" and "We are patriots because we are afraid to be cosmopolitan. We are cosmopolitan because we are afraid to be patriots." They summarize the major theme of her husband's life and the pathetic duality that pulls his insecure psychology in opposite directions.

If Mary has been deceived, and more often mystified, by her enigmatic husband, she realizes by the time he disappears that he has built his whole life upon the shifting sands of deceit. "All his life he's been inventing versions of himself that are untrue. Now the truth is coming to get him," she muses (72). She is hardly surprised when, looking for clues to his mystery, she finds in his diary the Scripture "He who is faithful in a little is faithful in much, he who is dishonest in a little is dishonest in much" (94). Here lies the heart of the novel. A spy is a spy in all: a dishonest tree must ultimately bring forth diseased fruit. Magnus's motivation—sometimes his compulsion—to betray is obscure, at times almost perverse. His first betrayal of Axel, when he turns his wretched friend over to the authorities without any need to except the possibility of winning Jack Brotherhood's approval, seems to border on the sadistic, as do his prep school "jokes." Since the foreground of the novel is Magnus's disappearance in the present, the unnecessary suffering of his wife, Mary, is evident throughout the action of the novel. Her pain over her missing husband, whom she genuinely loves, is very real: her sad internal monologues begging Magnus to return, her humiliating abuse by Brotherhood and the Firm searching for him, and her desperate attempts to find him are a picture of a soul in agony. These are counterpointed by the sketches of Magnus, perfectly calm if somber, as he hides in Devon and selfishly comes to terms with himself, as he always has, without regard to the cost to other people.

Magnus himself often seems to have a perception of the evil of his duplicity, even as he does it. Certainly, he is aware of his mistreatment of his first wife, Belinda, of his inability to return Mary's unequivocal love, of his betrayal of his American friend and colleague Grant Lederer, whose wife he seduces almost out of instinct rather than love or even lust. Even when his spying is detached from individual relationships, he senses the magnitude of his duplicity, if not the wrongness of it. With the United States, the longtime target of his and Axel's joint careers, he is particularly conscious that he is spying upon an essentially decent people. He cannot even bring himself to rationalize his betrayal.

> Pym set out, believe it or not, determined to disapprove of everything he saw. He found no holding point, no stern judgment to revolt against. These vulgar pleasure-seeking people, so frank and clamorous, were too uninhibited for his shielded and involuted life. They loved their prosperity

> too obviously, were too flexible and mobile, too little the
> slaves of place, origin and class. . . . when they mixed with
> one another they were American and loquacious and disarm-
> ing, and Pym was hard put to find a centre to betray. . . . Why
> had they done him no harm? Why had they not cramped
> him, frightened him, forced his limbs into impossible
> positions from the cradle up? He found himself longing for
> the empty, darkened streets of Prague and the reassuring
> embrace of chains. (455)

He wants punishment, "the reassuring embrace of chains," because his conscience calls for it, and a conscience is the mark of
a moral man.

Beyond Magnus's compulsion to betray is that moral voice
in him that demands self-destruction to atone for his unresolved
and evil nature. *A Perfect Spy* is the story of a man who has
everything going for him except himself. Charming, talented,
popular, successful, this is a man whose life should be a paradigm
of achievement. But he destroys it all, throwing away success
with both hands. Why does Magnus really become a double
agent? Not because he believes in anything, certainly, but, rather,
because he believes in nothing, least of all himself. He believes
in nothing, but that does not mean that he is inherently evil. After
all, as Smiley claimed in *Tinker, Tailor, Soldier, Spy,* "perhaps
treason is mainly a matter of habit" (332). A bad habit, and one
that the basically decent Magnus, who only wishes to please,
senses is one that ought to be subverted. What better way to
subvert it than to destroy the traitor, and that he does, not only
literally and physically at the end of *A Perfect Spy* but also step

by step, by making bad choices for reasons that only a psychologist might be able to explain.

The self-doubt, the self-hatred, and the central psychological themes of the novel are neatly wrapped up by Axel in a closing speech that is almost too neat.

> Sir Magnus, you have in the past betrayed me but, more important, you have betrayed yourself. Even when you are telling the truth, you lie. You have loyalty and you have affection. But to what? To whom? I don't know all the reasons for this. Your great father. Your aristocratic mother. One day maybe you will tell me. And maybe you have put your love in some bad places now and then. . . . Yet you also have morality. You search. What I am saying is, Sir Magnus: for once nature has produced a perfect match. You are a perfect spy. All you need is a cause. I have it. I know that our revolution is young and that sometimes the wrong people are running it. In the pursuit of peace we are making too much war. In the pursuit of freedom we are building too many prisons. But in the long run I don't mind. Because I know this. All the junk that made you what you are: the privileges, the snobbery, the hypocrisy, the churches, the schools, the fathers, the class systems, the historical lies, the little lords of the countryside, the little lords of big business, and all the greedy wars that result from them, we are sweeping that away for ever. For your sake. Because we are making a society that will never produce such sad little fellows as Sir Magnus. . . . So. I've said it. You are a good man and I love you." (430)

It is Axel's tragedy that he can claim that "in the long run I don't mind," that he still believes he and his people are sweeping away anything worse than they are ushering in. Sad as "Sir Magnus" may be, he is not nearly as sad as the products of the opposition. The opposition, though, doesn't really matter much in *A Perfect Spy,* and, as Axel perceptively notes, belief in one side or the other had little to do with the creation of Magnus Pym. Perhaps he really is a "good man," though—more than a psychotic at best with a deeply rooted need to deceive or a totally venal and conniving opportunist at worst. If he is a good man, as Axel claims, perhaps it is because something in him rejects the fact that he has "put . . . love in some bad places now and then" (332). People who have trusted their love to the likes of Rick Pym on the one side and the communist revolution on the other are not likely to have much respect for themselves, and such a lover is a good candidate for suicide, the expression of lack of self-respect of a corrupt psychology. In the end the harshest judge of Magnus's failure in his slippery struggle with love and loyalty, belief and betrayal, is himself.

Some critics, even recognizing the compelling and convincing achievement of Magnus as a character, have faulted the book on the grounds that the character lacks substantiality.[5] They claim that the novel is facile but morally lightweight, precisely because the protagonist does not so much betray his morality as simply lack one. Certainly, Magnus is a moral and personal failure, incapable of finding or holding himself to any code, incapable of any love that is not subject to the whims of his desperate insecurities. Why, then, should we take him seriously? This is a legitimate complaint, but it fails to take into account the overwhelming charm that makes Magnus important. Charm is a discredited concept in modern literature, particularly to American readers, smacking somehow of the shallowness of badly drawn Scott Fitzgerald characters. But one reason we still read Fitzgerald (even jejune Fitzgerald like *This Side of Paradise*) is that we recognize the importance of pure charm in an imperceptive world. From Jane Austen to Joseph Conrad (two of le Carré's favorite novelists and models) attractiveness of personality carries enough weight to qualify a character for social success or tragic damnation; Nostromo, after all, had little going for him but a good appearance and people's trust. Much of the brilliance, in all senses of the word, of *A Perfect Spy* goes into establishing the glittering richness of Magnus's personality. Le Carré builds with wonderful, convincing vignettes, like this opening image of Magnus cleverly doing parlor tricks for diplomatic society: "Herr Pym can put you a row of bottles in a line, and by pinging them with a table-knife, make them chime like the bells of the old Swiss railway, while he chants the stations between Interlaken and the Jungfraujoch in the tones of a local station-master and his audience collapses in tears of nostalgic mirth" (12); and even dying Magnus retains his fastidious concern for his cranky landlady, wrapping towels about his head when he shoots himself, "because if there was one thing Miss Dubber hated above another, it was mess" (474). Between these two details lies a wealth of tactile imagery demonstrating that Magnus is, indeed, not only an interesting, talented, substantial *character* but also an interesting, talented, substantial person—in short, *real*. A true tragedy, after all, is a story in which a substantial and psychologically convincing character comes to destruction through his flawed character.

But there are at least two Magnuses in *A Perfect Spy*. One is the insecure charlatan who picks his way through the world behind the mask of a gay deceiver. This is what he has learned from Rick, and his life might have been an amoral success were it not for the other Magnus—the one who writes an apologia to his son and shoots himself on the last page of the novel. This second Magnus is the moral Magnus who lurks behind the deceiver throughout the story and finally comes out of the closet to die a moral death instead of trying to get away with another charade. If Rick Pym is not a shallow character, he is one-sided, for he never changes. His son, however, goes through a dreadful transformation in being brought to the truth. It is the acceptance that his whole life has been a lie as well as the ethical consequences of that lie. His suicide is the act of a moral man rather than the inconsequential self-termination of a charming rogue who kills himself because his luck has run out and he can't get away with being himself any longer.

This duality in Magnus's psychology is at the heart of the enormous thematic, stylistic, and structural complexity of *A Perfect Spy*—a complexity not appreciated by all critics.[6] The almost psychotic fragmentation of Magnus's own damaged psychology is reflected in the multiple story lines, the frenzied shifting in and out of interior monologues, and the sudden time shifts, which often leave the reader disoriented. Some of the novel is openly told with Magnus serving as amanuensis, recording the events as he saw them. Other parts are flashbacks, colored by Magnus's sarcasm or wry perspective but whose narrative persona is unclear. Others, particularly those featuring cold-blooded realist Jack Brotherhood, seem to be simple objective recording of events, if such a thing is possible in so subjective a work.

Whose Name Was Writ in Water

Some of the subjectivity must be a result of le Carré's cutting the donnée of this novel from flesh very close to his own bone. With most of le Carré's fiction the reader is tempted to read too much of the author into the text. With much of *A Perfect Spy* it is almost impossible not to.[7] The critical figure of Rick Pym, Magnus's father, who is really a more significant character than his son through much of the book, is nearly directly lifted from le Carré's own father, Ronnie Cornwell, a mercurial con man, speculator, race track tout, skirt chaser, and high roller who served prison time for fraud, made a splashy and abortive run as a Liberal Party candidate for Parliament, and inflicted on his son a series of humiliations which lasted the boy a lifetime. Little in *A Perfect Spy* suggests that Rick Pym is not the fictional incarnation of Ronnie Cornwell. Le Carré, at first reticent about his father's moral defects as well as his grandiose "successes," admitted both openly at the time *A Perfect Spy* was published:

> Ronnie's life accomplishments, if unorthodox, were dazzling: a string of bankruptcies spread over nearly fifty years and accounting for several millions of pounds: literally hundreds of companies with grandiose letter paper and scarcely a speck of capital: a host of faithful friends who smiled on his business ventures even when they were themselves victims of them: four healthy and successful children: seven grandsons: an undimmed faith in his creator: spells of imprisonment on two continents which had left no discernible mark on everything.[8]

Up to a point the same might be said of Magnus—and le Carré himself. Up to a point. The celebrated author's unhappy childhood was certainly the origin of the "sad little Magnus," as Axel often called his friend/agent/victim, so like that other lonely little boy, Bill Roach in *Tinker, Tailor, Soldier, Spy.* At some point, however, David Cornwell and Magnus parted company, and the one went on to turn his intelligence and his powers of observation, his diffidence and his ability to detach from emotions, into art and thus into honesty. The other, Magnus, went on chewing on himself neurotically until he was gnawing on an empty bone. Just where the critical dividing point occurred will not be clear until Cornwell writes an autobiography or reveals enough for an objective biographer to write one for him.[9] Perhaps the turning point for Cornwell was when he became John le Carré and rejected espionage, a profession that must to a considerable degree be based on deceit.

CHAPTER TWELVE

The Cold War Wanes

The Russia House and *The Secret Pilgrim*

Smiley's People is the last of John le Carré's "pure" Cold War novels—studies of the monumental political, philosophical, and psychological struggle threatening the peace of the world for two generations. Certainly, le Carré painted that struggle as far more complex than simply a global cops-and-robbers thriller, for the novels from *Call for the Dead* through the "Karla trilogy" emphasized the subtle resemblances between the antagonists, the sordid techniques that compromised both East and West, and the depths of human psychology. Still, the epic confrontation hung over all the action, and le Carré was well aware of how central to his art the intelligence sector of the conflict had been. "Spying was the passion of my time," he said later. "I was there. I felt some of it on my own body. And as I grew away from it and recollected it in tranquility, I made it my bit of earth, my context, my way of looking at life."[1]

The Little Drummer Girl had been a foray into themes and plots; *A Perfect Spy* marked a personal exploration of the psychology of a single spy in the last days of the Cold War, but the focus was psychological rather than political. By the end of the decade of the 1980s, with the coming of glasnost and Gorbachev, le Carré returned to the old spying fields but recollected, perhaps not so much in "tranquility" as through the glass of time, more clearly and more personally than when the Cold War was hotter.

The result was two short novels, *The Russia House* (1989) and *The Secret Pilgrim* (1990), about closing doors upon the past and embracing the future. Both were elegiac and nostalgic.

The Russia House

With *The Russia House* le Carré moves directly into the post–Cold War world after two major novels in which he side-stepped dealing directly with the confrontation as he had in earlier fiction. *A Perfect Spy* focused inward on the psychology of a single player in the "great game." *The Little Drummer Girl,* like *The Honourable Schoolboy,* spotlighted a sideshow—the Middle East, rather than Southeast Asia—in which neither Soviet communism nor British/American capitalism were the major players. Both novels dealt brilliantly with material that had obvious implications for the communist/capitalist struggle, but both were primarily concerned with other issues. *The Russia House,* however, returns to the main axis of the East-West conflict but is directly focused on the question of how "decent" people can deal with the close of the Cold War and the possibility of true peace. Le Carré said of the novel, "We've got to enter a new era no matter how hard it is to give up the convenient attitudes of mutual animosity."[2] Accordingly, the principles of the novel are again the Russians and the West. It is le Carré's first, and so far finest, novel of reconciliation, and it was greeted by a friendly barrage of critical commentary treating the novelist of espionage as a conquering hero brooding benevolently over the body of his former prey, an enemy whose threat had been the subject of most of his previous work.[3] *The Russia House* suggests itself as the prologue to the last, synthetic act of le Carré's lifetime study in literature of the relationship of the individual to political institutions— the most important issue of the world in the second half of the twentieth century.

Le Carré's inspiration for the story represents one of those dramatic moments when literature and life intersect. Tentatively testing the limits of glasnost in 1987, the novelist cautiously applied for a visa to visit Russia for the first time. He was surprised when it was granted and even more surprised when he was greeted by the Russian intelligentsia not as an enemy but as a kindred spirit and apostle of cross-cultural amity. On a trip to Leningrad he met with one of his personal heroes, Andrey Sakharov, the dissident physicist who had created the hydrogen bomb for the communists then suffered decades of intense abuse for opposing the Party's tyranny. When Sakharov asked le Carré about the physicist Klaus Fuchs, who had given American atomic information to the Soviets because he rejected capitalist ideology, le Carré found himself wondering, "What would have happened if Sakharov had taken that route?" To paraphrase *The Russia House* that was the moment that "the Bluebird spread his wings" in the novelist's mind.[4]

The teller of the tale in the novel is Palfrey (a gentle, unspirited mount suitable for delivering a delicate load and, in this case, treating it with understanding). He is a self-confessed bureaucrat, a relatively neutral voice from within the ossified structure of the Western intelligence community, who serves the Circus, he modestly says, as "a fixer, bit-player and pleaser and finally as a chronicler." Le Carré carefully distinguishes him from the novel's other official and unofficial voices in that

Palfrey lacks passion, for good or ill. Also, as "legal advisor to the illegals," he represents both the establishment and the "antiestablishment." Compared to the punchy, slangy rhetoric of the CIA men like "Sheriton," the choppy but pushy muscular voices of the Russian literary crowd, or the deliberately formal voices of the British intelligence men, Palfrey is simple, direct, and artless. Palfrey's sympathetic role in *The Russia House* is particularly bittersweet considering his ultimate fate within the whole sweep of le Carré's canon, for he will be led astray by his allegiance to "the Service" in *The Night Manager* and unwittingly play a major part in betraying agent Jonathan Pine in that novel, then commit suicide out of guilt and remorse. He sets the tone for the novel, which is particularly significant because *The Russia House* was le Carré's deliberate attempt to return to "a much friskier, leaner style—more in the manner of *The Spy Who Came in from the Cold* but with all the experience I've picked up in the years between."[5] Palfrey represents "the good Circus," much as Smiley does in *The Spy Who Came in from the Cold* and *The Looking-Glass War,* and he stands ready to pick up the pieces after the bunglings of incompetence, much as Smiley does in those novels. He lacks the brutal cynicism of Leamas or the biting sarcasm of the narrative voice in *The Little Drummer Girl,* and Palfrey always seems to desire a kinder, gentler Circus, if such were possible. He deplores the new broom of slick bureaucracy, reporting, for example, the advent of secret cameras to monitor activities: "It was becoming that kind of an operation." Like Smiley, he is unlucky in love, uncomfortable with visible honors and the pomp of power, and disposed to view with compassion and understanding the human foibles of human agents. Smiley, however, must fight an implacable proclaimed enemy in Karla, deliberate treason in Haydon, and inexcusable hypocrisy and incompetence in the British bureaucracy. For Palfrey the "bungling" of *The Russia House* is open to interpretation, and we suspect that his attitude toward Barley Blair's "defection" is more forgiving than that of his superiors.[6]

The Bluebird whose marvelous tale of Russian unpreparedness triggers the tale is, of course, "Goethe," the symbolic sobriquet by which the character whom Sakharov inspired is known in the novel; again, as with the copy of *Simplicissimus* carried by Smiley and Axel, le Carré's academic roots in German romanticism assert themselves, for the original Goethe, the godfather of European romanticism, was the voice of international humanism and the concept of a community of minds which transcended the limits of chauvinist provincialism. The Russian "Goethe's" counterpart, and the novel's hero, is "Barley" Blair, a dissipated British publisher who, even less than previous le Carré heroes, has few credentials for heroism. Barley is straight out of Graham Greene's and Eric Ambler's stable of shoddy, reprobate candidates for sainthood, the alcoholic losers and leftovers of democracy's competitions. Like most Greene and Ambler protagonists, Barley has too much "liquidity" (to borrow Rick Pym's term in *A Perfect Spy*) and too little viciousness to qualify for either Dickensian poverty or naturalist savagery. He is simply the epitome of the meaningless twentieth-century man—alienated, frustrated, aimless, and desperately in need of a cause. Like Magnus Pym, Barley, too, is looking for love; unlike Magnus, he lacks an almost sociopathic inclination to compensate for his shortcomings by wallowing in sin and destructive social behavior. He is simply nowhere. Also, as far as British intelligence is concerned, he is most perceptive when he protests, "I'm the wrong man . . . and you're a fool for using me" (100).[7]

At which point two forces enter his life: the vision that "Goethe" has of a universal "decency" that transcends nationality and ideology and Katya. The first is essentially an expanded version of the second, presumably without the erotic element. "Behaving like a decent human being," which "Goethe" calls upon Barley to do, is really a generalizing of the intense primacy of individual love which Katya arouses in him. Both forces pressure Barley to renounce a matrix of formal allegiances that have shaped his meaningless life. His loyalty to his country, to firm, to the traditions of upper-class solidarity, even to his family—all go by the boards when "Goethe" and Katya offer him a vision of brotherly love, peace, and responsibility to a personal morality that transcends all the ties of society which Barley has felt before.

The "dialogue" between "Goethe" and Barley is a tricky duet for which le Carré's libretto is especially skillful. It begins, as Barley tells it, with Barley drunkenly warbling the main melody unthinkingly at a gathering of Soviet intellectuals with whom he parties after a Moscow fair. The scientific but romantic soul of "Goethe" is touched, he believing that he has found a kindred spirit, and later that same fuzzy evening he sings Barley's idealistic song back to him. Picking up on Barley's homily, "Today one must think like a hero to behave like a merely decent human being," "Goethe" demands a pledge: "Promise me that if ever I find the courage to think like a hero, you will act like a merely decent human being" (87). Barley hears this voice of idealism, but, even when "Goethe" sends his treasonous manuscript betraying the failure of Russian military technology ("The

Russian knight is dying inside his armor"), Barley is not yet
hooked. Still, his sleeping better self has been aroused, and,
ironically, it is an appeal to it which stirs him to accept Ned's
call to arms: "It's crude and un-English but I'll say it anyway.
Do you want to be a passive or an active player in the defence
of your country?" (100). The problem is that "Goethe's"
idealism is still framed in the abstract: it has no human face,
and for le Carré ideologies without faces are not only weak;
they are dangerous, for they destroy human beings without ever
acknowledging their humanity (no theory has the impact on
Leamas of the image of the faces of the doomed children which
closes *The Spy Who Came in from the Cold*).

The "human face" to "Goethe's" vision of universal humanism is, of course, Katya's. Her vulnerability lends her willingness
to sacrifice herself peculiarly Christian overtones. In contrast to
her former lover, "Goethe," with his highly intellectualized
conceptions of brotherhood and decency, Katya is uncerebral.
She doesn't even pretend to understand his physics or his philosophy. Her loyalties are fundamentally personal, and her commitment is first to him then later to Barley; her two children and
fumbling Uncle Matvey only add to le Carré's portrait of her
humanity, right down to her account of her first true awareness of
the greater political world, when she was caught up in her father's
and "Goethe's" passionate belief in the "Prague Spring" of
Czechoslovakia—"Democracy with a human face"—which first
inspired her to surrender her heart, and her virginity, to "Goethe."

Despite the fact, or perhaps because of it, that *The Russia
House* is a love story, Katya is not an impressive heroine from a
feminist perspective. She has courage aplenty and tremendous
warmth and vivacity, but she tends to be, as many of le Carré's

women do, a part of the moral and psychological environment in which men work out the imperatives of their lives. Although le Carré works hard to make her a viable alternative to the neurotic mental compulsions of men who are dedicated to ideas, she is too patently a symbol of heart over mind, and, were she drawn with less authority, she would be in danger of being simply a pathetic symbol of feeling humanity sacrificed on the altar of dedicated but heartless ideology. She is surely a more convincing and full-blooded character than, say, Maria in Hemingway's *For Whom the Bell Tolls,* who is in roughly the same position as Katya ideationally, but feminists may still be legitimately bothered by her lack of intellectual involvement in the conceptual progression of the novel. She has enormous influence on Barley but still relatively little input into his critical decision to opt for heart over head and risk trusting the Russians as opposed to his own people.[8]

The roles of the other players in the action of *The Russia House* are more ambiguous, and the novel lacks the clear villainy of most of le Carré's earlier books. Le Carré has never been one to resort to simplistic black hats and white hats, but in most of his fiction there are characters who are unequivocal embodiments of evils, if not of evil itself. Mundt, Haydon, and even Karla may have their virtues, or at least excuses for their brutality and dishonesty, but they quite clearly are running dogs for those plagues that Camus and the passive existentialists maintain it is our obligation not to side with. In *The Russia House* the real enemy is ideological inertia. The novel is a bit like one of those thrillers in which the bad guys have been killed off, but the heroes must race desperately to defuse a ticking time bomb that has been left behind. Most interesting in the novel is le Carré's handling of bureaucracy, which has always been a convenient whipping boy for him. Much of the strength of the Smiley fiction sprang from the wonderful satiric portraits of mendacious officials preening their feathers and scrambling up the greasy poles toward what they perceive as their proper stations in life. Percy Alliline, Miles Sercomb, Saul Enderby, Toby Esterhaze, and many lesser bureaucrats were often the jealous guardians of a complex structure of ritual, pomposity, jargon, and rigmarole that, even if they were not themselves deliberately villains, provided a fertile nest and shield for moral corruption, pride, and, ultimately, evil to thrive. In *The Russia House* the issue is more subtle. On both sides, of course, there are still the petty, self-important pencil pushers guarding their tiny paper fiefdoms, like Palmer Wellow, the low-level "resident clerk" of the service who appropriates the precious original manuscript of the Bluebird document which Katya passes to Niki Landau and sits on it for two days. The British and U.S. intelligence officers, notably Ned, whom Barley truly respects, are at times buffoons and caricatures, but they seem to be in the main well meaning. Naturally, le Carré gets in a few satiric shots: there's the British director of the operation, Clive, "who had one of those English faces that seemed to have been embalmed while he was still a boy king" and is "sleek, tight-lipped and groomed for television"; or Walter, "a teased out Falstaff of the richer common rooms" (57); and even Ned, who heads the Russia House, is pigeonholed by bits of telling jargon. But they're not really bad men, and, in contrast to bureaucrats like Marston or Enderby in other le Carré novels, they seem to be just doing their jobs.[9]

One of the most telling scenes in the novel is the fifteen-page section in which British intelligence and "the Cousins" from the CIA confront Barley and try to persuade him to help them verify and investigate the crucial "Goethe" manuscript revealing Soviet weakness. The scene has many parallels: the convoluted persuasions in *The Little Drummer Girl,* Smiley's interrogations of Karla (as well as his "friendly" probings of Connie Sachs and her remarkable will-o'-the-wisp memory), a half-dozen interrogation scenes in *The Night Manager.* With the Cousins, Barley plays the heavy, and for the most part the bureaucrats are, understandably, if a bit woodenly, frustrated by his attitude. When the senior CIA official says cavalierly: "Proud to meet you, Barley. Let's have fun. Let's do some good," and Barley replies sarcastically: "Now that *is* jolly. . . . If you want a Third World leader assassinated, I'm your man," Clive snaps: "We're as bad as Bob's lot and we do the same things. We also have an Official Secrets Act, which they don't, and we expect you to sign it" (59). This kind of candor is something new, and there is a sense that Barley has been properly reminded of his manners. Clive and Bob, Ned and Palfrey, may have their cute little mannerisms, and le Carré picks them up, but minor affectations do not make them vicious. Palfrey himself calls the Official Secrets Act, "a weasely document . . . designed to impress the signatory and no one else," and Barley "could grumble about Americans in general, but no sooner had he met them individually than he spoke of them as decent fellows all" (231).

Nobody in the book is vicious. The Russians are often befuddled and venal, like the ponderous "man of letters" Nezhdanov or comical Uncle Matvey (who crosses Mr. Micawber with the kindly grandfather in *Dr. Zhivago*), but not one of them exhibits the kind of cold-blooded visciousness of previous novels. The KGB, in particular, is conspicuous by its absence, although the overriding Russian fear of them is testimony to their former ruthlessness. Ironically, it is Barley himself who makes the strongest case against them but then only when describing his father's disillusionment: "He could have forgiven the Russians most things, but not the Terror, nor the camps and not the deportations. It broke his heart" (235). But where are these Russian thugs who ran the camps? They have simply disappeared.

This avoidance of dealing with the brutality of the Russian system is the greatest weakness of *The Russia House,* and yet it is also the key to the book. The implications of "Goethe's" volatile manuscript are clear: a "Russian knight . . . dying inside his armor" doesn't make a very convincing villain, and le Carré's picture of the "evil empire" scarcely peoples it with heavies, much less demons. A few clumsy *apparatchniks* are about as close as the novel comes to an appearance by the "other side," despite the paranoia of the Russia House and the CIA. The KGB hardly appears at all, and it would be difficult to find anything threatening in people like Uncle Matvey or the literary camp followers Nezhdanov and Zapadny. What is very much alive in the novel is the pervasive fear that generations of brutal oppression have left. From Katya's desperate fear at her first meeting with Nikki Landau to Barley's wistful hopes in Lisbon on the last page that the Russians will do something "decent" for a change and let Katya go, it is always implicit in *The Russia House,* as in all le Carré's fiction, that the Russian record on treating human beings decently is atrocious.

Le Carré reminds the reader repeatedly that "spying is waiting"; "spying is hoping"; spying is prolonged terrified apprehension not necessarily of what *is* dangerous but of what might be. Always, Barley is aware of the brooding legacy of communist terror—in the apartments of Moscow, on the streets of Leningrad, in his anxious contacts with "Goethe," and especially in his love affair with Katya. Barley's whole relationship with her after they first meet in Moscow is suffused with fear. Hers pervades everything about their initial contact, including her refusal to give him her address. Only during their second meeting—on a clandestine rooftop hideaway watched over by the vigilant spook Wicklow—does she begin to trust him, as the depth of her apprehension becomes apparent. Much of the romance of this highly romantic novel is that of Tristan and Isolde or Lancelot and Guinevere—love stolen under the nose of an evil tyranny. Whether the lovers are right in their constant perception of threat or not, in view of the evidence of a lifetime of slaughter and deceit, is another matter. There is surely the possibility that all or most of the fear that hangs over the entire novel is simply paranoia, but that does not make it any less real to the characters or to the reader.

This paranoia is amplified halfway through the book, when Barley returns to England and then goes to the United States for "the Island Conference" with the CIA. There the U.S. intelligence chief, Sheriton, ups the stakes by pointing out that "the entire American military might is invested in the belief that the Soviet hardware is accurate as hell" and raising the specter of an American congressional attitude summed up by his parody of "Deep South hillbilly": "Time we blew those mothers apart before they do the same to us" (236). Soon it is obvious that the Americans' suspicion extends beyond the fear that the "Goethe" manuscript is a deliberate plant; it extends to Barley as well. First, Barley is grilled by hostile interrogators, and then he is subjected to a lie detector test (for knowledge of which the scrupulous

The Cold War Wanes

researcher le Carré credits instruction by a former FBI member in the acknowledgments).

Finally, Barley is sent back to Russia to reconfirm the legitimacy of "Goethe's" report. Little wonder that his allegiances at this point are a bit shaky, for the murk of distrust and fear has thickened about him on all sides. He is afraid of the communists because of who they are and who they have been and, particularly, because Katya and "Goethe" are afraid of them. He is wary of his own people in the Russia House because of their bureaucratic lack of humanity, their manipulativeness, and their paranoia. It is hardly surprising that he is unsure about where he stands or whose interests he should defend as the novel moves toward resolution. That resolution is that Barley leaves the great game. The concept of individuals of conscience simply declaring a "farewell to arms" because the arms have become not only corrupt but irrelevant is new to le Carré's fiction. His great antagonists—Smiley, Leamas, Westerby, Dieter Frey, Karla—had been battered and abused and often driven from their callings, but they had all stayed the course, limping into port—whether it be death or exile—unrepentant and still committed. Even Karla, although he was forced to defect at the end of *Smiley's People,* showed no sign of apostasy. *The Russia House,* however, offers a philosophy akin to a popular pacifist poster slogan: "Suppose they gave a war and nobody came?"

The conclusion of *The Russia House* is one of the most ambiguous sections in all of le Carré's work. The novelist has often left his characters unresolved. Lack of closure and ambivalence about direction is the hallmark of the characters who survive at the end of his books, and there is not one of them that leaves the reader without a sense that all parties to espionage compromise themselves in the practice of their trade. Seldom, though, is the actual plot of the resolution unclear, yet the conclusion of *The Russia House* is rife with questions.

The most important is the singular silence of the KGB. Despite his manifest criticisms of British and U.S. intelligence, le Carré has never been coy about the repulsiveness of the Russian counterparts of MI5 and the CIA. Some Russian security personnel are genuine swine, like Connie Sachs's "Ginger Pig" Kirov, others complex but ruthless intellectuals like Karla or Dieter Frey; all are unequivocally savage when the chips are down. The marks of KGB brutality scar the bodies and psychologies of all whose lives are touched by them, whether in the form of the uniformed thugs who shoot Leamas or the faceless gray men who haunt "Goethe's" imagination. Yet this grim host simply disappears in *The Russia House.* Barley, Katya, and "Goethe" slink about in terror of them through most of the novel, but when Barley decides to deal with them they simply don't exist, at least for the reader. After Barley asks the jack-of-all-trades go-between Alik Zapadny to put him in touch with "the proper authorities" (who out of deference to his heritage Barley still calls "the pigs who think they own you" [331]), the rest of the activity inside Russia is seen, and related, through a glass darkly by Palfrey, describing what seems to be happening as Barley seems to be turning traitor. "The elusive truth that Ned was speaking of came out slowly and in a series of distorted perceptions, which is generally the case in our secret overworld" (334). Palfrey reports the sketchy observations of various allied intelligence legmen—Wicklow, Henziger, Paddy—who make contact with the renegade agent in his last visible moments, and then he disappears. Everything else between that point and his reticent and uninformative last meeting in Lisbon with Palfrey, which closes the book, is deliberately vague and suggestive.

Even the one significant piece of information which would seem to indicate the sinister hand of the KGB—the official Soviet announcement of "the death after illness of the distinguished physicist Professor Yakov Savelyev ["Goethe"] . . . of natural causes," is immediately followed by Palfrey's report that "the conspiracy theorists had a ball," speculating that "Savelyev was not dead" and that "his material was vindicated, was not vindicated. . . . It was worthless. . . . It was pure gold. . . . It was smoke." "In short, there was enough for everyone to get his teeth into" (343). Even the apparent "termination" of "Goethe" is ambiguous, and he may have died naturally, for Katya was quick to verify "Goethe's" sickness earlier in the book. In short, the dreadful KGB, the deviltry of which had been one of the few givens of le Carré's picture of the Cold War, is still unseen, lurking in the shadows of this novel, even if its presence is often suggested by the characters' fear.

If the KGB's vile works are not manifest to the reader, however, the threat of them obviously obsesses Barley (who has every reason to believe, through Katya's evidence, that this modern Gestapo is killing or has killed "Goethe." This dreadful KGB is the one that Barley trusts to keep its side of the unholy bargain by which he has sold himself to the Russians for Katya's life or freedom or happiness—or something undefined. Why does he do this? The novel's answer is that because of his love for Katya he is willing to take a terrible risk and trust the KGB, hoping that the organization will trade her and her family for whatever information Barley has about British and American reactions to "Goethe's" analysis of Soviet technology. (The "laundry list" of questions posed by Western technicians is supposed to reveal much about Western technology.) This does make a kind of perverse sense, if the only thing that matters to Barley is Katya. If his own safety, patriotism, his country's defense, and his honor mean nothing to him in the balance with his love of her, then offering the KGB himself with no collateral may be a bad deal, but it is the only deal he can get. Still, it is far from clear that it makes sense. It is most significant that le Carré did not write the sentimental ending so tempting to any reader (or writer) who believes that Barley's deal is justified—the reunion of Barley and Katya in Lisbon at the very end of the novel (which the makers of the film based on *The Russia House* could not resist). There is nothing but wistful thinking to suggest that Katya will ever show up at the end of the novel, and a much more realistic reading of the novel, as well as the rest of the author's fiction, suggests quite the opposite: that Barley may have done a noble deed but that, glasnost or no glasnost, little in twentieth-century Russian behavior should lead anyone to expect that they will ever let her out of Russia. If the gray men killed the Bluebird, as there is every reason to believe that they did, they are unlikely to let his consort fly away to a new happiness.

This hope for the Russians carrying out their side of Barley's deal and letting Katya go lies behind the standard reading of *The Russia House.* Most critics hold that it is finally the story of a courageous man who is empowered by love enough to trust his instincts and break with the confining myths of Cold War confrontation. There is an alternate interpretation, and that is that he is a sentimentalist who lets his desire for the world that he wants affect his judgment of the world as it clearly is. Unlike Smiley, who hoped that Bill Haydon did not seduce his wife but had the professionalism and the tough-mindedness to proceed as if he did, Barley, who has always taken the slothful path of least resistance, is naive enough to trust the Russians because he desperately wants them to be trustworthy. Sadly, everything suggests that they are not.[10]

Such a cynical reading of the novel suggests an even more cynical interpretation of the book's resolution. There is a sinister possible explanation for Palfrey's observation that, "after a becoming period of withdrawal, her [Katya's] ebullience reasserted itself and she was seen about" (347). Evidently, Katya has not only not been punished for what even by the lenient standards of any Western democracy would be high treason; she has apparently thrived. Why have the Russians not punished her? The answer that "for once in his life Barley had hammered out a first-rate contract" is unconvincing, for Barley really had nothing to trade. Le Carré has a fine sense of sarcastic understatement and is not likely to drop a snide phrase like "after a becoming period of withdrawal" without implying hypocrisy. Might it not be possible that the whole of *The Russia House* is a description of an elaborate Russian "honey trap" in which the amateur English spy is snared by a beautiful but unscrupulous Russian agent far more skillful at using romance than her untrained and vulnerable English target is at detecting such callous deception? To carry such an interpretation a step further, might it not be possible that Barley himself was "turned"—truly "turned" and not just making a single deal for overriding humane concerns. Palfrey says, after all, that there were rumors of Barley being seen in Moscow and of singular happenings in Russians prisons as he was being "debriefed" by the KGB. Perhaps he did, indeed, "take his place among the other shadows that haunt the darker byways of Moscow society—the trodden-out defectors and spies, the traded ones and the untrusted ones with their pathetic wives and pallid minders, sharing out their dwindling rations of Western treats and Western memories" (348–49). Of course, Barley does not end up "haunting the darker byways of Moscow society" as a declared traitor, like Kim Philby, whom le Carré himself called "loathsome." Barley ends up in a comfortable pied-à-terre in Lisbon, where he is conveniently available to old Palfrey, who is more than eager to serve as his amanuensis. Which may explain why, as Palfrey tells it, Barley "seemed concerned to make me a gift of his story, so that I would have something to take home to my masters" (353).

So it is that le Carré closes *The Russia House* with tantalizing alternatives in the final chapter. As with the story of the lady and the tiger, the reader may decide that the brooding fear that hangs over the action of this novel—the record of atrocity in reality and in John le Carré's fiction of the Russians and the ambiguity with which the novel resolves itself—implies that Barley is a brave but foolish Quixote who made a bad deal and got burned. Then again, he may be seen, as so many readers have, as an apostle of the new era of human cooperation who had the vision not only to love his enemies but to trust them and is rewarded for his farsightedness by having them return to him the woman he loves. Isn't it pretty to think so?

The Secret Pilgrim

The Secret Pilgrim, published in 1990, was the slightest of John le Carré's full-length novels in twenty-eight years and the one with the least thematic integrity. Not since *A Murder of Quality* in 1962 had he produced anything so short, and at least that early novella had the virtue of unity. *The Secret Pilgrim* is essentially a collection of short stories, a grab bag of "tales of the Circus."[11] Although the writer's formidable reputation and the skill he demonstrates in some of its individual stories earned it favorable reviews, overall it must be seen as a capable five-finger literary exercise, breathing space between the hefty substantiality of the fifteen years of continuous artistic achievement which preceded it and the remarkable redirection of *The Night Manager,* a very big book in every way, which was to follow. Apologetic commentators on *The Secret Pilgrim* can maintain that the almost enervated structure of the novel is a function of its narrative—that of two old men chewing over the butt ends of their days and ways.[12]

The structural road map of *The Secret Pilgrim* is drawn by geography, and the book is useful as a reminder of the considerable spatial stretch of le Carré's work in terms of setting. Despite the distant and exotic locales of *The Little Drummer Girl, The Honourable Schoolboy,* and bits and pieces of other novels, we still tend to think of le Carré as a fly on the Berlin Wall, observing the *mano a mano* struggle in central Europe of two intransigent adversaries. In *The Secret Pilgrim* the locus of action is constantly changing, and the East and West German border is not even the center of most of the European stories in the collection, much less such exotic settings as the tale set in the Cambodian jungle. London, Munich, and Hamburg, and the wild coasts of the Baltic are only the more important scenes of the stories in *The Secret Pilgrim.* After the critical debacle of *The Naive and Sentimental Lover* le Carré's fictional world stretched out until it included the whole world, and *The Secret Pilgrim* represents all of it.

For his structure le Carré borrowed the old Kipling and Conrad trick of the cigars-and-brandy-men's-club framing action. Ned, who came to grief as head of the Russia House when Barley Blair defected under his nose, has now been farmed out to run Sarratt, the Circus's training school for budding young spies. He invites the redoubtable Smiley (perhaps here in his last appearance) to address the current graduating class, and, to his surprise, Smiley accepts. After exchanging formalities, the two old colleagues sit lugubriously ruminating as the mists of their long past swirl about them. It's formed the framing action of a dozen British empire films: "I say, old boy, whatever happened to . . . ?" The stories of "what happened" fill the rest of the book and constitute a file of Circus operations as diverse and fascinating as the span of le Carré's espionage and intelligence novels of the previous three decades. These particular stories tend to be a bit more adventurous, melodramatic, and emotional than many of le Carré's novels, but perhaps this is because they are more compressed. Most of the fundamental action in le Carré's novels can be summarized in a page or so of essential incident. Each of the stories in *The Secret Pilgrim* could be the basis for a complete novel, and there is a sense of speed here as opposed to the more deliberate development, with pages of qualification, of *A Perfect Spy* or *The Honourable Schoolboy.*

The Cold War Wanes

The man who dredges these stories out of his memory is not Smiley but Ned, interrupted here and there by Smiley's prompts and interpolations. Ned is a very different breed of cat from his distinguished guest. A professional administrator in a way that Smiley never was, he is a more conventional leader figure, more a man of action, and particularly more active in love and friendship with both women and men. If not exactly more lucky in love than Smiley, he is at least less vulnerable. Smiley's prolonged dedication to the deceitful and willful Ann, after all, bordered on infatuation, and for all that it did credit to his loyalty that he was capable of such steadfast human commitment, the obsessive clinging to Ann bordered on a neurosis and finally on masochism. Ned is hardly—fortunately, for the artistic worth of these tales— a romantic swordsman of the Bondian stripe, but he has been around. He recounts one youthful passionate affair with the hot-blooded young mistress of a fishing boat captain who doubles as a Circus spy, and he seduces (or "shares") the girlfriend of another agent, ostensibly to pry information out of the girl but without giving the reader the sense that he is making a sacrifice in doing so. Stephanie, Bella, Britta, Mary: the novel is a litany of women for whom Ned has modulated the rigors of professional absolutism, with mixed results. Even the comic vignette with which the novel begins reminds the reader of what people will do for love: Ned recalls a job when he was babysitter for "the Panda," the beloved chief wife of an oil-rich sheik, whose husband paid stores to ignore her dishonesty because she loved to shoplift.

The "Panda" story serves as a prologue to the true action of *The Secret Pilgrim* and suggests that the collection has far more comic resonance than most of le Carré's fiction. Indeed, each of the tales has a quality of the humorous grotesque which highlights the absurdity of espionage in strokes reminiscent of Graham Greene's burlesques, like *Our Man in Havana* (in which "secret plans" turn out to be the schematic diagram of a vacuum cleaner). Ned's Rabelaisian account of his youthful fling with Junoesque Bella, the oversexed paramour of the Baltic captain, is a retelling of Chaucer's tale of May and January, with overtones of the "Miller's Tale." Another reminiscence concerns the clever way the Circus passes off a particularly mercenary Hungarian professor, Teodor, on the rich but gullible Cousins, the CIA. The Polish agent and torturer, who could easily become as horrible as the torturers in *The Night Manager,* is simply a bizarre local-color character in *The Secret Pilgrim.*[13] Even the tragic tale of how Ned's interrogation of a cipher clerk, Cyril Frewin, for a suspected liaison with a male Russian contact drives the poor man to suicide has comic overtones: le Carré deftly sketches the fateful interrogation as a delicate pas de deux of ritual absurdity.

Some of this comic absurdity is inherent in espionage itself, as the very oxymoron of the title suggests. A "pilgrim" on the one hand is an openly dedicated person, committed to a cause with at least quasireligious overtones. A "secret" pilgrim, however, is by very nature one who hides that commitment in veils of deceit, who pretends somehow not to be a pilgrim at all, shunning and disguising his or her cause. Such, of course, is practically the definition of a spy. *The Secret Pilgrim* joins a distinguished list of such oxymoronic le Carré titles, inherent in each of which is the ambiguous tension that characterizes espionage: *Call for the Dead; A Murder of Quality; The Looking-Glass War; Tinker, Tailor, Soldier, Spy; A Perfect Spy;* and the next novel le Carré would write, *The Night Manager.* Each posits a fundamental contradiction: the dead do not speak, murder is crude and brutal, war is not a cosmetic ritual, spying is not a children's game, a spy is by nature flawed, and the anarchy of the night defies management. Like F. Scott Fitzgerald's definition of a first-rate intelligence as one that could embrace two contradictory ideas at the same time and still retain the ability to function, the spying mind is one that subsumes two contradictory states simultaneously—and makes the combination believable.

In some way all the stories of *The Secret Pilgrim* are about passion, or at least about the effects of love in its many manifestations, as they are in much of le Carré's fiction. Of this novel LynnDianne Beene claims, "To his credit he makes love and individuality—not spy fiction's superficial patriotism or modern literature's manifested self-awareness—determine a protagonist's fate."[14] In the first story Ben remembers his first assignment as a fledgling spy, when his best friend and companion accidentally compromised a network and tried to run away from the terrible consequences of discovery to "blown" spies. Torn between loyalty and professionalism, Ned pursues his friend and ends up, also accidentally, betraying the guilty man to his doom. In this case the doom is ironically represented by gentle George Smiley, who performs a singular function for so gentle a man—as an understated executioner for the intelligence establishment; Smiley plays similar roles in *The Spy Who Came in from the Cold, The Looking-Glass War,* and *The Honourable Schoolboy.* The moral of this particular tale, and in a sense of the whole collection, is explicit in Ned's analysis of the significance of a beautiful woman he has incorrectly supposed to be Ben's mistress: "she was the first of the siren voices that sounded in my ear, warning me that my mission was an ambiguous one" (71).[15]

At the center of the stories that make up *The Secret Pilgrim* is a powerful tale of a "failed" agent who gives his life for love. This is Hansen, a "perfect" spy in Southeast Asia. Brilliant at languages, passionate in his application to any job, and possessing a capacity for losing himself in any identity that is invaluable in the simmering mixture of Asian nationalities, Hansen has the instincts of a predatory animal and strong commitment to his trade, until his Eurasian daughter, hooked on drugs, is captured by communist guerrillas. From this point the story is that of patient Griselda in reverse. Hansen pursues his daughter at great risk and finally retrieves her from the communists. But her mind and will are shot, and she settles finally in a Bangkok brothel. Instead of deserting her, Hansen abandons the spy game and lives with her in the whorehouse, staring into her vacant and uncaring eyes and doing petty services for her between her tricks. If this seems insane, Ned makes it clear that it is done out of love, and his telling of the pathetic story invests Hansen's dedication with a humane dignity. Like Smiley's love for Ann. Each of the stories in this collection is a story of espionage and the Circus, but each is also a story of individuals who have managed to act as *more* than simply spies but as human beings too.

It is Ned's voice that makes the collection work and which binds it together with a tenuous integrity. There is considerable character development between the young Ned of the opening stories and the cynical but kindly Ned who sits in the smoking room talking with Smiley. The young Ned was all flash and fire, and the old Ned gives a wonderful picture of his youthful callow but emotional self: "The mythic island—it should have been Ossian's—the swirling clouds and tossing sea, the priestess in her solitary castle—I could not get enough of it" (59). The blatant romanticism of this eager young player in "the great game" is neatly contrasted to the old Ned of the last story, in which he appeals unsuccessfully to the decency and patriotism of a rich aristocrat who has neither and is threatening both innocent human lives and indirectly England herself by illicit arms trade (a premonition of the plot of *The Night Manager,* le Carré's next book). This older Ned is jaded and bruised after a lifetime in the Circus, but his idealism is not so sublimated that he is not shocked by the mendacity of the man, who simply refuses to see that what he is doing is wrong.

This story of the arms dealer Bradshaw in particular looks forward to le Carré's new world of fiction beyond the institutional struggles of the Cold War. Ned's closing meditation on the West winning points the way.

> All my life I had battled against an institutionalized evil. It had a name, and most often a country as well. It had a corporate purpose, and had met a corporate end. But the evil that stood before me now was a wrecking infant in our midst. . . . For a moment, it was as if my whole life had been fought against the wrong enemy. . . . I remembered Smiley's aphorism about the right people losing the Cold War and the wrong people winning it. I thought of telling him that now we had defeated Communism, we were going to have to set about defeating capitalism, but that wasn't really my point: the evil was not in the system, but in the man. (374)

Bradshaw is ghastly fulfillment of Smiley's earlier observation that "the privately educated Englishman—and Englishwoman, if you will allow me—is the greatest dissembler on earth" (30). This one is more than a dissembler; he's a monster without shame and the hypocrisy to try to justify his evil.

The application of this judgment to Bradshaw demonstrates the purpose of Smiley in *The Secret Pilgrim,* which is to remind the reader that the most important struggle in the postwar world was the Cold War and that how it turned out mattered deeply. Smiley opens *The Secret Pilgrim* by stressing this, saying: "The purpose of *my* life was to end the time I lived in. So if my past were still around today, you could say I'd failed. But it's not around. We won. . . . What matters is that a long war is over. What matters is the hope" (11). Yet step by step, through the often charming tales of this collection, there are also echoes of Smiley's cynicism sounding more like Stendhal than George Orwell, reminding all the young spies manqué that the Cold War was a true and deadly moral struggle in which lives were lost and genuine issues of morality embraced; it was also in many ways a burlesque battle created to satisfy the inflated egos of the nations and people who waged it:[16] "Spying is eternal. . . . If governments *could* do without it, they never would. They adore it. If the day ever comes when there are no enemies left in the world, governments will invent them for us, so don't worry. Besides—who says we only spy on enemies? All history teaches us that today's allies are tomorrow's rivals. . . . For as long as there are bullies and liars and madmen in the world, we shall spy" (193).

In a sense Smiley is framing here the conundrum of the serious spy novelist as well as the serious spy. On the one hand, for reasonable critics as well as for reasonable writers, espionage fiction *is* "entertainment"—smoke and mirrors produced to titillate readers searching for casual stimulation rather than real arousal of thought and feeling. On the other hand, serious spy fiction, like serious spying, takes for its metier matters of life and death and embraces issues of psychology, ideology, and morality which have cost lives and determined—to use a phrase John le Carré might find both melodramatic and appropriate—the history of the world. As le Carré himself said of *The Secret Pilgrim,* "I use the secret world [of the book] really as a theatre for describing the big world, the overt world."[17]

CHAPTER THIRTEEN

Better than Bond

The Night Manager

Perhaps discriminating readers should not enjoy *The Night Manager* (1993) as much as they have.[1] With the exception of *The Secret Pilgrim*—really a collection of well-turned short stories— no le Carré novel since *The Honourable Schoolboy,* written nearly a generation earlier, had combined such craftsmanship in writing with weaknesses of characterization and plotting. But le Carré seems to lead a charmed life among popular reviewers, as opposed to academic reviewers, who for the most part simply ignore him. The worst judgments of the novel in the popular media called it highly entertaining—worthy fluff reading for intellectuals. *Newsweek* labeled *The Night Manager,* "The best James Bond novel in thirty years,"[2] a gross simplification that still cut disturbingly close to the bone. Most other commentary dripped encomium, invariably noting le Carré's dexterous ability to adjust to the loss of the Cold War as a subject. Of course, the "real" Cold War had effectively been over for a decade, and le Carré had adjusted to that with little difficulty. First, in *The Little Drummer Girl* (1983) he had dealt with a conflict that was only tangentially linked to the East-West standoff of Central Europe, then in *The Russia House* (1989) he returned to that standoff but only in terms of its ending. Finally, *The Secret Pilgrim* (1990) provided an elegiac retrospective of the circus's role in the Cold War. Of le Carré's fiction in the fifteen years following the conclusion of the "Karla trilogy" (*Smiley's People* [1980]), only

A Perfect Spy (1986) dealt primarily with the meat of the East-West conflict, but the focus of that novel turned entirely inward on the psychology of an individual spy rather than his actual spying. In short, Karla's defection at the end of *Smiley's People* closed the door not only on le Carré's two classic combatants but on the undeclared war in which they met as well. Le Carré himself was quite explicit about staking out new subjects: "I was heartily sick of the cold war and seriously concerned about how I'd get more juice out of it," he said. Still, he was confident of his ability to find new material: "To say the spy writer has had his toys taken away from him is ridiculous. . . . Anybody writing now will have to work a little harder and think a little harder, but the world's his oyster."[3]

Most of the oysters in *The Night Manager* are served at the high table of the novel's villain, Dickey Roper, who is almost an Antichrist set against the ascetic villainy of ideological dinosaurs like Karla. For *The Night Manager* the "us-them" is no longer "British spies–communist spies" but, rather, a few decent British intelligence personnel versus international arms dealers. Reading more deeply into the novel, even that dichotomy is not exact. The enemy this time is a loose consortium of shadowy manipulators involved in an intricate complex of arms trades and drug deals. Corrupt intelligence officers, stupid intelligence officers, Machiavellian politicians, and venal businessmen all have a vested interest in promoting and maintaining the international flow of illegal arms and drugs which fuels wars and lines their pockets. Put together, they are the underside of that military/industrial complex that President Eisenhower warned the United States about in his last major address to the nation.

Understanding John le Carré

In a sense the whole subject of *The Night Manager* is the business of defining this amorphous enemy. To be sure, the "Karla/Smiley" novels and the stories of the Circus's forty-year struggle with the communists was also about "knowing" the antagonist. Mainly, however, that knowing consisted of finding out what the enemy was doing and how. Often implicit in the process of detection was the discovery that in a symbolic, psychological, and often literal sense the enemy *was* yourself: Karla turns out to be an alter ego of Smiley; Leamas finds that his service's rules for playing the espionage game are as unprincipled as the enemy's; the presumably treasonous fugitive in *A Small Town in Germany* is actually a revealer of truth just as is his pursuer, Turner. Still, at the heart of these novels is a fundamental distinction between "us" and "them." "We" believed certain things about the way life should be lived, and "they" believed something different. If cowardice, venality, greed, and hypocrisy muddied the waters—as they always did—obscuring the possibility of a "clean hunt" and a "clean kill," it was not because such a resolution was not conceivable.

There is a fundamental polarity in *The Night Manager,* too, but the focus of the novel's development has shifted. In this book there is never any question about "right" and "wrong." High roller Roper, robber baron Anthony Bradshaw, and éminence grise political schemer Geoffrey Darker are only the most visible demons in a world full of evil men and women, and there is never the slightest question that Jonathan Pine and the brave little band of brothers in British intelligence who back him *should* destroy all three, if possible. What, then, are the issues of the novel? What sort of a novel is it, beyond a classily handled cat-and-mouse adventure?

Better than Bond

The single major focus of *The Night Manager* is style. Not the style of the prose—although le Carré's skirting the trap of self-indulgence in that area is indicative of the overall theme of the book. The "issue," as in Tom Wolfe's *Bonfire of the Vanities,* is lifestyle—the *way* people live—and much of the novel is an account of one man's exhaustive delineation of what it means to live, as Dickey Rope does, with much style and no morals. All three of the villains in *The Night Manager,* but Roper in particular, are successful men in a sense that no characters in the author's earlier fiction are. They live *well* by doing evil, and in this way they are distinct from earlier le Carré villains like Karla, Mundt, and even Haydon, whose lives are not notably more attractive than those of their enemies and are often less appealing. Roper, however, represents two concepts that are new for the le Carré canon: evil that is purely individual and evil that prospers mightily. The prospering is particularly significant, because it is of a particular kind: establishment prospering. Le Carré might have chosen for the epigraph of this novel, as Mario Puzo did for *The Godfather,* Balzac's aphorism "Behind every great fortune there is a crime."[4] Dickey Roper is not just evil; he is evil trying rather successfully to pass himself off—not as good, for that would be preposterous, but as simply another method of dealing with life on life's terms. And, except for the fact that his "trade" produces massive death and suffering, there is little about him to let the world know that he is a greedy thug and a world-class criminal.

Well, there is something that hints at his sinister trade. That "something" is the sick, almost psychotic nature of his life, but that sickness is well hidden. Beneath the nouvelle cuisine, the tailored white dinner jackets, the elegant mistress, and the richly and tastefully appointed yacht lurks a perverted world of slavery, sadism, and most of all inordinate pride on a truly sinful scale. Roper's mistress, Jed, is virtually chattel, his "friends" are degenerates or psychopaths, and his social Darwinism is hand-book pap. It is the study of this lifestyle which is at the heart of *The Night Manager,* for the novel is essentially a bildungsroman with a very adult hero being built. Jonathan Pine is, of course, the hero, and he is on an odyssey of discovery, examining and then imitating step by step how the rich, powerful, and evil people of the world live—so that he may bring at least one of them down.

One serious problem with using the international trade in illegal arms as a villain is that it is without redeeming virtue, unlike Karla and the communists, whose brutality was at least theoretically practiced in the service of idealism. For all his ruthlessness Karla had honesty and conviction. He believed in something, as did Axel of *A Perfect Spy* and the Arab (and Israeli) terrorists of *The Little Drummer Girl.* Dickey Roper, the antagonist of *The Night Manager,* mouths parodies of social Darwinism, claiming that if he doesn't supply arms someone else will and that guns keep the peace. "Armed power's what keeps the peace, while unarmed power doesn't last five minutes," Roper rationalizes in defense of his filthy trade. "Who are the killers? . . . not the chaps that make the guns. It's the chaps who don't open the granary doors" (371). But the "bottom line," a term he often uses in his slick version of Orwellian "newspeak," is that his only motivation is an inordinate greed, and he has no compunction about the human cost of satisfying it.

Dropped into the middle of this intricate tangle of bureaucracy and malevolence is Jonathan Pine, "the night manager." Le

Better than Bond

Carré has always had a gift for titles, and *The Night Manager* is one of his best, rich with implication and innuendo. Pine is a second-level administrator of first-rate European hotels, English by birth but multinational by inclination. It is his job to "manage" the monied clients who parade before him, cleaning up their messes and covering up their scandals. An orphan from the working class, Pine is acutely aware not only of his own place in the social pecking order but also of how to manipulate that order to his own, or anyone else's, advantage. Further, as night manager, he is an observer of the dark and tawdry underside of the glittering upper class. Knowing what trash the rich can be, he is both a servant and a silent judge, but basic to his job is lack of involvement, and much of *The Night Manager* is about his accepting commitment. Involvement with the high-class Egyptian whore Sophie leads him to abandon servility, for she is gruesomely slaughtered by her arms dealer boyfriend, indirectly because of Pine's intelligence connections. Having given, through love, this hostage to fortune, Pine determines to take control not only of his own life but of the slimy power brokers who murdered her, the most sinister of whom is "Dickey" Roper, "the worst man in the world." With the help of a small and decent branch of British intelligence (significantly not the one that got Sophie killed), Pine orchestrates an elaborate deception, creating a false identity for himself. Rather as Leamas did in *The Spy Who Came in from the Cold,* Pine builds himself a criminal persona, stages a dramatic rescue of Roper's young son, and insinuates himself deeply into Roper's trust and organization, ultimately getting close enough to the flamboyant arms dealer to betray him, just as Roper is mounting a monumental guns-for-drugs deal in Central

America. In doing so, Pine truly becomes "the Manager of the Night"—the manipulator and director of those dark forces he wants to destroy. He also becomes something very close to the killer double agents of le Carré's traditional Cold War novels.

In the process of assimilating into Roper's world, Pine faces the dilemma of every spy. He must become the thing he loathes to fight it. Step by step Pine trains himself to fit in with the ostentatious but brutal lifestyle of the group he must penetrate. At this chameleon adaptation Pine is singularly adept, and the whole process of his infiltration is fascinating but also perilously close to being unbelievable, although it never teeters too far over the line. Were le Carré not so extraordinarily facile in spinning a web of realistic particulars in establishing Pine's authenticity, the reader might have a little trouble accepting the authenticity of this lady killer who cooks like Paul Bocuse, kills effortlessly with his bare hands, and has the sailing skills of an America's Cup yachtsman. Pine also has that instinctive appreciation of "the good" which has obsessed creators of masculine heroes ever since Jake Barnes laid down the rule of "true" bullfight appreciation for aspiring aficionados in *The Sun Also Rises*. So finely honed are Pine's powers of discrimination that he is able to sense every sleazy nuance of Dickey Roper's fantastic lifestyle.[5]

Delineating and deftly parodying that lush lifestyle, and that of several other characters less flamboyant but still loathsome, is what much of *The Night Manager* is about. Dickey Roper's imitation of Hugh Hefner programmed by Ayn Rand is only the most extensive of the biting social caricatures that brighten the novel and make it a witheringly funny picture of several demimondes thriving in the modern world despite being totally lacking in virtue. Around Roper is a wonderful crowd of the morally wretched but materially blessed of the earth: Roper's satiric business manager Lord Langbourne, who seems to be in a drugged lethargy except when copulating with every housemaid he can grab and buying and selling guns; the personal bodyguard and man Friday Major Corkoran, a velvety homosexual retired marine killer; Frisky and Tabby, two sadistic homosexual torturers, distressingly close to parodies of much less serious forms of popular spy fiction; assorted brutal South American military/politico drug dealers and facilitators, both silky and crude but all exuding a faint odor of brimstone.[6]

Above and beyond all the jet set scum of the novel, even Roper, is Sir Anthony Joyston Bradshaw, left over from the last chapter of *The Secret Pilgrim,* in which the narrator of that book, Ned, revealed that Bradshaw's monumental power and wealth made him an ultimate power broker. This robber baron represents the ne plus ultra of the military/industrial complex, a man with apparently bottomless ties to power, money, and social acceptability. Bradshaw gives new meaning, as does Roper, to the term *friends in high places,* although he apparently gets hoisted to some degree on Dickey Roper's petard at the end of *The Night Manager,* when the guns-for-drugs deal goes awry due to Pine's information implicating many of the influential people involved. Were le Carré a true naturalist as an artist, rather than an occasional writer of naturalism, he would have cut one of *The Night Manager*'s weakest scene: Bradshaw's comeuppance, humiliated by Leonard Burr, the "good" intelligence officer of the novel and loyal recruiter and friend to Pine. But le Carré indulges himself and the virtue-hungry reader by allowing Burr to tell Bradshaw off. "You see, I really hate you. There's lots of people I want to put behind bars and never shall, it's true. But you're in a category of your own, you are; always have been" (399). Bradshaw cringes, capitulates, puts the heat on his dependent Roper, and Pine is saved—to the artistic detriment of the novel, for in the real world courageous policemen seldom get the last laugh on the robber barons.

Roper's "crowd" includes one character who not only is the weakest in the novel but who represents all *The Night Manager*'s weaknesses—Roper's mistress Jed, a predictably gorgeous courtesan of the very highest caliber. She is, by count, the fourth stunning beauty in *The Night Manager* who finds herself irresistibly drawn to Jonathan Pine, and she is nicely done but totally unconvincing, at least by the high standards of "convincing" in most of le Carré's fiction. What is most unbelievable of all is that Pine, the consummate professional, is so taken with this woman that he unnecessarily confesses to her out of the blue who he is and that his mission is to destroy Roper. Wild with passion and the chance of release from Dickey Roper's sinful gilded cage, Jed not only doesn't betray Pine but persists in throwing herself at him in ways that accidentally accomplish the same end. Roper, presumably recognizing in the new glow in Jed's cheeks a deflection of passion, tracks her change in behavior to Pine and uncovers the agent's true identity.

Were *The Night Manager* to close with the very believable natural consequences of Roper's discovery, it would be a better book and not "Goldfinger for grown-ups," as David Remnick called it in a perceptive and objective review in the *New York Review of Books*.[7] The novel would also be closer to the kind of depressing verisimilitude which *The Spy Who Came in from the*

Better than Bond

Cold was. Had le Carré left Roper tied to his chair being tortured to death by Tabby and Frisky, the novel would have presented the unpleasant but logical conclusion of a world populated by people like Dickey Roper and his friends in government and industry. For whatever reasons le Carré decided on a deus ex machina salvation, with Pine's friends in the "good" branch of intelligence offering Roper almost *anything* to let Pine go and throw in Jed for lagniappe.

This deus ex machina rescue of Pine at the end of *The Night Manager* is surely the most unconvincing aspect of the novel, and it is representative of its overall weakness. Ironically, *The Night Manager,* which offers the most sinister presentation of evil in all of le Carré, can be accused of being more delightful than substantial. Were it not so gruesomely dark in terms of its depiction of unmitigated villainy, the novel might invite Graham Greene's label for his own tales of espionage: "entertainments." But even when Greene dealt with pure evil in thrillers (as he did in *The Third Man,* in which adulterated drugs poisoned little children) he managed to make the tone less lurid and melodramatic; Greene's real monsters were the demons of moral ambivalence haunting the psychological landscape of novels like *The Heart of the Matter,* and most critics would agree with R. H. Miller that "Greene's portrayal of the British intelligence system, which hovers on the edge of farce, provides comic relief to the high seriousness of writers like John Le [*sic*] Carré and Len Deighton."[8] On the one hand, *The Night Manager* is a pure thriller, with an energized superspy of awesome skill and attractiveness who tilts against romanticized villains. On the other hand, it is a serious study of the structure of evil in the postwar world, and the author's clear intention is to lay out the convoluted channels by which power corrupts at all the upper levels of society. Much of the novel is devoted to establishing the interlocking power structure by which private entrepreneurs and governmental bureaucracies either inflict suffering upon innocent victims or allow it to be inflicted. Le Carré is very deliberate, for example, in devoting pages to establishing the character Geoffrey Darker, the sinister director of "Pure Intelligence," by which le Carré means intelligence without a human face—abstract, institutionalized intelligence, as opposed to the kind of pragmatic, individualized information gathering that respects human beings. This "darker" agency is the English equivalent of the CIA, and it represents a concept diametrically juxtaposed to Burr's small, practical subbranch of British intelligence which launches Pine against Roper and then idealistically bails him out at considerable cost at the end of the book. Neither does le Carré leave any ambiguity about the character of Darker's American counterpart, Ed Prescott. In an inflamed little diatribe to Prescott, Joe Strelski, the field manager of the anti-Roper mission, "Operation Limpet," defines Prescott's jet set venality.

> Don't change, Ed. America needs you as you are. Don't give up any of your friends in high places or your connections with the Agency or your wife's arm's-length lucrative directorships of certain companies. Keep fixing things for us. The decent citizen knows too much already, Ed. Any more knowledge could seriously endanger his health. Think television. Five seconds of any subject is enough for anybody. People have to be normalized, Ed, not destabilized. And you're the man to do it for us. (392)[9]

Better than Bond

What Strelski is also defining here is the nature of evil in a world in which the simplistic polarities of the Cold War no longer have even a semblance of validity. Of course, they never did, as le Carré went to great lengths to explore in all his fiction through *The Secret Pilgrim*. Still, there was some accuracy before glasnost to framing major questions of social morality in terms of the struggle between East and West. Without that standoff, however, there seems to be little reduction in evil. If anything, it is more sinister without the mitigating virtue of arising, at least initially, from idealism and ideology, rather than self-interest and self-indulgence. Dieter Frey, Karla, Axel, Control, and even Bill Haydon were all men whose virtue corrupted through circumstance and who came to evil out of a misguided sense of the good. Dickey Roper, the country club politicians, the bureaucrats, the bribed officials, and all the rest of his despicable ilk are virtually without redeeming virtue, and le Carré's attempt to define that hydra-headed monster as it preys on the postwar world is a very serious attempt indeed.

And yet there is that unfortunate deus ex machina salvation, those pneumatic nymphets rolling into Pine's bed, his Bondian physical and social skills, and the whole superheated, "bluefire" melodrama that tinges the atmosphere of the book, in parts almost bordering on purple prose. In contrast to *The Spy Who Came in from the Cold* and other earlier, "leaner" novels, le Carré almost succumbs in *The Night Manager* to the lure of romantic lushness:

> Sophie too has her back to him, and it is as beautiful as he always knew it was, white against the whiteness of her evening gown. She is gazing, not at the snow, but at the

huge wet stars of the Cairene night, at the quarter-moon
that hangs from its points above the soundless city. The
doors to her roof garden are open; she grows nothing but
white flowers—oleander, bougainvillea, agapanthus. The
scene of Arabian jasmine drifts past her into the room. (26)

This is not the florid prose (and plotting) of the tabloids, but it still
compromises *The Night Manager* in a way that is unusual in le
Carré's fiction. The cartoon quality of the rescue of Pine is
particularly disturbing, and it is tempting to interpret it almost as
a cynical parody of Ian Fleming's cliffhanger salvations. Similarly, le Carré's tongue-in-cheek naming of characters in this
novel is droll but skates dangerously close to the self-conscious
rococo archness of Restoration comedy: sinister Geoffrey Darker,
stout Jonathan Pine, stuffy snob Mrs. Katharine Handyside
Dulling, aristocratic worker-for-the-right Rex Goodhew! Complex as le Carré often is, though, such subtlety of self-mocking
tone is not in his rhetorical arsenal, and, if *The Night Manager*
succumbs to the spy novel's Achilles' heels of implausibility and
dramatic hyperbole, it may be an understandable fault but unfortunate, nevertheless.

Yet, all in all, there are far worse critical epithets than
"entertaining,"[10] and boring is one; even Henry James admitted
that there was no critical criterion of a work of art more important
than that of simply liking it. *The Night Manager* may not be as
good a novel in terms of formal artistic merit as many of le Carré's
books, but, perhaps more important, it is a wonderful, readable,
ambitious, *big* book that may well be read lovingly long after
smaller formal successes—le Carré's and other writers'—are

forgotten. Dickens was self-indulgent, too, particularly when it came to providing upbeat resolutions. Considering that le Carré has often been criticized for writing highbrow and impenetrable prose, he can hardly be accused of wanton self-indulgence if he provides one spy with a happy ending. Surely the lives of *all* spies are not nasty, brutish, and short.

CHAPTER FOURTEEN

All Sorts and Conditions of Men
Our Game

When le Carré published *Our Game* in the early spring of 1995, much of the critical commentary focused on the astonishing timeliness of the novel. Here was a story of Russian brutality suppressing nationalist freedom fighters in the Caucasus which topped the best-seller lists literally as Soviet tanks swept through the streets of Grozny in newly independent Chechnya,[1] less than a hundred miles from the critical final action of *Our Game*. A few critics even speculated that it was le Carré's bad luck to have chosen Ingushetia for the setting of the novel rather than neighboring Chechnya, but most saluted his prescient realization that the Caucasus had the most potential for becoming the Balkans of the post–Cold War world. There is, indeed, a slightly eldritch quality about a major novel the violent action of which is echoed by today's headlines.

Our Game is the second, and most recent, of le Carré's purely "post–Cold War" novels, defining and examining a new international world replete with new dangers and, less obviously, new potential. Like *The Night Manager, Our Game* moves his fiction into different territory thematically and stylistically. If the evil of *The Night Manager* is vicious and greedy individualism, the evil of *Our Game* is vicious and mindless nationalism, and the intrepid English who wind up fighting it are a team of spies whose ultimate united front against totalitarian brutality suggests that *Our Game* is essentially a male bonding story. Except, in this case, one member of the central team never actually appears in the story.

The focus of the novel, if not its primary locale, is a tiny semiautonomous region of the Caucasus Mountains called Ingushetia, one of several such geographic tidbits in this ethnically scrambled area. Compared to the Caucasus, the Balkans are a monolith of ethnic integrity.[2] Le Carré has always been far more a writer of locale—almost at times a "travel writer"—than most critics have acknowledged; even his comparatively weak novels, like *The Honourable Schoolboy* and *The Secret Pilgrim,* have been distinguished by marvelously graphic tours de force of geographical description; the sketches of Hong Kong and Thailand in the former and a half-dozen scenes in the latter are superb. Similarly, the scraps of physical description of Ingushetia, mainly at the close of *Our Game,* are stirringly graphic: "The weather changed as wildly as the landscape; giant insects hummed around my face, nudged my cheeks, and danced away. One moment friendly white clouds drifted sweetly across the blue alpine sky, the next I was cringing in the lee of enormous eucalyptus trees in onslaughts of torrential rain. Then it was a sweltering June day in Somerset, with scents of cowslip and mown grass, and warm cattle from the valley" (291–92). And the landscape is only the start. There's a vivid page on the history of the Ingush (presented, of course, from the Ingush side [268]) and another on Ingush values (270–71), but the best sections are the descriptions of lifestyle of the *goretz,* or mountain people. Their code is simple: "Greed makes a man stupid . . . manhood and honour are all that count" (57).[3] As one of their leaders describes his folk, "We're a bunch of unruly mountaineers who love God, drink, fight, boast, steal, forge a little money, push a little gold, wage blood feuds, and can't be organized into groups of more than one" (282).

Caught up as it is in a desperate war for cultural and personal identity, and abandoned by the "civilized" world to the brutality of Russian imperialism, the region is no Shrangri-la. To understand Ingushetia is also to realize that such an Eden, though beautiful, may be a violent place where life is frequently cruel and ugly. As the Ingush leader Cheecheyev puts it, "We don't play cricket here" (291). This is a masterpiece of sardonic understatement, since *Our Game* is John le Carré's most violent novel, certainly since *The Little Drummer Girl,* containing as it does one of the most grisly torture murder sequences in recent thrillers and a plethora of other scenes resonant with physical violence, from slapping to maiming. Entering such a savage proving ground in hope of redemption is not to be idyllic for the English intelligence agents, Cranmer and Larry, or any outsiders who might follow them. Le Carré makes this exotic region come alive, and for the sensitive reader, in the words of another Ingush leader, Ingushetia becomes "a tragedy and not a statistic." This personalization is perhaps the real purpose of the novel, for, as the small lush pieces of physical description may indicate, Ingushetia is not a spot on the map for le Carré or even a symbolic never-never land where values lost in youth may be reclaimed. It *is* Eden—primitive, beautiful, and an arena in which people may once again make choices that are not only moral but also spiritual.

As for spirituality, John le Carré does not name his characters casually, and the protagonist and narrator of *Our Game* is not accidentally named Cranmer. He is a modern version of that complex Elizabethan bureaucrat who wrote the poetry of the

Book of Common Prayer but experienced spiritual agony because he compromised his moral instincts in the service of Henry VIII, the king who executed him for "politic reasons." That analogue Cranmer (Sir Thomas) died in the fires of Smithfield recanting his pusillanimous betrayal of his own conscience and doubtless wishing that he had a chance for the kind of spiritual redemption which le Carré's protagonist finds by trudging his own tortuous stations of the cross in his search for his missing friend Larry. That *Our Game* recounts this as a journey of the soul is clear but not obtrusive. The novel is replete with spiritual touchstones—from Cranmer's "safe house," a made-over church with a secret priesthole, to his reading of Larry's pamphlet on the agony of the Ingush titled "The People's Calvary" to his own apotheosis when he finds himself strangely party to the creation of an Ingush shrine to the memory of his atheistic friend Larry. The novel ends with the Ingush ritual of *tauba,* a ceremony of repentance which Cranmer realizes is more applicable to himself than the sinless Ingush who practice it (301). After all, it is he, rather than they, who is in need of redemption, since "Cranmer in his criminally negligent myopia had consigned the Ingush cause to the dustbin of history" (193).

Cranmer's diffidence is characteristic of the bureaucrats and administrators of the institutions and governments who have been the ultimate villains of le Carré novels since *Call for the Dead.* In the conflict between the potentially feeling individual and the soulless institution, le Carré most closely reveals his affinities with Conrad and Dostoyevsky. Cranmer and Larry's farewell to arms, and to the duplicity of covert action, marks their readiness to embark on a spiritual journey away from the callous functionalism of the bureaucrat and the civil servant. They are candidates for *feeling,* as Alec Leamas was in *The Spy Who Came in from the Cold,* written a third of a century before *Our Game.* But, whereas Leamas, too deeply enmeshed in duplicity to escape, could get no farther than the dream of the doomed children trapped in a traffic accident and forlorn hope that Liz's love could help him care about life's little moments, Cranmer *can* still be saved, if he survives the trial by fire of his pilgrimage to the perilous castle of Ingushetia's mountain fastness.

Those who didn't like *Kim,* or more likely didn't read *Kim,* as most people sadly don't these days, probably won't either like or understand much of *Our Game.* Kipling's master novel of the British Empire, published at the dawn of the twentieth century, managed somehow to summarize the greatness of imperialism, record and mock its shortcomings, and implicitly prophesy the coming age of Balkanization after the departed imperialists had left "the subject peoples" to deal with the anarchy and brutality of a world without clearly defined superpowers.[4] Readers of *Kim,* lost in an appreciation of the richness of Kipling's verbal portrait of Indian life, sometimes forget that the novel is very explicitly about the training of a spy, and the spying that he is training for is what Kipling calls "the Great Game," the gathering of intelligence for the empire in those romantic mountain fastnesses that marked the edges of the "civilized" world (meaning the boundaries of British control). The "game" of *Our Game,* like *Kim*'s, is the thwarting of the Russians in their attempt to subvert feisty, independence-minded mountain peoples, and much of the local color is similar too. Dramatic tension, exotic setting, primitive violence, and the lure of the exotic give both novels the flavor of fantasy.

All Sorts and Conditions of Men

As often with le Carré, the deceptively simple title of *Our Game* is subtly evocative of the whole, complex import of the work. Tim Cranmer, the narrator, is of course a spy—or, at least, he *was* a spy. Much of *Our Game* is about his "un-becoming" a spy, learning to live, like Ned Barley and Smiley in *The Secret Pilgrim,* in the real world. Still, the bitter irony of *Our Game* is that to escape from the "spy game" Cranmer must go through an elaborate process of detection and spying on his best friend which is more furtive than anything he actually did in the service. Further, virtually every character in the novel is some sort of spy too. Some, like Cranmer or his Russian counterpart Zorin, are card-carrying intelligence officers from England or Russia or from the obscure little postage-stamp regions of the Caucasus which pop up with perplexing regularity on the evening news: Chechnya, Ingushetia, Ossetia, Nagorno Karabakh, and many more. Other characters, like the Mutt-and-Jeff team of thuggish cops who grill Cranmer in the first chapter, are simply *acting* as spies, trying to extract information by subterfuge and intimidation.

Cranmer is a forcibly retired member of the service, gently put out to pasture by his age and the end of the Cold War. This is George Smiley on the shelf and going through a low-key withdrawal and rather unsuccessful recovery from a lifetime of spy work. One might think that Cranmer would find the pain of being cut off from espionage relatively mild, since he has inherited wealth and a gourmet vineyard to occupy him and has a ravishingly beautiful mistress whom he believes that he adores. But his life is empty, as it always has been, and for a different reason than Smiley's. Smiley, at least, could truly love, but Cranmer's love life has been "a parade of misalliances . . . the clear consequence of never allowing my heart to leave its box" (126). His alter ego, Larry, suggests that Cranmer's malaise is a result of being "square" in the old fuddy-duddy sense of the term (perhaps as *John le Carré* is French for "John the Square"). For Larry, says Cranmer, "I epitomize the shortcomings of the morally torpid West" (187). No question Cranmer is middle-class. The Ingush freedom fighter Cheecheyev is being sarcastic, but not inaccurate, when he mocks him as "Larry's middle-class destiny" (277).[5]

The comment about having kept his heart in a box may be the key to Cranmer's problem. A lifetime of spying has made him a spy psychologically, morally, and aesthetically. He himself feels acutely the corrupting effect of the trade: "What good had it ever done us, this cloak-and-dagger rigmarole." More important is the question "What harm had it done us, this endless wrapping up and hiding our identities?" (30). As le Carré has been saying for decades, even though there may be moral preferences between one side or another, the deceitful practice of espionage compromises *anybody* who does it. Like Smiley after the Quest for Karla trilogy, Charlie at the end of *The Little Drummer Girl,* and that ultimate victim of the spy mentality, Magnus Pym, whose life demonstrates that the "perfect spy" is a moral and psychological mess, Cranmer needs rehabilitation—a moral redirection beyond simple tradecraft. The cause of Ingushetia is such a redirection, and it is represented in the novel not by an Ingush but by another English spy, Cranmer's protégé and field agent, brilliant Larry Pettifer, a pyrotechnic character.

Because le Carré, through Cranmer, often portrays Larry in outrageous poster-paint colors, it is easy to believe that he is the center of the novel and that "Cranmer was the box that Pettifer came in" (299). This is to ignore the fact that Larry, whose lifelong espionage role is playing the field agent to Cranmer's controller, is, as a spy, and perhaps as a person too, the creation of Cranmer, who snatched him out of a random life as an undirected intellectual malcontent and made him a spy. Larry literally does not appear in *Our Game*. Presumably, he has been killed in the Caucasus and lives only in the memory of his friend, yet not only does Cranmer never find him, but it is not even absolutely clear that he finds proof of his death. The novel is not *about* Larry any more than *Waiting for Godot* is about Godot: it is about Vladimir and Estragon. The will-o'-the-wisp Larry is, like Harvey the ectoplasmic white rabbit, not just elusive; he may not even exist, or at least it seems that way through much of *Our Game*. He also may be dead through the entire action or insane or just off on a drunk. At no point in the novel can any of the characters, much less the reader, definitively prove *anything* about Larry. Wisely, le Carré presents him largely through the narrative psychology of his mentor, friend, rival, and ultimately disciple, Tim Cranmer. This renders the portrait of the shadowy agent not just impressionistic but often surrealistic. Because of the complexity of his sensibility, the opacity of his rhetoric, and the understandable confusion of his perilous situation, Cranmer is neither trustworthy nor sometimes even coherent when it comes to Larry. Deliberately playing games with time shift, syntax, and rhetoric, le Carré often invites speculation—particularly early in the novel—about whether scenes involving the fugitive spy are in the present, the past, or purely imagined in the mind of the narrator. Even two-thirds of the way through *Our Game,* when a section begins, "I drove, with Larry beside me in the passenger seat" (209),[6] it is completely unclear about whether

Cranmer is remembering such a moment, imagining it, describing Larry's literal presence, or speaking metaphorically. In this case it's a memory, but even the most perceptive reader will not be sure for several paragraphs.

There is another reason why the portrait of Larry as presented by Cranmer is suspect, and that is that Larry has betrayed his mentor in every possible way, particularly in stealing from him the one thing in life he truly loves, Emma. Larry has also—almost incidentally, it seems—officially betrayed his country and his profession to the KGB, as Cranmer eventually learns from his Russian counterpart, Zorin (255). It would not have been unbelievable for *Our Game* to have ended with a dramatic confrontation scene in which Cranmer finds the rogue agent and kills him out of revenge; such a volte-face might have made a stronger ending, as John Updike suggested in the *New Yorker*.[7]

Even given the unreliability of Cranmer's perception of Larry and of his presentation of that perception, the ambience of the missing spy is fairly clear. Larry is one of James M. Barrie's "Lost Boys," for whom the collapse of the Soviet Union meant discovering that Captain Hook was a painted pirate with a rubber claw. Left-leaning Larry was a longtime double agent, recruited by those vanquished Russians but still apparently loyal to his British roots and now out of work as a spy for either side. With the Cold War gone this puckish Iago has lost his profession. He is a Byronic hero, even more dangerously close than Jonathan Pine to becoming an unbelievable romantic stereotype. Still an adolescent in midlife (Larry is only three years younger than Cranmer),[8] this "love thief on a seesaw" (59) displays a scathing contempt for the British establishment, which pays his bills and for whom he demeans himself in a lifetime of spying. Larry took a first in languages at Oxford (as le Carré did) and is a recognized scholarly authority on both art and politics. Emma does not seem to be just gushing when she says that in college "on the radical stuff . . . Pettifer on practically *anything* was absolutely *mandatory* . . . metaphorically he's a *god"* (28).

The only reason that Larry, this "beautiful, lawless extrovert," works as a character is that he appears only in Cranmer's often romanticized memories, and the most brilliant thing about *Our Game* is le Carré's decision not only to keep Larry in the wings[9] but also to make sure that the reader never is really sure whether he's even *there,* alive or dead. His real importance is for Cranmer, who realizes, "He was the risk I would never take" (28), and he is also all the people Cranmer never was. Both romantic and a parody of romanticism, Larry is legion, popping in and out of the novel as Cranmer's agitated psyche dictates. One moment he is straight from Conrad and Kipling's "The Man Who Would Be King": "I dreamed of Larry as a latter-day Lord Jim, the enthroned monarch of all the Caucasus, and Emma as his somewhat startled consort" (273). And this is where Larry most truly exists—in the imagination not only of Cranmer but also of the freedom-hungry people for whom he becomes a symbol. In real life, if Larry could ever have been said to have led such a thing, he is a cartoon, but in the imagination of other people Larry can have meaning.

The key to that meaning is suggested by Cranmer's impromptu eulogy for Larry delivered on the spot where Larry may or may not have been massacred for the cause of Ingush freedom.

> I said that Larry was an Englishman who had loved freedom above everything. He had loved the courage of the

Ingush and shared their hatred of the bully. And that Larry
would live because he had cared, and that it was those who
cared too little who died the death. And that since courage
went hand in hand with honour, and both with loyalty, it
was necessary also to record that, in a world where loyalty
was increasingly difficult to define, Larry had contrived to
remain a man of honour even if the necessary consequence
of this was to go out and find his death like a warrior. . . .
For it occurred to me as I spoke—though I was careful not
to say it in so many words—that if Larry had led the wrong
life, he had at least found the right death. (297–98)

What is interesting in this apparently bombastic bit of puffery is
not only its ironic tone—for Cranmer is well aware of the stuffy
"nothing in his life became him like the leaving of it" bombast—
but also the remarkable detail that follows it. Now that Cranmer
knows he is part of a deliberate myth-making process, he picks up
a bit of straw that *may* have been part of Larry's trademark straw
boater (his "strat") and pronounces it a relic of the incipient saint,
who will be enshrined by the Ingush as a martyr to the cause of
freedom. The old, worldly wise Ingush guerrilla Cheecheyev
knows what's going on and says of Larry, "He's found his
Byronic death" (284), and Cranmer muses on the irony of the
atheistic iconoclast Larry's apotheosis: "to be named ghost in a
holy shrine" (298). Critics who feel that this is a patronizing
treatment of the superstition of primitive peoples—"Lo, the poor
Indian"—might remember, as le Carré undoubtedly does, that
Western Europe is dotted with Christian shrines housing vener-
ated reliquaries containing bits and pieces of "saints" not much

more grotesque than the wisp of straw that *may* have circled the brow of St. Lawrence Pettifer.[10]

Characters like Larry have appeared in le Carré's fiction before—the dashing, mercurial, bohemian sexual athlete Bill Haydon of *Tinker, Tailor, Soldier, Spy;* the Steppenwolf Dieter Frey in *Call for the Dead;* and most dramatically Jonathan Pine in *The Night Manager.* In a less self-assured form the Puckish but insecure Magnus Pym in *A Perfect Spy* is a version of Larry. These are le Carré's lizard people, all beautiful lively writhers who slither through the world on charm and chutzpah, glittering as they walk.[11] It is only in two late novels, *The Night Manager* and *Our Game,* that le Carré finds any possibility of redemption for such characters, for in the earlier books their social facility invariably masks a moral vacuity and corruptibility.

The character of Larry poses a fascinating puzzle for followers of the le Carré canon. One way to read *Our Game* is to see him as a mocking portrait of the British "hero" whom le Carré has most publicly rejected, and with good reason—Kim Philby. It was Philby, named self-consciously by his romantic father St. John after Kipling's spy-child, who was the model for Bill Haydon, "our latter-day Lawrence of Arabia," as Peter Guillam calls him in *Tinker, Tailor, Soldier, Spy.* But, of course, Larry is not absent, because he is consistently present throughout the novel as Cranmer's alter ego. Perhaps more thoroughly than in any other novel, le Carré presents the world of espionage as one of divided personalities, in which not only do the ally and the enemy become one, but each spy is aware of his incompleteness and the degree to which he and both his partner and his enemy may become one. Cranmer is always aware of this, for his friend and enemy Larry haunts him continually. Cranmer looks in the mirror, and "sometimes the face was Larry's and sometimes mine" (77), and he drives "with Larry beside me" (209). "That was the way with doubles the world over. If you were on the right side the wrong side looked absurd." When, at one particularly confused moment in his ambivalent love-hate relationship with Larry, he actually thinks he has killed his friend in rage, he screams to Larry (and himself): "Die, and then they'll be only one of us to live my life. Because two of us, Larry, old boy, is actually a crowd" (87). Even so early in the novel Cranmer has realized that, in searching for Larry, he is searching for himself, and he is hardly surprised near the end when Emma's guardian, Dee, tells him, "Maybe you don't want to find your friend but become him" (299).

As in all le Carré novels, there is more than one case of doubling. Like Larry, who has literally extended into adulthood the cute college trick of snatching hats off other people's heads and wearing them, virtually everyone in the novel seems to be wearing more than one hat. The Ingush leader Cheecheyev is "a Caucasian werewolf. . . . Rational spy by day, *gorets* by night. By six in the evening you can see his fangs appear" (95). This is the same man whom Larry describes as "half noble, half savage, all Mensch, and bloody funny" (92). Then there's Sally, the mysterious beauty with the raven hair who helps Larry steal Russian money and who turns out to be Emma, Cranmer's mistress, who turns out to be Larry's lover—a psychotically damaged ex–flower child who turns out to be an elaborate honey trap for Cranmer but who is really a dedicated political activist who. . . . But, as Cranmer ruefully observes after he realizes the depth of disguises and personae that surround him: "That was the way with doubles the world over. If you were on the right side the wrong side looked absurd" (95).

Part of the effect of the emphasis on doubling in *Our Game* is to make it the most personal and psychological of le Carré's novels since *A Perfect Spy,* a story that is a true companion piece to *Our Game* and anticipates it in many ways. That was the novel in which le Carré turned inward with a vengeance, virtually negating the importance of the actual *world* of spying in deference to focusing upon the psychology of the spy. In *Our Game* the external world is very much there, but it is almost exclusively filtered through a psychology so subjective as to suggest in almost Wittgensteinian terms that all knowledge is subject to the perception and interpretation of the human mind. One indication of the narrowed focus of the novel—particularly since it is a novel of doubling—is le Carré's willingness to abandon almost completely his career-long effort to give the Russians their due. He has occasionally been accused, particularly by conservative commentators such as William F. Buckley,[12] of treating the evil of communism unduly gently, if not romanticizing the Russians or even presenting them as morally equivalent to the forces of democracy. In *Our Game* the Russians are unequivocally the villains. Even the Russian KGB agent Zorin, in a blatantly sympathetic moment, when he cradles his dying mistress in his arms "with pain and adoration," is manifestly a racist bully as he tries to justify Russian atrocities to Cranmer by dismissing the Ingush yearning for freedom as "the national aspirations of a tribe of savages" (254). Le Carré finally seems to have discovered, after years of indicating that the Russians are not as bad as we

think they are—or, at least, we're almost as bad as they are—that
they really are a despicable lot, a bit more civilized than the Huns
but not much. Cranmer, at least, seems to speak for the author at
the end of the novel, when he admits that the Russian treatment
of the Ingush has made him feel that "they were enemy to me in
a way they'd never been before" (285).

Nit-picking formalists may find much to criticize in *Our
Game,* and some already have. Le Carré can be accused, as he has
been, of mocking gays, such as the swishy bureaucrats in the new
intelligence establishment who bedevil Cranmer and delay his
quest for Larry; le Carré's novels often suggest that open homosexuality such as Roddy Martindale's and covert tendencies such
as Bill Haydon's mark a susceptibility to evil.[13] The United
States, at least with regard to its politics and foreign policy,
remains in le Carré's fiction a land of cartoon belligerence intent
upon *la cocacolazation du monde* and obtuse even beyond the
stupidity of the British Foreign Office; one of le Carré's wry shots
at the Americans is to have Larry, imprisoned in a Cuban jail,
feign outrage at the suggestion that he is the scummiest creature
imaginable, "a Yanqui spy" (265). As always, some of le Carré's
sketches of characters are acidly etched with an ear for class
distinctions which shows superb characterization but is hardly
politically correct, as when a Cockney police sergeant pronounces *intaglio* as "entirely-o" (144).

These, however, are petty complaints. Le Carré has taken
risks in this novel, as he did in *The Night Manager.* In both he has
moved far closer to the traditional "thriller" genre, with its tales
of derring-do, superheroes, violent action, shocking stimulation,
and the unfashionable Victorian suggestion that "life is real, life

is earnest, and the grave is not the goal." The melodramatic Bondian flame that lit the more sensational parts of *The Night Manager* is still ablaze in *Our Game,* although a bit less luridly. Still, connoisseurs of the frumpy low-key school of espionage writing represented by Smiley will wince at even Cranmer's character, much less Larry's. Unlike Smiley, who fades into several retirements by disappearing into musty tomes of linguistic scholarship, cuckolded, befuddled, and alone, Cranmer "retires" to an inherited vineyard of gourmet grapes and a gamin raven-haired mistress half his age with concert-level skills as a classical pianist. Then he launches himself on a brilliant trail of detective work, bamboozles the entire British intelligence service and the police, and successfully completes a perilous odyssey that would have destroyed most men half his age. And Cranmer is the codger of the *two;* the sex appeal is supplied by, Larry, who is Jonathan Pine of *The Night Manager,* with a dollop of "Peck's Bad Boy" thrown in for spice.

One of le Carré's largest risks is portraying a moral conflict in which the heroes and the villains are clearly polarized. Despite an occasional softening touch such as the Russian Zorin's love for his dying mistress and an infrequent acknowledgment that the dissolution of the Soviet empire has been a bitter pill for Russia to swallow, the brutality of the Russians and their allies, the Ossetians, is without mitigation. In *Our Game,* as Cheecheyev says, the only real danger to humanity is "the Soviet Empire not even dead in its grave, and the Russian Empire already climbing out" (285). On a theoretical plane political scientists may find the novel's simplistic solution to the world's problems—self-determination for all peoples, no matter how insignificant—as naive as the suggestion that the Cold War was simply a half-century of saber rattling by two equally morally deficient bullying superpowers.

Fortunately, *Our Game* is not an important and worthy novel because of the validity of its political theory or the formal accuracy of its description of the physical and behavioral world. It is important because it creates a compelling myth of human thought and behavior. Cranmer's journey is a journey of the mind, and le Carré paints the landscape with a brush similar to that of the "magical realism" writers of South America. In doing so, he has broken new ground for the last promising phase of an already substantial career. Having defined the moral and spiritual wasteland of the Cold War in a series of distinguished novels in the first thirty years of his productive life as a writer, he has moved to exploring the possibilities of redemption, commitment, and meaningful moral action in a world in which "good" and "evil" have definite meaning, rather than the gray resemblance that they came to have in the sad world of George Smiley.

CHAPTER FIFTEEN

The Captains
and the Kings Depant
The Tailor of Panama

Critics have been writing "after the Cold War" reviews of John le Carré's work since 1980. *The Tailor of Panama* (1996) is the author's seventh full-length novel focused on the winding down and aftermath of that monumental struggle, rather than just the waging of it. The East/West confrontation with its outcome in doubt has not been the main concern of le Carré's fiction since he retired George Smiley as a central character in *Smiley's People* (1980). That novel ended with Peter Guillam's judgment of his mentor's symbolic struggle with Karla: "George, you won." Disingenuously, Smiley replies, "Did I? . . . Yes. Yes, well, I suppose I did." Indeed he did, and so did the West, even if Smiley's introspective masochism makes it difficult for him to accept the victory.

After *Smiley's People* the Cold War festered for years in the wings of le Carré's fiction, as it did in reality in the world. In the headlines communist Russia sputtered and fumbled its way toward Third World chaos and abdicated its position as a major player on the international stage. In the novelist's later fiction Russia serves primarily as a backdrop for the individual psychological struggles in *The Little Drummer Girl* and *A Perfect Spy* and as a vanquished enemy recollected in tranquillity in the memory of old spies in *The Secret Pilgrim.* There might still be noble deeds left undone for would-be knights-errant such as Pine in *The Night Manager* and Cranmer in *Our Game,* but true espionage in the classic sense of "spying for one's country" was dead.

It is on the corpse of "true espionage" that the maggot characters of *The Tailor of Panama* feed. The Panamanians themselves are bad enough: a motley collection of tin-pot militarists, brutal thugs, drunken "diplomats," and on-the-take politicians. There may be one or two decent, if confused, Panamanians, like the protagonist's devoted girlfriend—mistress would be too strong a word, since they never go beyond cuddling—Marta, whose face has been smashed by the local militia, but for the most part corruption is universal. Le Carré made five extended visits to Panama researching the novel, and in a blistering article in the *New York Times Magazine* he wrote, "Everybody knows that in Panama even the best of men find it hard to get rich without a little white powder sticking to their fingers."[1]

If the Panamanians in the novel are bad, the British—and their local lackeys—are bad *and* ridiculous. The only sympathetic one of these, and by far the most important for the novel, is the tailor himself, Harry Pendel, the only begetter of the fanciful cock-and-bull stories which become the "product" of intelligence and ultimately render themselves into violent historical fact. Pendel, an expatriate "branded on the tongue" by his slum childhood, is a British "hybrid" orphan who has concocted an identity for himself out of whole cloth (and his fertile imagination) as a former Savile Row arbiter of aristocratic fashion, now catering to the Panamanian nouveau riche. Half Irish and half Jewish—le Carré's background in German literature suggests the Wandering Jew of many Germanic stories, including

The Captains and Kings Depant

Goethe's poem "The Wandering Jew"—Pendel has fled a squalid and suspect past that includes prison for arson. He has emerged phoenixlike in Panama by representing himself as the appointed heir to the property and tradition of a bespoke London tailoring establishment. Harry is a fascinating composite—a whole gallery of commonplaces drawn together from the rich history of literary characterization. In what may be le Carré's drollest and most pharisaical joke, Harry, who has visions of himself as tailor to royalty, is equipped like Willy Loman in *Death of a Salesman* with an almost mythic Uncle Ben who appears ghostlike in Harry's memory to chide him for failure: ". . . the chutzpah is yours and so is the blarney, if you could only ditch the guilt."[2] As with many picaresque protagonists there is an innocent quality to Harry. Like Candide he is a naïf among scoundrels, and like Tom Jones and Huckleberry Finn, more a mischievous storyteller than a true liar. Harry is an actor, a dreamer, an impersonator, and a fabricator who is constantly inventing himself as well as his friends, clients, and "contacts" in his own imagination. As he creates clothes for the recently gentrified scoundrels of Panama, he creates fictions for himself: "And as he went on cutting to the music his back began to arch in empathy until he became Admiral Pendel descending the great staircase of the Presidential palace for his inaugural ball. Such harmless imaginings in no way impaired his tailor's skills. Your ideal cutter, he liked to maintain . . . is your born impersonator. His job is to place himself in the clothes of whoever he is cutting for and become that person. . . ." (15). But the analogy of the good tailor as impersonator goes farther for Harry. In his romantic mind he sees himself as the creator of character, both in dressing his clients and in imagining fictional worlds for them—and for himself with them, or *as* them.

Harry even has a neologism for what he does—"fluence": "It was tailoring. . . . It was improving on people. . . . It was cutting and shaping them until they became understandable members of his internal universe. . . . It was fluence. It was running ahead of events and waiting for them to catch up. It was life as art. It was fiction. . . . It was a system of survival that Pendel had developed in prison and perfected in marriage, and its purpose was to provide a hostile world with whatever made it feel at ease with itself" (52).

This is the clothes-closet romantic and daydream deceiver that British Intelligence—through a combination of duplicity and incompetence—manages to recruit as a spy, a British "ear to the ground" of volatile Panama during the confused period when the United States is preparing for the transfer of the canal to Panamanian control. "Intelligence" at the level of Harry's control is Andrew Osnard, the totally unscrupulous young operative whose inspiration it is to transform this social-climbing tailor to banana republic martinets and politicos into a "secret agent." When opportunity presents itself for romanticizing on this grander, and more profitable, scale, Harry is primed to transfer fantasizing from his daydreams to the pages of espionage reports which he sells to British intelligence. Realizing that he has a chimera by the tail, Osnard scrambles, first to advance, then to salvage his career. In doing so Osnard becomes a malevolent coconspirator with Harry in the creation of BUCHAN, the codename for a fictitious data source touted by Osnard as the ultimate "espiocrat."

To the bamboozled British bureaucracy, BUCHAN seems not only a superspy, but the possessor of a mental key that seems to unlock the murky political and psychological psyche of Panama. As one of the few honest characters in *The Tailor of Panama* observes, "There seemed to be no one worth knowing in Panama that BUCHAN didn't know, and it was extraordinary . . . *eerie* in fact, that Andy in such a short time had succeeded in getting to the very heart of Panama" (156). It is not eerie at all, because Osnard understands what Harry instinctively (and less calculatingly) feels—that virtually everyone of "importance" in the country is a fake. Less a fraud than simply pathetic is the drunken Panamanian aristo Mickie Abraxas, whom Harry "invents"—without the poor sot's knowledge—as the leader of a fictitious guerrilla underground about to revolt. Some characters may have substance in themselves but become fantasies in Harry's creative interpretation of them. The inscrutable Japanese multibillionaires who really wheel and deal in the bizarre Panamanian economy figure in Harry's lurid nightmares as bogeymen somewhere between the Grand Poohbah and Ming the Merciless, and he "reports" through Osnard that they are ready to buy the country so they can build an alternate canal to subvert world trade.

The parade of burlesque characters winds its way through the world of *The Tailor of Panama,* and le Carré casts a wide net of contempt for the spheres of governments and politics. There is a cynical and sarcastic Restoration-comedy quality to the novel's scorn for the shoddy incarnations of the boast of heraldry and pomp of power. American politicians, Japanese businessmen, Scottish bureaucrats, and the whole panoply of Central American military poseurs are all targets for le Carré's biting social satire, and what is common to them all is their inflated egos spewing inflated lies about themselves and their places in the world.

Deflating these egos is the thematic and stylistic tone of *The Tailor of Panama,* and if there is a comic image that eponymously represents all the deflations of the novel, it is that of the "stately hide mounting horse" that Harry keeps in his shop, so that "A sporting gentleman could test the comfort of his breeches, confident that his mount would not disgrace him" (37).

The concept of fabrication is central to *The Tailor of Panama.* Every character, every subplot, every aspect of the Panamanian world, is deliberately created, as the country of Panama was itself deliberately created by imperialist America's need for a nation to wrap around the strategic canal. Everyone in the novel makes up stories: stories about themselves and who and how important they are; stories about other people, which are either malicious lies or self-seeking schemes; stories that are lies designed to cover up other lies. In one of le Carré's cleverest and most complex puns, he has British intelligence, which is listening to fairy tales about nonexistent Panamanian subversion, name the "intelligence gathering" operation after British spy novelist John Buchan, who wrote thrillers such as *The Thirty-Nine Steps* about ordinary people caught in the tangled webs of intelligence deception. This "clever" labeling gives British Intelligence "wits" the opportunity—ironically, as it turns out—to call those who create this hyped-up junk "Buccaneers," an appropriate term for just the sort of melodramatic pirates they are. Le Carré's clever use of John Buchan's name here seems to involve some subtle dissembling on the part of the author as well as his characters. Le Carré has always been reticent about attributing influences and sources for his work and his inspiration, even in the case of obvious influences such as Joseph Conrad and Graham Greene. However, in a fascinating and out-of-character recent foray on the Internet, he responded to a series of questions by readers through E-mail, and one of his responses was particularly relevant to *The Tailor of Panama.* "I don't really know much about the tradition of spy-writing. Kipling, Conrad, Buchan and Greene are probably the main players. Then there are awful, mercifully-forgotten chauvinistic writers like Peter Cheyney and Co. And an anti-German rabble-rouser called E. Phillips Oppenheim who practically launched World War One singlehanded. And of course there's the Bible, which shows how good the Israelis were even before they got the Mossad. When I was younger, I read the big adventure stories: H. Rider Haggard, Dumas, P. C. Wren, [Robert Louis] Stevenson. Then the big historians, first English, then French. My taste was always for big-soul stuff: large context, man as pawn, courage in adversity, etc. It just sort of grew out of all that. But the other tutor was experience itself."[3]

At the heart of this cutting satire is the principle that history may not be bunk, but the people who deliberately try to write it (in contrast to those who create it by their deeds) are. "Truth" is invented by spies and "diplomats," and the resulting product is manufactured by morally fallible humans rather than written in stone by God. The only tenable attitude toward "truth" in such a world is a bitter and comic cynicism. Erudite readers may remember Barth's *The Sot Weed Factor,* in which the founding of colonial America is recounted as a parody of eighteenth-century scholarship; Stendhal's debunking of European romanticism in *The Charterhouse of Parma*; or Shakespeare's Falstaff and his meditations on honor in *Henry IV.*

Casting Harry as the tailor who retailors, le Carré draws on one of the novel's most important literary models: Thomas Carlyle's *Sartor Resartus* (1836), translated in English as "The

Tailor Retailored." Not only the leitmotiv of the artist remaking himself, but also le Carré's sometimes inflated style, the creation of a world of grotesque caricatures, and the use of arcane and often extreme literary allusions and conceits are out of the Carlylean heritage. Carlyle's message to Englishmen seeking to "remake" themselves was to look to Germanic models. "Open thy Goethe!" Carlyle thundered ponderously, advising his admirers to find inspiration in German romanticism. Le Carré's thorough knowledge of German language and literature may well have inclined him toward Carlyle when he was a young scholar of German literature, just as in later life his experience of the real world and his intelligent sophistication would have produced a cynical and sarcastic rejection of the naïveté of Carlylean idealism. All too well does le Carré appreciate the perverse path followed by many Germans and Germanic followers of superheated romanticizing in a century that produced the vicious pomposities of Hitler in Germany and Noriega in Panama.

The Cuban equivalent of Noriega was Fulgencio Batista, and a novel of bizarre espionage in Batista's Cuba is another model for *The Tailor of Panama.* Harry Pendel is directly drawn on Jim Wormold, Graham Greene's comic inventor of spies and spy stories for greedy British intelligence in *Our Man in Havana* (1958). Le Carré closes *The Tailor of Panama*'s "Acknowledgements" with "And lastly, without Graham Greene this book would never have come about. After Greene's *Our Man in Havana,* the notion of an intelligencer fabricator would not leave me alone" (336). The debt to Greene is evident repeatedly within *The Tailor of Panama,* both directly and indirectly, including a particularly sly comparison of the awkward decoding device slapped on Harry's telephone to "a kind of reconstructed vacuum cleaner"—exactly the mundane appliance upon which Greene's spy bases his bogus atomic-pile drawings. Wormold is a British vacuum-cleaner salesman in Cuba who needs money and deliberately manufactures a phony spy ring with phony intelligence (conveniently generating a need for its real payroll, which he pockets). Although Wormold is amiable, his mockery of the melodramatic hocus-pocus of espionage is also mendacious. Greene classified *Our Man in Havana* as one of his "entertainments," but in addition to satirizing the frivolous rituals of intelligence, Greene makes it quite clear that Wormold's "entertainment" costs several lives and is indulged against a backdrop of violence, torture, and suffering.

Violence, torturing, and suffering are business-as-usual in Panama, although le Carré's portrait of this "non-nation nation" is usually more comic than savagely caustic. Certainly the picture is almost unequivocally damning. Superficially there is an eclectic, almost democratic quality to le Carré's Panama: "The faces on the pavement are African, Indian, Chinese and every mixture in between. Panama boasts as many varieties of human being as birds, a thing that daily gladdens the hybrid Pendel's heart." (8) Although the parade of human diversity may gladden Harry's social-climbing heart, the human parade in *The Tailor of Panama* is hardly either democratic or culturally inspirational. Behind the ephemeral facade of cocktails on the veranda and the whiff of frangipani lurks an ugly societal picture. "Gossip is what Panama has instead of culture" (49) is the kindest judgment le Carré has for this rotten, artificial mishmash of opportunism, oppression, and corruption, which he sees as a condemnation of the worst evils of capitalism and materialism. Le Carré's traditional bête noire, communism, is actually about the only social and political evil not prevalent in this phony nation where "freedom" only means the right of the strong and vicious to loot and despoil and where every aspect of society shows the worst face of capitalistic excess. Describing the world of the novel, le Carré says, "The mere fact that communism doesn't work doesn't mean that capitalism does. In many parts of the globe it's a wrecking, terrible force, displacing people, ruining lifestyles, traditions, ecologies and stable systems with the same ruthlessness as communism."

Le Carré's "fin-de-twentieth-siècle" Panama has little to be said for it, but what can decidedly not be said against it is that it is a hotbed of conspiracy or a threat to the "Free World," a term that le Carré makes clear has far less meaning than it used to in the wake of the Cold War's demise. Central to the zeitgeist of *The Tailor of Panama* is the lack of war, in fact the lack of any true international confrontation at all. The "spies" of the novel invent nonexistent conflicts and threats, alarms, and excursions to enhance their egos, mask their insecurities, or advance their careers in a torpid world that encourages them to be spies because spies are more dramatically satisfying than the banality of reality.

Without the Cold War the "art" of intelligence becomes a silly rather than sullen craft, and the appropriate literary expression of it no longer the bitter Hobbesian naturalism or fatalistic existentialism that set the tone of le Carré's early fiction. The "appropriate" form for the restless international peace of the new fin de siècle is sarcastic parody—and less the sarcasm of Swift than that of Gilbert and Sullivan. War in this murky New Age is not Hell: it is a chimerical charade. Also appropriately, the stage is no longer the Old World with its old codes, but the New World, which may have borrowed the traditions of the Old but has rewritten them in serio-comic style to fit the hemisphere of Disneyland and Evita Perón.

It is the matter of tone and style that separates *The Tailor of Panama* from le Carré's two previous "international novels," *The Night Manager* and *Our Game*. It is tempting critically to consider the three together as representing a geographic expansion of the author's horizons late in his career, a shift in viewpoint to regard a post–Cold War world no longer Eurocentric. But whereas the psychologies of Pine and Cranmer are critical to the two earlier novels, still in both cases the essential focus is on the *action*—the battle to defeat arms trader Dicky Roper in *The Night Manager* and the struggle for a people's freedom in *Our Game*. But the heart of *The Tailor of Panama* is the character of Harry Pendel, and the novel is his just as a good nightclub monologue belongs to the comic who speaks it. The novel is *about* Harry.

Emphasis on character rather than—or, more exactly, in addition to plot development—is nothing new for John le Carré. At the center of all his fiction lurks the psychology of the individual spy juxtaposed to unfeeling political and social systems. Often these spies are psychologically damaged and morally compromised. but even if they struggle futilely and absurdly, their pain is real and not without meaning; they have dignity, even if they do not respect themselves. Similarly the systems within which or against which they work—communist or democratic, nationalist or ideological—have substance even if it is often an evil substance.

In *The Tailor of Panama* neither characters nor countries, beliefs nor appearances, have any such firm substance. All is smoke and mirrors. It is all a joke; the people, the plot and the absurdities of modern geopolitics upon which that plot is built, the novel itself, all constitute a shaggy dog story, alternately droll and burlesque, told tongue-in-cheek by the form's consummate master, John le Carré, now become its parodist.

And as to the author himself, ultimately the novel is a sardonic comment on spy fiction, the "artists" who create it, and perhaps on readers who believe that in the "toughness" and excitement of the spy novel they are apprehending the real world as opposed to the world of "virtual reality." There may be a message here, too, for critics, book reviewers, academics, and the pedants who study spy fiction and couch their analyses in esoteric language appropriate to study of the form as High Art rather vulgar Popular Culture. Charmingly this least serious of le Carré's novels is also the most forcedly, if playfully, literary. From the book's deliberate model—Greene's *Our Man in Havana*—to its incessant flow of subtle literary puns, le Carré walks a delicate stylistic tightrope like a vaudeville acrobat, weaving a compelling tale of skulduggery and derring-do while mocking the genre with arch stylistics and subtle intellectual witticisms.

The dominant motif of *The Tailor of Panama* is the idea of the creation of fiction—the spy as a morally compromised but creatively ambiguous artist who spins an intricate web of fact, fiction, and suggestive innuendo. In doing so, the spy—and his creator, the author—creates himself as a narrative persona within the novel, whether he recounts it as a first-person narration or not. This image of the author/spy as a corrupt artist who writes a

The Captains and Kings Depant

creative lie with an artificially created self as the protagonist is hardly new to le Carré's fiction. Almost by definition a spy is an inventive teller of lies, and le Carré's spies are writers of fictions featuring themselves. From Leamas with his charade as a vulnerable turncoat to Jonathan Pine and his elaborate masquerade in *The Night Manager,* they have all been liars creating themselves as characters in the fictions which are their trade. As such, they are psychologically divided from themselves, and in novel after novel le Carré has probed the themes of "doubling," of doppelgängers, of alter egos, and of spies' searches for lost or never-found selves. The archetype of this tension is Magnus Pym of *A Perfect Spy,* who is "perfect" as a spy—and a perversely clever "artist" in creating himself—exactly because he is so *imperfect* as a moral human being.

There is a complex authorial cynicism about the concept of the artist implicit in *The Tailor of Panama.* In its simplest form, the novel seems to imply, the spy is automatically an author, and vice versa. The difference between the two, of course, is that it is the acknowledged and honest business of the author to fabricate and entertain, whereas the supposed ultimate "business" of the spy is to ferret out the truth. Le Carré is candid about his recognition of his moral ambivalence as an artist, as he confessed in interview with *Salon* in November 1996 after *The Tailor of Panama* was published: "I find a secret sharer [in Harry Pendel], a real companion who took me through the book. And I think it may have something to do with a latent guilt which is in creative people about the way they misuse the truth themselves, particularly if they're writers, fiction writers, the way they seize anything that comes to hand, adapt it and distort it and so on. Thomas

Mann was always pursued by the guilt of creativity, wrote short and long stories about it and expressed it in the form of disease in novels like *The Magic Mountain*."

The idea of le Carré seeing himself as Harry may provide the ultimate key to *The Tailor of Panama*'s unique position in his canon. Coming as it does near the end of le Carré's spectacularly successful career, the novel may stand as a kind of personal authorial commentary on his own narrative persona. Just as in *A Perfect Spy* le Carré limned in what must have been considerable exactitude of psychological detail the forces that shaped David Cornwell—and which that troubled youth resisted with great integrity—perhaps *The Tailor of Panama* presents a corresponding portrait of John le Carré the narrative persona of the author. After all, le Carré is the creation of that remarkable young man, David Cornwell, who *did not* become the traitor Magnus Pym. Instead he created an alter ego, John le Carré, out of the tenuous insecurity of living with the shams and scams of his father, Ronnie Cornwell. Similarly Harry Pendel fashions himself out of the singular formative disasters of his childhood to become a spinner of intelligence fantasies. As in Harry's psychology there is always "the part of him that played spectator to his more theatrical actions," (14) so there is the ability in le Carré to see himself as a character. Both men are somewhat bemused by their success and self-effacing—almost deferential—in embracing it. Harry is initially delighted but insecure in his prosperity and people's willingness to see him as a man of substance and significance. Le Carré, who often describes himself as "dull," finds himself in middle age a celebrated media figure (at the level of trading questions and answers with Mikail Gorbachev), and is virtually the only practicing thriller writer universally acclaimed critically as an artist.

At sixty-five John le Carré is as productive as at any period in his career, as the publication of three major novels in four years indicates. Still, even if he moves into a new phase of post–Cold War fiction with as much finesse as he has shown in adapting to the decline of communism, *The Tailor of Panama* will stand as a unique and charming testimony to the novelist's ability to create a work genuinely distinct from the mainstream of his fiction in style and focus. In *The Tailor of Panama* he has created an envoi for himself and his work, and in it Harry Pendel stands as an emblem for the role of the spy-novel author. He is a masterly creation as a character, rich and deep in his own right, but Harry is also a gentle mockery, not of David Cornwell but of John le Carré, that formidable authorial persona of a writer who can claim not only to be the greatest figure in the important and exciting genre of spy literature, but one of the major writers of modern English fiction.

NOTES

Chapter 1: Biography and Career

1. John le Carré, quoted in Joan DelFattore, "John le Carré (David John Moore Cornwell)," in *Dictionary of Literary Biography: British Mystery and Thriller Writers since 1940,* no. 87, ed. Bernard Benstock and Thomas F. Staley (Detroit: Bruccoli, Clark, Layman/Gale, 1989), 240–55, 332.

2. Ibid., 241.

3. James Cameron, "Schoolmaster Who Came in from the Cold," *Daily Telegraph Magazine,* 503, 28 June 1974, 27.

4. DelFattore, "John le Carré," 242.

5. Ibid.

6. Peter Lewis, *John le Carré* (New York: Ungar, 1985), 4.

7. John le Carré, quoted in the frontispiece to *John le Carré Sampler* (New York: Bantam, 1987). This is a small collection of exerpts from le Carré's novels, designed for promotional distribution rather than sales.

8. A quarter of a century after the sensational success of *The Spy Who Came in from the Cold,* le Carré wrote: "[It] changed my life and put me on bare-knuckle terms with my abilities. Until its publication I had written literally in secret, from inside the walls of the secret world, under another name, and free of serious critical attention. Once this book hit the stands, my time of quiet and gradual development was over for good, however much I tried to recreate it" (John le Carré, foreword to the Lamplighter Edition of *The Spy Who Came in from the Cold* [London: Hodder and Stoughton, 1989], 5).

9. Television interview with Charlie Rose on National Public Radio (NPR), 27 June 1993.

10. Introduction to *John le Carré Sampler,* frontispiece.

Chapter 2: Overview

1. Joseph Conrad, quoted by John le Carré in his introduction to *Hearts of Darkness: Photographs by Don McCullin* (New York: Alfred A. Knopf, 1981), 20.

Chapter 3: Loomings

1. John le Carré, foreword to the Lamplighter Edition of *Call for the Dead* (London: Hodder and Stoughton, 1992), 5.

2. Le Carré suggests three immediate models for his creation of Smiley: his Oxford tutor, "totally inconspicuous" Vivian Green; Sir John Bingham, a senior intelligence officer and writer whom le Carré knew as a "young spook"; and "myself" (television interview on NPR with Charlie Rose, 27 June 1993).

Chapter 4: *The Spy Who Came in from the Cold*

1. In addition to Eric Ambler and Graham Greene, the most successful espionage writer of the 1960s besides le Carré was probably Len Deighton, who published *Funeral in Berlin* in the same year as *The Spy Who Came in from the Cold.*

2. Graham Greene, quoted in the *Economist* (10 July 1993): 84. This encomium has been reprinted whenever the book is mentioned and has been widely quoted, notably on the cover of the U.S. editions of the novel.

3. All quoted from the dust jacket of John le Carré, *The Spy Who Came in from the Cold* (London: Victor Gollancz, 1963; New York: Coward-McCann, 1964). All further quotations and references are to the Coward-McCann text.

4. See John G. Cawelti, "The Complex Vision of John le Carré," *The Spy Story* (Chicago: University of Chicago Press, 1987), 156–86. "Leamas is also, as are so many of the characters of Graham Greene, a 'burnt-out case'" (162).

5. Joseph Heller, *Catch-22* (New York: Simon and Schuster, 1961), 430.

6. John le Carré, quoted by Peter Lewis, *John le Carré* (New York: Frederick Ungar, 1985), 77.

7. Miriam Gross, "The Secret World of John le Carré," *London Observer,* 3 February 1980, 33, 35.

8. Le Carré, foreword to the Lamplighter Edition of *The Spy Who Came in from the Cold,* 6.

Chapter 5: The Coldest War

1. John le Carré, foreword to the Lamplighter Edition of *The Looking-Glass War* (London: Hodder and Stoughton, 1991), vii.

2. D. B. Hughes, defending the novel against criticism that *The Looking-Glass War* did not measure up to *The Spy Who Came in from the Cold,* claimed that this second major le Carré novel was "the novel its predecessor was blown up to be" ("John le Carre's *The Looking - Glass War," Book Week* [25 July 1965]: 3).

3. Le Carré, foreword to the Lamplighter Edition of *The Looking-Glass War,* vii.

4. Significantly, le Carré wrote *The Looking-Glass War* as his own marriage was dissolving. "I wrote it on the island of Crete, whither I had fled after the clamour of *The Spy,* in the hope of repairing a marriage that had suffered too much from the blows of success. Stuck on a solitary Cretan peninsula, and feeling somewhat directionless myself, I suppose I naturally identified with the forlorn loves of my two male protagonists: Avery's, for his estranged wife, and Leiser's for a world that no longer existed" (foreword to the Lamplighter Edition of *The Looking-Glass War,* ix).

5. John le Carré, *The Looking-Glass War* (London: Heinemann, 1965; New York: Coward-McCann, 1965), 220. All quotations (and references) are from the Coward-McCann text.

6. John le Carré, foreword to the Lamplighter Edition of *A Small Town in Germany* (London: Hodder and Stoughton, 1991), 5–6. Of all the excellent forewords that le Carré wrote for the Lamplighter editions of his works, this and the one for *The Little Drummer Girl* stand out not only as perceptive literary commentary but as illuminating windows on the processes of the author's remarkable mind. His sketch of the gestalt of Bonn as well as of the psychological condition of postwar Germany is one of the finest mini-essays in le Carré's writings.

7. See Peter Lewis, *John le Carré* (New York: Frederick Ungar, 1985), 96.

8. Le Carré, who took an Oxford first specializing in German romanticism, was familiar with Coleridge's description of Cologne.

9. See LynnDiane Beene, *John le Carré* (New York: Twayne, 1992), on the image of Bonn in *A Small Town in Germany*. "These nightmarish images central to Bonn's identity signal the empty morality that Bradfield and his ilk recommend" (66).

10. John le Carré, foreword to the Lamplighter Edition of *A Small Town in Germany,* 8.

11. John le Carré, *A Small Town in Germany* (London: Heinemann, 1968; New York: Coward-McCann, 1968), 259. All quotations (and references) are from the Coward-McCann text.

12. Malcolm Muggeridge, review of *A Small Town in Germany, Book World* (20 October 1968): 3.

Chapter 6: Interlude

1. Tony Barley, *Taking Sides: The Fiction of John le Carré* (Milton Keynes: Open University Press, 1986), 3. As a political leftist, Barley's attack on the novel is predictable. Barley finds it virtually impossible to regard any novel seriously which is not focused on social or political issues.

2. One exception to the barrage of critical assault on the novel is

LynnDianne Beene (*John le Carré* [New York: Twayne, 1992]). Her chapter on *The Naive and Sentimental Lover* (71–87) is the most thorough and objective treatment of the novel.

3. The reluctance of British and American fiction to deal success-fully with business and businessmen as the focus of major literature is singular and little remarked by critics. The Continental "novel of commerce" epitomized by Thomas Mann and Balzac has no real parallel in English—certainly not in *The Naive and Sentimental Lover.*

4. Without explicitly delineating le Carré's affinities with and debt to Joyce, David Monaghan suggests it in his book-length study *The Novels of John le Carré: The Art of Survival* (New York: Basil Blackwell, 1985). In his chapter on le Carré's use of language, "A World Grown Old and Cold and Weary: Description as Metaphor," Monaghan points to Shamus's quoting of Joyce and interweaving Joycean metaphor into his own poetic speech. See Monaghan, "Description as Metaphor," in *John le Carré,* ed. Harold Bloom (New York: Chelsea House, 1987), 134.

5. Edward Dudley Owens, "The Clues of the Great Tradi-tion," in *The Quest for John le Carré,* ed. Alan Bold (London: Vision Press, 1988), 65. Owens's discussion is a witty and provoca-tive review of *The Naive and Sentimental Lover* which charmingly deals, as too few reviewers do, with the enormous importance of class in le Carré's fiction and career. "Mr. le Carré in *The Naive and Sentimental Lover* on the one hand defied the Establishment by doing the unexpected, entering the forbidden territory and finally having as a thriller writer the impudence to try his hand at an unclassifiable novel. On the other hand, he virtually laid himself before it as a candidate for acceptance by coming forward for his examination in Serious Fiction. He was sharply reminded that Trespass-ers Will Be Persecuted. He had not, after all, taken the precaution of clothing himself in something like Catholicism which would immunize him by acknowledging he could never hope to be taken absolutely seriously" (66).

Chapter 7: *Tinker, Tailor, Soldier, Spy*

1. Richard Locke, "The Spy Who Spies on Spies," *New York Times Book Review* (18 July 1974): 30.

2. Roger Sale, "Fooling Around and Serious Business," *Hudson Review* 27, no. 4 (Winter 1974–75): 626.

3. Pearl K. Bell, "Coming in from the Cold War," *New Leader* 74 (24 July 1974): 15–16.

4. John le Carré, foreword to the Lamplighter Edition of *Tinker, Tailor, Soldier, Spy* (London: Hodder and Stoughton, 1991), 7.

5. See Peter Lewis, *John le Carré,* 116, for an interview with le Carré on this point.

6. See Beene, *John le Carré.* She notes that, of all spies, "only Smiley struggles with the human consequences of the act" (97).

7. David Monaghan, *Smiley's Circus: A Guide to the Secret World of John le Carré* (New York: St. Martin's, 1986), 161.

8. Anthony Blunt, a member of the Cambridge Apostles and friend of (and likely field contact for) Kim Philby. See Barrie Penrose and Simon Freeman, *Conspiracy of Silence* (New York: Vintage, 1986). The most recent study of Philby is Anthony Cave Brown, *Treason in the Blood: H. St. John Philby, Kim Philby and the Spy Case of the Century* (New York: Macmillan, 1995), which stresses the sinister influence of St. John Philby on his son. *Treason in the Blood* also explores the friendship between Philby and the head of counterespionage at the CIA, James Angleton. This friendship survived Philby's treason, which may be relevant to le Carré's caustic portraits of senior CIA personnel in *The Russia House, The Night Manager,* and other novels.

9. Le Carré, quoted in Tom Matthews, "In from the Cold," *Newsweek* 113, 5 June 1989, 55.

10. John le Carré, "Introduction," *The Philby Conspiracy,* by Bruce Page, David Leitch, and Phillip Knightley (London: André Deutsch, 1968), 1–16. This unequivocal attack disabused Philby supporters, who felt that le Carré was sympathetic to Philby. Le Carré wrote: "Deceit was

Philby's life's work; deceit, as I understand it, his nature. 'I have come home,' he said in Moscow. Philby has no home, no woman, no faith. Behind the political label, behind the inbred upper-class arrogance, the taste for adventure, lies the self-hate of a vain misfit for whom nothing will ever be worthy of his loyalty. In the last instance, Philby is driven by the incurable drug of deceit itself" (7).

11. Information about Greene's introduction to Philby's autobiography *My Silent War* is taken from R. H. Miller, *Understanding Graham Greene* (Columbia: University of South Carolina Press, 1990). "His preface to Kim Philby's memoir, *My Silent War,* attests to that sense of personal loyalty that has always been a mark of Greene's style" (171). Some might suggest that, in this case, it is a sign of Greene's inability to recognize a traitor. Greene served under Philby in MI5 in World War II and continued to defend him until his death in Russia in 1988. See Miller, *Understanding Graham Greene,* 5.

12. *Newsweek,* 113, 5 June 1989, 54.

13. Interview with Charlie Rose on NPR, 27 June 1993.

14. John le Carré, foreword to the Lamplighter Edition of *Tinker, Tailor, Soldier, Spy,* 8–9.

15. Barley, *Taking Sides,* 88.

16. See Lewis, *John le Carré,* 119.

17. See Margaret Moan Rowe, "Women's Place in John le Carré's Man's World," in *The Quest for le Carré,* ed. Alan Bold (New York: St. Martin's Press, 1988), 69–86. "Just as the machinations of the Secret Service are an enigma to all concerned and one agent is constantly watching the other, so the running of the school is a secretive affair to the boys and it is also an institution where one watches the other" (174).

18. See discussion of the "Great Game" and Rudyard Kipling's *Kim* in the chapter on le Carré's *Our Game.*

19. See Holly Beth King, "Child's Play in John le Carré's *Tinker, Tailor, Soldier, Spy,*" in Bloom, *John le Carré,* 65–71, for a discussion of children's games in the novel and the book as a novel of manners.

20. See Lewis, *John le Carré*, 117. Lewis, of course, is considering each of le Carré's work as part of a full-length study of his canon and tends to put each novel in that context. Lewis also maintains that le Carré had not projected the trilogy as such when he began writing *Tinker, Tailor, Soldier, Spy.*

21. The Russian "Matrushka" (nesting doll), which Smiley decides is symbolic of Bill Haydon, and by extension of the whole Tinker/Tailor case, is one of le Carré's most deliberate and complex symbols. It became the graphic logo for the highly successful British Broadcasting Corporation (BBC) film treatment of *Tinker, Tailor, Soldier, Spy,* on which the author collaborated closely. "He [Smiley] settled instead for a picture of one of those wooden Russian dolls that open up, revealing one person inside the other, and another inside him. Of all men living, only Karla had seen the last little doll inside Bill Haydon" (353).

Chapter 8: Cold War in the Wings

1. Stefen Kanfer and Dean Fischer, "The Spy Who Came in for the Gold: John le Carre's Honourable Schoolboy," *Time* 105, no. 49, 3 October 1977, 56–60, 67–68, 72.

2. Anthony Burgess, "Peking Drugs, Moscow Gold." *New York Times Book Review* (25 September 1977): 9.

3. John le Carré, foreword to the Lamplighter Edition of *The Honourable Schoolboy* (London: Hodder and Stoughton, 1989), 7.

4. *The Honourable Schoolboy* (London: Hodder and Stoughton, 1977; New York: Alfred A. Knopf, 1977). All quotations (and references) are from the Knopf text.

5. Burgess, "Peking Drugs, Moscow Gold," 10.

6. John le Carré, quoted in *Time* 105, no. 49, 3 October 1977, 60. He also said in this interview, "I keep promising them a treat in the next book if they'll just keep quiet now."

7. LynnDianne Beene goes a bit farther in seeing *The Honourable Schoolboy* as a study of Smiley's moral deterioration. "Smiley becomes Westerby's executioner as he takes on the role of the uncaring bureaucrat who steals people's anima and exploits their humaneness" (*John le Carré*, 104).

Chapter 9: Last Illusions

1. For representative serious reviews of *Smiley's People* at the time of publication, see V. S. Pritchett, "A Spy Romance" *New York Review of Books* (7 February 1980): 22–24; Anatole Broyard, *New York Times*, 12 December 1979, C29; Michael Wood, "Spy Fiction, Spy Fact," *New York Times Book Review* (6 January 1980): 1, 16, 17. The decade and a half since the publication of *Smiley's People* has seen considerable growth in the reputation of the novel, and it is now recognized as one of le Carré's finest works.

2. For a discussion of the relationship of "the Circus" as an institution and questions of institutional conscience in le Carré, see S. S. Power, "The Circus and Its Conscience," *Times Literary Supplement* (8 February 1980): 131.

3. Cf. Frederic Henry's discussion of the "biological trap" of pregnancy in *A Farewell to Arms*, one of the purest statements of literary naturalism in American literature.

4. See Rowe, "Women's Place," 69–86. See also Brenda Silver, "Woman as Agent: The Case of le Carré's *Little Drummer Girl*," *Contemporary Literature* 28, no. 1 (1987): 14–40.

5. Gregory Stokes: "The Reluctant Cowboy," *Village Voice* 25, no. 2, 14 January 1980. "In le Carré's masterpiece, *Tinker, Tailor, Soldier, Spy*, Smiley is merely the protagonist; bureaucracy itself is the hero" (33).

6. Barley, *Taking Sides*, 132.

7. John le Carré, *Smiley's People* (London: Hodder and Stoughton, 1980; New York: Alfred A. Knopf, 1980), 205. All quotations are from the Knopf text.

8. Although le Carré has not, to my knowledge, commented upon the matter, one of the great ironies of the final days of the Cold War is that it was only in its dying gasps that a head of the KGB—Andropov—became head of the Soviet Union.

9. For a discussion of this point, see Lewis, *John le Carré,* 171–72.

10. LynnDianne Beene, so sensible in most of her analysis of Smiley, is off in exaggerating the diminishment of Smiley in the novel: "Smiley, the rational man, realizes that his final victory has lost him more than it won. The anticlimactic surrender places Smiley in a Sisyphean struggle with the ethical contradictions of his dubious victory" (*John le Carré,* 126). John G. Cawelti's hyperbole is worse: "In *Smiley's People,* Smiley has achieved a balance between thought and action in which his imagination and his intellect have become totally devoted to the destruction of Karla. But in the process he becomes as 'spiritually dead' as Aldo Cassidy" (*The Spy Story* [Chicago: University of Chicago Press, 1987], 185).

11. Barley (*Taking Sides,* 121) discusses le Carré's probable use of the grisly Hoffmann tale rather than the softer Grimm version.

Chapter 10: "The Theatre of the Real"

1. "I found that writing Smiley after Smiley, through Guiness, had entered the public domain was very difficult, and I was beginning in my mind to caricature myself and him," said le Carré in a television interview (qtd. in Lewis, *John le Carré,* 117).

2. Alexis Gelber and Edward Behr, "A Stellar Spymaster Returns," *Newsweek,* 7 March 1983, 44.

3. Some feminist critics might claim his *only* effectively drawn

female. See Rowe, "Women's Place," 69–86. Also see chapter 10 on the failure of female characterization in *The Russia House.*

4. John le Carré, *The Little Drummer Girl* (London: Hodder and Stoughton, 1983; New York: Alfred A. Knopf, 1983), 48. All quotations are from the Knopf text.

5. See James Walcott, "The Secret Sharers," *New York Review of Books* (14 April 1983): 19–21; Jonathan Yardley, *Washington Post,* 14 March 1983, B1, for representative reviews by respected critics. Yardley has always been partial to le Carré, but the esoteric *New York Review of Books* has occasionally looked with fashionable condescension upon popular writers, particularly of specialized genres.

6. William F. Buckley, "Terror and a Woman," *New York Times Book Review* (13 March 1983): 1, 23. This essay is reprinted in Bloom, *John le Carré.*

7. Bloom, intro., *John le Carré, 4.*

8. "But le Carré is now, like the later Greene, a bit preoccupied with profundities, so that while he is undoubtedly the best of a class group, he is not truly in the tradition [of thriller/detective fiction], content to let the tale carry its own convictions" (Robin W. Winks, *Modus Operandi: An Excursion into Detective Fiction* [Boston: David R. Godine], 63). Winks wrote this in response to the completion of the "Smiley trilogy" and just before the publication of *The Little Drummer Girl.*

9. Tony Barley, in *Taking Sides,* writes extensively of the political ambience of *The Little Drummer Girl* from a leftist perspective: "Apart from the necessity of giving the reader sufficient historical information to invite a more than stereotyped understanding of the political motivations of both sides, le Carré's main narrative difficulty is to find a way of presenting the issue through Western eyes while retaining both a sense of spectating as a foreigner and a sense of Western 'conscience,' of complicity in the problem. The character of Charlie provides the solution. As an English

actress, recruited to play a fictional part, she participates from a distance; as a confused and guilt-ridden radical-liberal, she has mixed feelings of sympathy for both sides and, whatever her former abstract romanticized loyalties, she will swing in the direction of the side that is able at any point to exert the most powerful moral pressure upon her" (148).

10. Quoted in Melvyn Bragg, "*The Little Drummer Girl:* An Interview with John le Carré," *The Southbank Show,* London Weekend Television, 27 March 1983 ; reprinted in Bold, *Quest for John le Carré,* 131.

11. David Pryce-Jones, "A Demonological Function," *New Republic,* 18 April 1983, 27–30. See also Gerald Kaufman, "John le Carré's Israeli Thriller," *Jewish Chronicle,* 1 April 1983, 17.

12. Bragg, "*The Little Drummer Girl,*" 135.

13. Ibid., 134.

14. See T. J. Binyon, "Theatre of Terror," *Times Literary Supplement,* 25 March 1983, 289.

15. Le Carré, quoted in Bragg, "*The Little Drummer Girl,*" 134.

16. Bloom, intro., *John le Carré,* 4.

17. See Auberon Waugh, "Mixed Up by a Master," *London Daily Mail,* 31 March 1983, 7.

Chapter 11: Whose Name Was Writ in Water

1. John le Carré, *A Perfect Spy* (New York: Alfred A. Knopf, 1986), 72. All quotations (and references) are from this text.

2. Beene, *John le Carré.* Beene, usually extremely perceptive on psychological issues, gives short shrift to *A Perfect Spy,* in part because she treats Ricky Pym completely as a separate character rather than as the most significant element in Magnus's composite psychology. Beene claims that, "although Magnus is the novel's title character, Rick Pym is its protagonist" (123).

3. See R. Z. Sheppard, "A Tale of the Acorn and the Tree," *Time* 114, no. 17, 28 April 1986, 71–72.

4. For a discussion of the effect of Rick on Magnus, see Frank Conroy, "Sins of the Father," *New York Times Book Review,* 13 April 1986, 1, 24.

5. See Anne Barnes, "A Perfect Mess of Spies," *London Times,* 2 May 1987, 17a.

6. DelFattore, in "John le Carré," claims that needless complexity is the besetting sin of much of le Carré's fiction. She protests that "his persistence in writing lengthy novels that include verbose and apparently pointless descriptive passages, innumerable tangents, and a plethora of poorly defined minor characters is intriguing if not perverse" (255).

7. See Vivian Green, "*A Perfect Spy:* A Personal Reminiscence," in Bold, *Quest for le Carré,* 25–40. "Are we not tempted to read too much into a novel which is above all a fine piece of entertainment . . . ?" Green asks and decides, "I doubt whether he [le Carré] may ever come as close to the bone as in *A Perfect Spy*" (39).

8. John le Carré, "Spying on My Father," *London Sunday Times,* 16 March 1986, 33–35.

9. This may not be for some time. In 1994 le Carré brought suit against a would-be biographer for defamation of character and has indicated to the author of this study that it is a policy of his not to communicate with writers before they produce critical analyses of either le Carré or his work.

Chapter 12: The Cold War Wanes

1. John le Carré, in a speech to the Boston Bar Association, May 1993; quoted by David Remnick, "Le Carré's New War," *New York Review of Books* (12 August 1993): 20.

2. John le Carré, interview with Charlie Rose on NPR, 27 June 1993.

3. See Charles Trueheart, "John le Carré: The Spy Spinner after the Thaw," *Washington Post,* 25 May 1989, D1–3; Harriet Waugh, "The Spy Who Went Out to the Warm," *Spectator,* 1 July 1989, 26–27; Craig Whitney, "Now the Other Side Warms to le Carré," *New York Times,* 22 May 1989, C13, C18.

4. Tom Matthews, "In from the Cold," *Newsweek* 113, 5 June 1989, 56. This overview of le Carré's standing vis-à-vis the Soviet bloc marked a real beginning of consideration of him as a "post–Cold War novelist." See also Waugh, "Spy Who Went Out to the Warm," 26–27; Whitney, "Now the Other Side Warms to le Carré," C13, C18; Jonathan Yardley, "From Russia, with Love," *Washington Post Book Review* (4 June 1989): 3. Whitney's article, particularly, has an account of le Carré's use of Sakharov as the inspiration for "the Bluebird" (C13).

5. Le Carré, quoted in Alvin P. Sanoff, "The Thawing of the Old Spymaster," *U.S. News and World Report* 106, no. 24, 19 June 1989, 61.

6. John le Carré, *The Russia House* (New York: Alfred A. Knopf, 1989). All quotations are from this text.

7. Ibid.

8. In terms of a feminist reading *The Russia House* represents a step backward for le Carré, negating some of the increasing complexity exhibited by characters such as Mary Pym, Connie Sachs, and Charlie of *The Little Drummer Girl*—le Carré's most complex and believable character in all his fiction. See Rowe, "Women's Place in John le Carré's Man's World," 69–86. Rowe maintains that "in the '80's John le Carré's fiction is still centered on men, but women characters grow more complex" (84). See also Waugh, "Spy Who Went Out to the Warm," 26–27.

9. Predictably, le Carré is more popular with British intelligence personnel than with the American ones, whom he has often cruelly satirized. American Miles Copeland, a former United States intelligence officer and professional writer and analyst of intelligence operations, says of the British professionals' attitude toward le Carré: "They like the way he captures the mood of their world, its internal rivalries and the

personal problems that get tangled up with their professional lives."
Copeland stresses that this is in contrast to the American attitude,
particularly of CIA director Richard Helms, who called *The Spy Who
Came in from the Cold* "a bitter and cynical story of violence, betrayal,
and spiritual exhaustion" (qtd. in Donald McCormick and Katy Fletcher,
Spy Fiction [London: Oxford University Press, 1990], 66).

10. Interestingly, there are indications that Russians tend to read le
Carré with considerably more cynicism than Westerners and that they
are correspondingly less likely to accept simplistic portrayals of the
KGB as either effective devils or benevolent converts to glasnost. See
Sergi Petrov, "The Little Drummer Boy: What John le Carré Does Not
Know about Russia," *New Republic,* 21 August 1989, 30–33.

11. Le Carré himself seems to have recognized the fragmented
quality of the "novel." He discusses some of the structural problems in
William Boyd, "Oh, What a Lovely Cold War," *New York Times Book
Review* (6 January 1991): 3. A short but revealing sidebar to this article
is an account of an interview with le Carré, "I Was Heartily Sick of It,"
by Craig R. Whitney. See also Frederic Raphael, *Sunday Times,* 13
January 1991, 1.

12. The date of the foreground action of *The Secret Pilgrim* (Smiley's
fireside talk with Ned) is vague. Presumably, they meet in the early days
of glasnost in the early 1980s. By this time Smiley is older than seventy
but probably less than eighty. David Monaghan, in *Smiley's Circus,*
dates his birth at around 1907 (161).

13. "Local Color" is not an inaccurate grouping for the tales in *The
Secret Pilgrim.* All of le Carré's fiction has strong geographic orientation, but even as eclectic a travelogue as *The Honourable Schoolboy*
tends to be focused on a single locale. *The Secret Pilgrim* is not only set
all over the globe, but it runs out a series of almost grotesque character-
izations that often border on exaggeration. For a biased discussion of the
novel in general and characterization in particular, see Ian Buruma,
"After the Fall," *New York Review of Books* (28 March 1991): 8–9.

14. Beene, *John le Carré,* 137. Beene's discussion of *The Secret Pilgrim* is cursory in comparison with the depth of her analysis of other fictional works by le Carré, since her book went to press just after the novel was published.

15. John le Carré, *The Secret Pilgrim* (New York: Alfred A. Knopf, 1991). All quotations are from this text.

16. LynnDianne Beene takes a darker view of *The Secret Pilgrim,* claiming that the informing theme of the stories is not so much that the West won the Cold War as that the *wrong* people in the West prevailed. "The Caricatures of *The Secret Pilgrim* do not exploit ambiguity as much as they lament that the wrong people—Smiley's embittered dons and, in the 1990's, England's lower-middle-class noveaux riches [*sic*]—continually set the moral standards" (*John le Carré,* 137).

17. John le Carré, interview with Charlie Rose on NPR, 27 June 1993.

Chapter 13: Better than Bond

1. By the time of the publication of *The Night Manager* in early summer of 1973, le Carré had reached a stage of highbrow lionization which apparently made him almost immune to real critical attack, except by arcane academic critics. Even an objective commentator like Julian Symons, although acknowledging the novel's weaknesses, insisted on putting at least some of it in a class with the author's masterpieces, writing: "Is *The Night Manager* up to the best of le Carré? The equivocal answer has to be yes, but only where it concerns the worlds of Roper and the London and Washington agencies" ("Our Man in Zurich," *New York Times Book Review* [27 June 1993]: 3). See also reviews by Merle Rubin, "A Master of Spy Tales Uncovers a New Plot," *Christian Science Monitor,* 14 July 1993, 14; and Sean O'Brien, "A War against Principle," *Times Literary Supplement* (July 1993): 1.

2. Malcolm Jones, "A Summer Book Bag: *The Night Manager*," *Newsweek* 122, 5 July 1993, 54.

3. John le Carré, interview with Craig R. Whitney, *New York Times Book Review* (6 January 1991): 3.

4. Honoré Balzac, quoted by Mario Puzo, *The Godfather* (New York: Putnam, 1969), 10.

5. Poor boy Pine is not only a bit too comfortable with the lifestyle of the jet set but a bit too discriminating as well. Le Carré's scathing picture of parvenu Roper is deft social satire, but Pine's appreciation of the subtleties of it is as if Huck Finn were not awed by the pretentious Grangerford house but had the aesthetic taste to mock it. Of course, unlike Huck, Pine's background as a manager of social pretention contributes to his believability as a critic of taste.

6. For a thorough discussion of the problem in *The Night Manager* of le Carré's's presenting sleaziness of lifestyle as metaphysical evil, see Paul Berman, "Puttin' on the Ritz: *The Night Manager* by John le Carré," *New Republic* 209, 9 August 1993, 35–38. Berman is also one of the few commentators on the novel to grasp the ideological connection between communism and gangsterism: "in every country where Marxist guerrillas have been defeated but where social conditions remain bad, the same circumstances that used to push young people into the guerrilla armies will now push them into gangster armies. . . . Instead of Soviet imperialism, internal rot" (37).

7. David Remnick, "Le Carré's New War," *New York Review of Books* (12 January 1993): 23. This essay presents the best balance between acknowledging le Carré's contribution to the "anti-Bond" spy novel and the problem of the "Bondian" elements in *The Night Manager.* Remnick writes, "At a time when Ian Fleming's eroto-nuclear fantasies were the favorite reading of John Kennedy, le Carré had the moral decency to deglamorize a war that pretended to glamour" (20).

8. Miller, *Understanding Graham Greene,* 114.

9. John le Carré, *The Night Manager* (New York: Alfred A. Knopf, 1993), 392. All references are to this text.

10. One of the most interesting was the charge that the book was "inaccurate," a word seldom used about le Carré except by leftist or rightist ideologues. Walter Laqueur, chairman of the Research Council of the Center for Strategic and International Studies in Washington, D.C., writing of *The Night Manager,* claimed that "the whole genre of the spy novel is in trouble, le Carré included." Laqueur maintains that le Carré has never really understood the Russians and that the Russian intelligentsia, in return, has little respect for le Carré's attempts to find a "human side" to Russian tyranny ("Le Carré in Russian Eyes," *Commentary* 95 [September 1993]: 54).

Chapter 14: All Sorts and Conditions of Men

1. Le Carré spells the country *Cechenia* throughout *Our Game,* apparently the preferred British spelling. The standard American spelling, observed here, is *Cechnya.*

2. The endpapers of *Our Game* are a map of the Caucasus showing an area of perhaps only fifty thousand square miles (*linear* miles, that is) in which some fifteen countries or potential countries jostle one another in a dizzying checkerboard of borders and holdings.

3. What is particularly interesting about this code is its aggressive contempt for materialism, which runs strongly as a theme of both *Our Game* and *The Night Manager.* With the closing of the Cold War, depriving le Carré of ideological villains, it seems that economic and spiritual—or, rather, antispiritual—ones will fill the gap. Cranmers's reaction to Moscow is significant, for he sees the city no longer as the Cold War center of alien ideology but, rather, as simply another materialist, capitalist dump (251).

4. For a good discussion—albeit a snide one—of *Our Game's* place in the tradition of the imperial British spy novel, see the review of the novel by Michael Dirda in the *Washington Post Book World* (26 February 1995): "All gone [the era of the Great Game] except in the

pages of Kipling's *Kim* and John Buchan's thrillers about Richard Hannay. Our spies, as we have learned from Graham Greene and John le Carré live drab, broken lives, their souls eaten up by despair and doubt" (1).

5. Cheecheyev's judgment may be clouded here by his prejudices about the bourgeoisie, particularly when he can identify it as such. When he first meets Cranmer in Moscow he cynically—and incorrectly—accuses him of being "here to represent market forces" (279), and, when he realizes the courage and skill of this "bourgeois" spy in tracking Larry so far, his backhanded compliment is: "Not bad for a middle-class destiny, not bad. Maybe you're more of an artist than you know" (281).

6. John le Carré, *Our Game* (New York: Alfred A. Knopf, 1995). All quotations are from this text.

7. John Updike, review of *Our Game, New Yorker* 61, 4 April 1995, 54.

8. The Book-of-the-Month Club, which selected *Our Game* for a main selection for spring 1995, describes Pettifer in relationship to Cranmer as "the younger Larry," although three years difference between two men in their fifties is usually unimportant. The impression is understandable (W. David Atwood, *BOMC News* [Spring 1995]: 2).

9. One of the most endearing things about Updike's review is his admission that he finds the character of Larry thoroughly unlikable. Larry's egotism, willfulness, and willingness to betray his friends may be excusable to Cranmer, who has, like George Smiley in his tolerance for Ann's bitchiness, a saintly and almost fatuous tolerance for Larry's objectionable showing off and capacity for ingratitude. Some critics obviously find such qualities beyond the pale and unbalanced by Larry's notorious charm.

10. Le Carré may be playing games here with the idea that one of those saints was St. Lawrence O'Toole, and Peter O'Toole played Lawrence of Arabia in David Lean's film.

11. Michael Dirda suggests that "Larry, the possible traitor, is more obviously one of le Carré's 'honourable schoolboys,' a man who amid the looking-glass universe of the clandestine actually believes in something" ("Through a Spyglass, Darkly," *Washington Post Book World* [6 February 1995]: 10). Such an interpretation of Larry suggests a shallow understanding of either *Our Game* or *The Honourable Schoolboy* or both. Jerry Westerby is a bit like Tigger in *Winnie the Pooh*—somehow bouncy and stolid at the same time and not very bright. There are several such characters in le Carré: Felix Leiser in *The Looking-Glass War,* Strelski in *The Night Manager,* and perhaps even Barley Blair in *The Russia House.* The most obvious one is Jim Prideaux in *Tinker, Tailor, Soldier, Spy,* whose plodding bourgeois "Rhino" personality could not be much farther from Larry's volatile intellectualism.

12. Buckley has long been both an admirer of le Carré's writing and a critic of his tolerance for the communists. See, particularly, Buckley, "Terror and a Woman," 1, 23.

13. On the other hand, it must be said in le Carré's defense that he cannot be accused of aggressive homophobia and associates it with tasteless, often cruel characters. In *Our Game* the prejudiced thug Okie Hedges includes homosexuals among his bête noirs: "Ockie dismissed intellectuals, Jews, blacks, the Yellow Peril, and homosexuals with a benign and universal hatred" (216).

Chapter 15: The Captains and Kings Depant

1. John le Carré, "Quel Panama!," *New York Times Magazine* (20 October 1980) 17.

2. John le Carré, *The Tailor of Panama* (New York: Alfred A. Knopf, 1996), 82. All references are to this text.

3. John le Carré, "John le Carré Answers his E-mail." *Salon* 1999.com, 22 November 1996, 10 pp. Online. Internet.

BIBLIOGRAPHY

Works by le Carré

Novels

Call for the Dead. London: Victor Gollancz, 1961; New York: Walker, 1962. Lamplighter Edition, London: Hodder and Stoughton, 1992.

A Murder of Quality. London: Victor Gollancz, 1962; New York: Walker, 1963. Lamplighter Edition, London: Hodder and Stoughton, 1990.

The Spy Who Came in from the Cold. London: Victor Gollancz, 1963; New York: Coward-McCann, 1964. Lamplighter Edition, London: Hodder and Stoughton, 1990.

The Looking-Glass War. London: Heinemann, 1965; New York: Coward-McCann, 1965. Lamplighter Edition, London: Hodder and Stoughton, 1991.

A Small Town in Germany. London: Heinemann, 1968; New York: Coward-McCann, 1968. Lamplighter Edition, London: Hodder and Stoughton, 1991.

The Naive and Sentimental Lover. London: Hodder and Stoughton, 1971; New York: Alfred A. Knopf, 1972.

Tinker, Tailor, Soldier, Spy. London: Hodder and Stoughton, 1974; New York: Alfred A. Knopf, 1974. Lamplighter Edition, London: Hodder and Stoughton, 1991.

The Honourable Schoolboy. London: Hodder and Stoughton, 1977; New York: Alfred A. Knopf, 1977. Lamplighter Edition, London: Hodder and Stoughton, 1990.

Smiley's People. London: Hodder and Stoughton, 1980; New York: Alfred A. Knopf, 1980.

Bibliography

The Quest for Karla. New York: Alfred A. Knopf, 1982. (The Smiley trilogy includes: *Tinker, Tailor, Soldier, Spy; The Honourable Schoolboy; Smiley's People.*)

The Little Drummer Girl. London: Hodder and Stoughton, 1983; New York: Alfred A. Knopf, 1983. Lamplighter Edition, London: Hodder and Stoughton, 1993.

A Perfect Spy. London: Hodder and Stoughton, 1986; New York: Alfred A. Knopf, 1986.

The Russia House. London: Hodder and Stoughton, 1989; New York: Alfred A. Knopf, 1989.

The Secret Pilgrim. London: Hodder and Stoughton, 1991; New York: Alfred A. Knopf, 1991.

The Night Manager. London: Hodder and Stoughton, 1993; New York: Alfred A. Knopf, 1993.

Our Game. London: Hodder and Stoughton, 1995; New York: Alfred A. Knopf, 1995.

The Tailor of Panama. London: Hodder and Stoughton, 1996; New York: Alfred A. Knopf, 1996.

Short Fiction

"You Can't Sack a College Boy." *Spectator* 27 (November 1964): 699–700.

"What Ritual Is Being Observed Tonight?" *Saturday Evening Post* 241, 2 November 1968, 60–62, 64–65.

Selected Nonfiction

"The Writer and the Spy." *London Daily Telegraph,* 29 March 1964, 18.

"What Every Writer Wants to Know." *Harper's* 231, November 1965, 142–45.

"Wrong Man on Crete." *Holiday* 38 (December 1965): 74–75.

"To Russia, with Greetings: An Open Letter to the Moscow *Literary Gazette.*" *Encounter* 26 (May 1966): 3–6.

Bibliography

"The Spy to End Spies: On Richard Sorge." *Encounter* 27 (November 1966): 88–89.

"A Writer and a Gentleman." *Saturday Review* 51, 30 November 1968, 4, 6.

"Vocation in a World of Pain." *London Sunday Times,* 25 October 1970, 35.

"Well Played, Wodehouse." *London Sunday Times,* 10 October 1971, 35.

"In a Small Place in Cornwall." *London Daily Telegraph Magazine* (6 September 1974): 39, 40, 45, 46.

"England Made Me." *London Observer,* 13 November 1977, 25.

"In England Now." *New York Times Magazine* (23 October 1977): 34–35, 86–87.

"An American Spy Story." Review of *The Man Who Kept the Secrets: Richard Helms and the CIA,* by Thomas Powers. *New York Times Book Review* (14 October 1979): 1, 46–48.

"At Last, It's Smiley." *London Sunday Telegraph Magazine* (21 October 1979): 105, 106, 111, 112.

"Tinker, Tailor, and the Mole That Never Was." *Manchester Guardian,* 7 November 1979, 14.

Introduction to *Hearts of Darkness,* by Don McCullin. London: Secker and Warburg, 1980; New York: Alfred A. Knopf, 1981. Social commentary accompanying a collection by one of England's best-known photographers of social realism, emphasizing the sad and degraded lives of men on relief and living in doss houses.

"Siege." *London Observer,* 1 June 1980, 25.

"Unlicensed to Quote." *London Times,* 17 March 1981, 13.

"Optical Illusion." *London Times,* 22 March 1982, 11.

"World Service." *London Times,* 1 July 1981, 15.

Introduction to *The Philby Conspiracy,* by Bruce Page, David Leitch, and Philip Knightley, 1–16. London: André Deutsch, 1968; New

Bibliography

York: Doubleday, 1968. One of le Carré's most important nonfiction writings, detailing his opinion of Kim Philby, a critical figure for the novelist's espionage fiction: "Philby is the price we pay for being moderately free."

"Memories of a Vanished Land." *London Observer,* 13 June 1982, 9–10.

"Exiles in the White House." *London Observer,* 26 June 1983, 25–26.

"Betrayal." *London Observer,* 3 July 1983, 23–24.

"Hughes of Hong Kong." *London Sunday Times,* 8 January 1984, 9a–b. A report on le Carré's research for *The Honourable Schoolboy.*

"Don't Be Beastly to Your Secret Service." *London Sunday Times,* 8 January 1984, 9a–b. A humorous "defense" of intelligence operations.

"Spying on My Father." *London Sunday Times,* 16 March 1986, 33–35. A particularly interesting article, since it confronts le Carré's father's checkered life and paves the way for the writing of *A Perfect Spy.*

"The Clandestine Muse." *Johns Hopkins Magazine* 38 (August 1986): 11–16.

"Inside Books: John le Carré on Perfect Spies and Other Characters." *Writer's Digest* 67 (February 1987): 20–21.

Works about John le Carré

Book-length Critical Studies and Collections

Barley, Tony. *Taking Sides: The Fiction of John le Carré.* Milton Keynes, Eng.: Open University Press, 1986. Le Carré from a political point of view. A provocative study compromised by the author's didactic leftist slant.

Beene, LynnDianne, *John le Carré.* New York: Twayne, 1992. Far and away the most intelligent and perceptive full-length study of le Carré. Approaches close textual reading of many novels but requires in-depth knowledge of le Carré for full understanding.

Bibliography

Bloom, Harold, ed. and intro. *John le Carré*. New York: Chelsea House, 1987. "Our Impudent Crimes," by Stefan Kanfer; "The Spy as Hero: Le Carré and the Cold War," by Andrew Rutherford; "Espionage Fiction and the Human Condition," by LeRoy L. Panek; "The Decline and Fall of George Smiley: John le Carré and English Decency," by Abraham Rothberg; "Child's Play in John le Carré's *Tinker, Tailor, Soldier, Spy,* by Holly Beth King; "Enter George Smiley: Le Carré's *Call for the Dead,* by Helen S. Garson; "The Hippocratic Smile: John le Carré and the Traditions of the Detective Novel," by Glenn W. Most; "Fear of Extremes: England's Relationship with Germany and America," by Lars Ole Sauerberg; "Terror and a Woman: *The Little Drummer Girl,"* by William F. Buckley; "'A World Grown Old and Cold and Weary': Description as Metaphor," by David Monaghan; "'The Second Burden of a Former Child': Doubling and Repetition in *A Perfect Spy,"* by Susan Laity. An idiosyncratic collection touching on some odd corners of the le Carré canon and ignoring main themes. The King and Monaghan essays are excellent and the Buckley essay highly readable. Laity's essay is useful for its discussion of the doppelgänger motif, pervasive in le Carré's fiction.

Bold, Alan, ed. *The Quest for John le Carré*. New York: St. Martin's Press, 1988. "A Perfect Spy: A Personal Reminiscence," by Vivian Green; "The Clues of the Great Tradition," by Owen Dudley Edwards; "Women's Place in John le Carré's Man's World," by Margaret Moan Rowe; "Le Carré and the Idea of Espionage," by Trevor Royle; "Information, Power and the Reader: Textual Strategies in le Carré," by Stewart Crehan; *"The Litter Drummer Girl:* An Interview with John le Carré," by Melvyn Bragg; "The Hippocratic Smile: Le Carré and Detection," by Glenn W. Most; "Le Carré: Faith and Dreams," by Philip O'Neill; "The Writing on Igloo Walls: Narrative Technique in *The Spy Who Came in from the Cold,"* by Robert Giddings. Bold's introduction is perfunctory.

Bibliography

Homberger, Eric. *John le Carré*. Contemporary Writers Series. London and New York: Methuen, 1986. A brief treatment, useful for collected comments of other critics.

Lewis, Peter. *John le Carré*. New York: Frederick Ungar, 1985. A thoroughly intelligent capsule summary of le Carré's novels, providing workmanlike commentary. The first major full-length treatment of le Carré, therefore lacking coverage of works after *The Little Drummer Girl* (1983).

Monaghan, David, *The Novels of John le Carré: The Art of Survival.* New York: Basil Blackwell, 1985. More a series of essays than a comprehensive treatment of the novelist's career or canon. Coverage only through the "Karla trilogy."

Monaghan, David, *Smiley's Circus: A Guide to the Secret World of John le Carré*. New York: St. Martin's Press, 1986. An invaluable handbook that systematically traces the operations of the "Circus" in novels concerning its activities, provides thumbnail chronologies of its activities, brief biographies of major and minor characters, and—particularly useful—definitions of jargon terms applicable to le Carré's presentation of espionage. Complete only through the "Karla trilogy."

Wolfe, Peter. *Corridors of Deceit: The World of John le Carré*. Bowling Green, Ohio: Bowling Green Popular Press, 1987. An academic treatment of political and sociological implications of the major themes and narrative technique through *The Little Drummer Girl.*

Selected Articles

(Information on articles relevant to particular parts of this book will also be found in the endnotes to each chapter.)

Ambler, Eric. "John le Carré Escapes the Follow-up Jinx." *Life* 58, no. 29, 30 July 1965, 8. A favorable review of *The Looking-Glass War* and a gracious pat on the back from a fellow spy writer.

Bibliography

Barzun, Jacques. "Spies and le Carré: A Response to Walter Laqueur." *Commentary* 76 (October 1983) 16–17. An important defense of le Carré in response to Laqueur's leftist attack on le Carré in the June 1983 *Commentary,* in which Laqueur accused le Carré of writing fascist "fantasies."

Burgess, Anthony. "Peking Drugs, Moscow Gold." *New York Times Book Review,* 25 September 1977, 9. Review of *The Honourable Schoolboy* at the time of the novel's publication.

Cameron, James. "Schoolmaster Who Came in from the Cold," *London Daily Telegraph Magazine* 503 (28 June 1974): 23–29. A readable and intelligent précis of le Carré's "revival" at the time of the publication of *Tinker, Tailor, Soldier, Spy.*

Cawelti, John G. "The Complex Vision of John le Carré," *The Spy Story,* 156–86. Chicago: University of Chicago Press, 1987. A chapter in Cawelti's study of the fiction of espionage, placing le Carré in the context of other spy fiction.

Conroy, Frank. "Sins of the Father." *New York Times Book Review* (13 April 1986): 1, 24. A review of *A Perfect Spy.*

DelFattore, Joan. "John le Carré (David John Moore Cornwell)," in *The Dictionary of Literary Biography: British Mystery and Thriller Writers since 1940,* no. 87, ed. Bernard Benstock and Thomas F. Staley,240–55. Detroit: Bruccoli, Clark, Layman/Gale, 1989.

Fenton, James. "Le Carré Goes East." *New Review* 4 (October 1977): 31–34. A review of *The Honourable Schoolboy.*

Freeling, Nicholas. "Crime Novels." *Times Literary Supplement* (24 June 1965): 39–40. A review of *The Looking-Glass War.* Encomium by a respected fellow mystery writer.

Garson, Helen. "Enter George Smiley: Le Carré's *Call for the Dead."* *Clues: A Journal of Detection* 3 (Fall–Winter 1982): 93–99. One of the first treatments of *Call for the Dead* to recognize the importance of the short novel within the overall canon of "Smiley" fiction. Extensive treatment of the character of George Smiley.

Halperin, John. "Between Two Worlds: The Novels of John le Carré." *South Atlantic Quarterly* 79 (Spring 1980): 17–37. An excellent long study of the state of le Carré's art at mid-career. Written at the time of the publication of the conclusion of the "Karla trilogy" with the publication of *Smiley's People.*

Hicks, Granville. "Spies without a Sense of Mission." *Saturday Review* 48, 24 July 1965, 39–40. Hicks believes that the literature of espionage should be more ideological.

Hunter, Evan."Spies and Moles and Other Entertainers." *New York Times Book Review* (24 January 1982): 12, 17. Points to the difficulty of professional literary critics in taking genre writers seriously, including le Carré; Hunter is a popular and respected writer of police process thrillers under the name Ed McBain.

Kanfer, Stefan, with Dean Fischer. "The Spy Who Came in for the Gold." *Time* 105, no. 49, 3 October 1977, 56–60, 67–68, 72. This article marked the popular acceptance of le Carré as a serious artist, written on the publication of *The Honourable Schoolboy.*

Laqueur, Walter. "Le Carré in Russian Eyes." *Commentary* 96 (September 1993): 54–55. A continuation of Laqueur's decade-long attack on the validity of le Carré's understanding of Russian psychology and the Cold War.

———. "Le Carré's Fantasies." *Commentary* 75 (June 1983): 62–67. A negative review of *The Little Drummer Girl* which provoked an ongoing critical dialogue in *Commentary.*

Lehmann-Haupt, Christopher. "Into the Age of Perestroika." *New York Times,* 18 May 1989, C28. A review of *The Russia House.*

Matthews, Tom. "In from the Cold." *Newsweek* 113, 5 June 1989, 52–57. At the publication of *The Russia House,* treats the irony of le Carré's "perestroika" with former Soviet readers after the Cold War.

Miller, Karl. "Gothic Guesswork." *New York Review of Books* (18 July 1974): 24–27. The best review of *Tinker, Tailor, Soldier, Spy* at the time of publication.

Monaghan, David. "John le Carré and England: A Spy's-eye View." *Modern Fiction Studies* 29 (Autumn 1983): 569–82. An attempt after the publication of *Smiley's People* to provide an overview of le Carré's career and, particularly, to put it in the context of English society.

Pritchett, V. S. "A Spy Romance." *New York Review of Books* (7 February 1980): 22–24. The best review of *Smiley's People.*

Remnick, David. "Le Carré's New War." *New York Review of Books* (12 August 1993): 20–23. A perceptive review of *The Night Manager.*

Rothberg, Abraham. "The Decline and Fall of George Smiley: John le Carré and English Decency." *Southwest Review* 66 (Autumn 1981): 377–93. A statement of the theory that the "Circus" novels show a moral decline in Smiley as he attempts to match the brutality of Karla.

Stout, Rex. "The Man Who Came in from the Cold." *Mademoiselle* 59, July 1964, 60, 61. A charming sketch of no great depth, but, written on the heels of the publication of *The Spy Who Came in from the Cold,* it forms an early appreciation by an urbane, knowledgeable, and eminent practitioner of the art of detective writing.

Updike, John. "Le Carré's Game," *New Yorker* 61, 20 March 1995, 102–3. A perceptive review of *Our Game.*

Waugh, Auberon. "Mixed Up by a Master." *London Daily Mail,* 31 March 1983, 7. A review of *The Little Drummer Girl.*

Will, George. "Le Carré's Unreal Mideast." *Washington Post,* 28 April 1983, 19–21. A review of *The Little Drummer Girl* praising le Carré's art but questioning his political picture of the region.

Selected Interviews

Assouline, Pierre. "John le Carré: Spying on the Spymaster." *World Press Review* 33 (August 1986): 59–60.

Barber, Michael. "John le Carré: An Interrogation." *New York Times Book Review* (25 September 1977): 9, 44, 45.

Bibliography

Bragg, Melvyn. "The Little Drummer Girl: An Interview with John le Carré," in *The Quest for le Carré,* ed. Alan Bold, 129–43. New York: St. Martin's Press, 1988.

———. "A Talk with John le Carré." *New York Times Book Review* (13 March 1983): 1, 22.

———. "The Things a Spy Can Do." *Listener,* 22 January 1976, 90. Le Carré's several interviews with Bragg, a close friend, are useful because the novelist is exceptionally candid about his personal life.

Chiu, Tony. "Behind the Best Sellers: John le Carré." *New York Review of Books* (6 January 1980): 30.

Dean, Michael. "John le Carré: The Writer Who Came in from the Cold." *Listener,* 5 September 1974, 306–7.

"The Fictional World of Espionage." *Listener,* 4 April 1966, 548–49.

Gross, Miriam. "A Labyrinth of Espionage: On the Trail of a Master Spy Novelist." *World Press Review* 27 (May 1980): 62.

———. "The Secret World of John le Carré." *London Observer,* 3 February 1980, 33, 35.

Hodgson, Godfrey. "The Secret Life of John le Carré." *Washington Post Book World* (9 October 1977): E1, E6.

Leitch, David. "The Ultimate Spy." *Sunday Times Magazine* (13 September 1987): 50–51.

Orlik, Viktor. "Spies Who Come in from the Cold War: A Session between John le Carré and the Soviets." *World Press Review* 36 (October 1989): 28–30.

Rose, Charlie. Interview with John le Carré on "The Charlie Rose Show," National Public Radio (NPR) Television, 27 June 1993.

Sanoff, Alvin. "The Thawing of an Old Spymaster." *U.S. News and World Report* 106, no. 24, 19 June 1989, 59–61.

Vaughn, Paul. "Le Carré's Circus: Lamplighters, Moles, and Others of That Ilk." *Listener,* 13 September 1979, 339–40.

Wapshott, Nicholas. "Tinker, Tailor, Soldier, Novelist." *London Times,* 6 September 1982, 7.

Bibliography

Whitney, Craig. "I Was Heartily Sick of It." *New York Times Book Review* (6 January 1991): 3, 7.

Yardley, Jonathan. "Le Carré's Drumbeat: Defending His 'Equation' on the Palestinians." *Washington Post,* 6 April 1983, B1. Discussion of the controversy surrounding the publication of *The Little Drummer Girl.*

Watson, Alan. "Violent Image." *Sunday Times,* 30 March 1969, 55, 57.

Index

Index

Index

Index

Index

Index

Index

Index

Index

Index